THE
GEEK
WAY

Also by Andrew McAfee

More from Less

Machine | Platform | Crowd (with Erik Brynjolfsson)

The Second Machine Age (with Erik Brynjolfsson)

Race Against the Machine (with Erik Brynjolfsson)

Enterprise 2.0

THE
GEEK
WAY

ANDREW McAFEE
FOREWORD BY REID HOFFMAN

The Radical Mindset
That Drives
Extraordinary Results

Little, Brown and Company
New York • Boston • London

Little, Brown and Company
Hachette Book Group
1290 Avenue of the Americas, New York, NY 10104
littlebrown.com

First North American Edition: November 2023
Published simultaneously in the United Kingdom by Pan Macmillan, November 2023

Little, Brown and Company is a division of Hachette Book Group, Inc. The Little, Brown name and logo are trademarks of Hachette Book Group, Inc.

The publisher is not responsible for websites (or their content) that are not owned by the publisher.

The Hachette Speakers Bureau provides a wide range of authors for speaking events. To find out more, go to hachettespeakersbureau.com or email hachettespeakers@hbgusa.com.

Little, Brown and Company books may be purchased in bulk for business, educational, or promotional use. For information, please contact your local bookseller or the Hachette Book Group Special Markets Department at special.markets@hbgusa.com.

ISBN 9780316436700
LCCN 2023935274

Printing 1, 2023

LSC-C

Printed in the United States of America

To my brother David McAfee, who has always been there

One will weave the canvas; another will fell a tree by the light of his ax. Yet another will forge nails, and there will be others who observe the stars to learn how to navigate. And yet all will be as one. Building a boat isn't about weaving canvas, forging nails, or reading the sky. It's about giving a shared taste for the sea, by the light of which you will see nothing contradictory but rather a community of love.

—*Antoine de Saint-Exupéry*

Contents

Foreword

by Reid Hoffman

I strongly believe that great technology entrepreneurs aren't just technology geeks, they're also business geeks. In the words of Apple's famous advertising campaign, they find ways to "think different." They apply their insatiable curiosity and love of experimentation to the challenge of building better products and companies. But while most people recognize that we now live in a veritable Age of Geekdom, no one seems to have analyzed and explained the core principles and mechanisms of business geekery. Even my own books, such as *The Alliance* and *Blitzscaling,* which definitely geek out on people management and building multibillion-dollar businesses respectively, don't examine the meta question of why the geeks have inherited the Earth.

With his new book, *The Geek Way,* Andrew McAfee (who is himself an alpha geek of the business variety) tackles the central questions of what geeks are, what they believe, and why they have been so successful in the past few decades. By combining management theory, competitive strategy, the science of evolution, psychology, military history, and cultural anthropology, he has produced a remarkable work of synthesis that finally explains, with a single unified theory (which he dubs "the geek way"), the reasons why the tech startup approach has taken over so much of the world.

While many of his conclusions come from an in-depth analysis of successful tech startups and tech giants such as Amazon, Google, Microsoft, and Netflix, he also draws lessons from grade-school children, military planners, and chimpanzees and explains why seemingly human frailties like

1

overconfidence, prestige, and gossip are actually essential to successful organizations.

Along the way, you'll learn why so many organizations descend into bureaucracy and unethical behavior, and the four key principles you can use to build a culture that combats these value-destroying villains. I predict that this book's greatest lasting contribution will be the way in which it presents a clear, detailed, evidence-based explanation of how culture works and why it is so important. Never again will you look at culture as a fuzzy, hand-waving management buzzword.

The Geek Way is a must-read for any leader who has wondered how to build a twenty-first-century organization. For those outside the technology industry, McAfee demystifies key concepts such as A/B testing and agile software development. But even technology veterans can benefit from understanding how so many industry best practices and articles of faith stem from underlying elements of human nature that evolved over millions of years. I consider myself a longtime student and chronicler of Silicon Valley, and I still took copious notes on the many new things I learned from reading this book. I think you'll have the same experience.

Introduction

The Misunderstood Revolution

> Here is an essential principal of education: to teach
> details is to bring confusion; to establish the relation-
> ship between things is to bring knowledge.
>
> —*Maria Montessori*

I'll never forget cross-examining my mother about punchcards.

It happened in 1978, when I was eleven years old. My parents had divorced the previous year and my mom had gone back to school to get an accounting degree so she could get a job. One of her required courses was computer programming, which at the time was still often done with punchcards. These were stiff paper cards, about 30 percent bigger than a dollar bill, which contained both the instructions and the data required to run a program.*

One night my mom brought home her homework: a box full of punchcards. I thought they were fascinating and asked what they were for. "They're for programming a computer," she said (while, I imagine, bracing herself for what she knew was coming).

"What's a computer?"

"It's a machine that does what you tell it."

"You mean like a robot does?"

---

* Many computers of that era didn't have disk drives or other storage media, because they were so expensive, so everything had to be stored on the cards.

"No, the computer that I'm working with doesn't move around."

"Then what good is it?"

"Well, you can get it to do things like print out a list of addresses."

"So a computer is just a typewriter?"

"No, it can do more than that. For example, it can alphabetize the addresses."

"So... it's a typewriter that alphabetizes?"

I forget how long this went on (a lot longer than my mom wanted, certainly), but I remember being hooked. This was *interesting*. This was *for me*. There are kids who immediately take to the violin or chess or fishing. I took to computers.

Portrait of the Author as a Young Geek

My interest in these strange new machines led me down a predictable path. Math team. Early video games. Subscriptions to *Byte* and *Omni*. Reading huge amounts of science fiction. Finding *Monty Python's Flying Circus,* and finding it hilarious. Attending computer camp. Not attending prom.

I was a geek.

That word came into English from Germanic languages, where it referred to "a fool or crazy person." Throughout much of the twentieth century it was mainly used in America to refer to a group of true outsiders: performers in circus sideshows who bit the heads off chickens and did other degrading and outré things. By the early 1980s, the term was also being used to refer to another set of outsiders: young people who were really into computers. So it was absolutely the right term for me.

In 1984, I got admitted to MIT. I immediately felt at home there and dug into my studies. I completed two undergraduate and two graduate degrees in six years, which felt like more than enough. When I got done with my master's degree, the one thing I knew for sure about myself was that I was done with higher education and ready to live in the real world. But it turns out that I didn't know myself very well. I got bored with my job, and when I thought about making a move, I realized that I missed academia. So in 1994 I started yet another degree, this one a doctorate at Harvard Business School.

Nineteen ninety-four was also the year that Netscape Navigator, the first commercial web browser, was released. It was the year, in other words, when computers and networks really started to come together and cover the planet. The birth of the World Wide Web kicked off one of humanity's biggest projects, and one that's still ongoing: interconnecting the world's people via technology and giving us on-demand access to both a decent chunk of our accumulated knowledge and huge amounts of computing power.

This project provided plenty of research opportunities for a business academic. I joined the HBS faculty in 1999 and devoted my professional life to investigating how digital innovations — e-commerce software, search engines, cloud computing, smartphones, and so on — were helping companies perform and compete better. As part of this work, I wrote many case studies: short documents describing a business situation that are used as the basis for class discussions at Harvard and other business schools.

These case studies covered a lot of terrain. I wrote about how the CVS drugstore chain rewrote its software to try to improve customer service, and how the global "fast fashion" retailer Zara used mobile technology to sense what people all over the world wanted to wear and quickly respond to this demand. I wrote about a European investment bank that was experimenting with an early internal blogging platform and about a strange new online reference called Wikipedia. I traveled to Argentina to look at an innovative soybean farmer; to Japan, where the owner of a taxi company built an automated ride-hailing service several years before Uber did; and to the port of Dubai, which wanted to better monitor all the cargo it received. And of course I went to Silicon Valley frequently. I wrote cases about online retailers, software and hardware startups, and entirely new kinds of companies like search engines and social networks. All of this work gave me a front-row seat to how digital technologies were reshaping the business world.

In 2009, after a decade on the faculty at HBS, I returned to the MIT

Sloan School of Management. I started collaborating with economist Erik Brynjolfsson, a great scholar of technology and information.* We shared a sense that something big was unfolding right in front of us—something as big as the Industrial Revolution. As we wrote in our 2014 book, *The Second Machine Age*, "The Industrial Revolution…allowed us to overcome the limitations of muscle power, human and animal, and generate massive amounts of useful energy at will…Now comes the second machine age. Computers and other digital advances are doing for mental power—the ability to use our brains to understand and shape our environments—what the steam engine and its descendants did for muscle power. They're allowing us to blow past previous limitations and taking us into new territory."

The Right Word

Erik and I also published two other books about digital transformation: *Race Against the Machine* (2011) and *Machine | Platform | Crowd* (2017). We were writing about the right topic at the right time, and our "machine trilogy" found a receptive audience. *The Economist* named *The Second Machine Age* "the most influential recent business book," and the *Financial Times* called me and Erik "the pinup boys of the Davos crowd."

That kind of attention didn't cause my modeling career to take off, but it did lead to a lot of offers to talk with leaders all over the world about the tectonic shifts taking place in industries, economies, and societies. And to keep learning. I rode in a Google self-driving car, watched robots scurry around an Amazon warehouse, talked with economists at Uber and Airbnb about using data and algorithms to dynamically balance supply and demand, and had countless other eye-opening experiences.

Lots of industrial-era companies were also having eye-opening experiences at the time, and not pleasant ones. The iconic American retailer Sears, which was founded in 1886, went bankrupt. So did household names like Kodak (1881), JCPenney (1902), Radio Shack (1921), and Polaroid (1937).

---

* And a great guy.

General Electric was one of the companies included when the Dow Jones Industrial Average was first calculated in 1896. In 2018 GE was delisted from the Dow because of its stock's poor performance.

As we moved deeper into the second machine age, entire industries collapsed. US newspaper advertising revenues declined by two-thirds between 2000 and 2015, erasing a full half century of growth. Magazines didn't fare much better; their ad revenue dropped by 40 percent between 2008 and 2018. The growing popularity of music streaming services hasn't come close to offsetting the near elimination of CDs and other physical media; revenues from recorded music fell by more 46 percent between 1999 and 2021.

These examples and plenty of others indicate that the digital transformation of industry after industry is dividing companies into two categories: those that can successfully participate in it, and those that can't. We hear a lot about "new economy" versus "old economy" companies, disrupters versus incumbents, the tech sector versus the rest of the economy, and Silicon Valley versus all the other regions of the US and world. In each case, the first category has the momentum; it's where the action is, where the value is being created, where the future is to be found, and so on.

All those categorizations made sense to me, and I used all of them, but none of them felt exactly right. Some of the companies that have excelled, for example, are in the "wrong" category. Amazon isn't in Silicon Valley. Apple was an incumbent computer maker until the iPhone turned it into one of the biggest disrupters the world has ever seen. Microsoft is both an incumbent *and* a non–Silicon Valley company; it seemed to have missed the "new economy" (whatever that is) entirely, until it came roaring back in recent years to become one of the most valuable firms in the world. And as time passed, the label "tech" stopped being a useful differentiator. As strategist Ben Thompson put it in 2021, we currently have "a problem of definition...Is Warby Parker a tech company? Is Carvana? Is DoorDash? The list goes on and on...Calling everything a tech company is like calling a shopping mall a car company; sure, it was enabled by and undergirded by the automobile, but what in that era wasn't?" Digital transformation was clearly creating winners and losers, but it didn't feel like we'd found the right way to talk about what distinguished the two groups.

And then my eagle-eyed literary agent, Rafe Sagalyn, spotted it. In *Machine | Platform | Crowd* Erik and I had included a few paragraphs about the "geeky" leadership style we'd observed at many successful tech companies. We used that adjective because the leaders we were talking about were classic computer geeks who had gone on to found companies. But Rafe said: "There's something big here. You're not just talking about the fact that some programmers founded companies. What you're hinting at is a whole new way to run a company."

Rafe sent me a bunch of articles to spur my thinking. One of them was a 2010 interview with Bill Gates where he expanded the definition of a geek: "Well, when geek means that you're willing to study things, . . . then I plead guilty, gladly." Geeks aren't always computer freaks, Gates is saying. Instead, they're obsessives of *any* kind (except, hopefully, the biting-the-heads-off-chickens kind): people who get fascinated by a topic and won't (or can't) let go of it, no matter what others think.

Geeks care about their passions a lot more than they care about mainstream opinion. As Dictionary.com puts it, a geek is "a peculiar person, especially one who is perceived to be overly intellectual, unfashionable, or socially awkward." Jeff Bezos embraced the unfashionable aspect of geekdom in Amazon's 2011 shareholder meeting. In response to a question about how the company innovates, he replied, "Very importantly, we are willing to be misunderstood for long periods of time." Geeks aren't concerned about going with the flow. They'll go wherever their inquiries take them.

During one of my conversations with Rafe, we were discussing the points that Gates, Bezos, and others were making. He asked me, "Are you saying that there's a new generation of business geeks out there?" It was like he'd removed a gag from my mouth. I started babbling at him, "Yes! *Absolutely!* Why do you think Bezos is always going on about Day 1 versus Day 2 companies? Have you heard about the Netflix culture deck? I've been learning about the birth of Agile programming, which works *so* much better. And

I was in this crazy meeting a while back at HubSpot where a new hire flatly contradicted the CEO to his face *and no one noticed.* Look, the company is getting an upgrade. And if you can't install that upgrade it'll be like you're running Windows 95…"

"Andy. Andy? *Andy.*" Rafe eventually got me to shut up. "That's the book. Write that book."

This is that book. It's not about what a bunch of computer geeks have created. It's instead about the creations and achievements of a bunch of business geeks: people who got properly obsessed with the hard problem of running a modern company, came up with unconventional solutions, and implemented them. A lot of these business geeks are found at companies within the high-tech sector, or in Silicon Valley. But not all of them. A lot of them are founders. But not all of them. What unites them isn't industry or geography or how big an ownership stake they have. What unites them is that they're geeks—obsessive mavericks—about business and companies. I finally found the word I was looking for. It more accurately described what was going on, and it had been hiding in plain sight. We've paid a lot of attention to the computer revolution kicked off by the geeks. But I think we've been misunderstanding the other revolution they initiated: a still-unfolding revolution in the company itself.

Rafe asked one other key question during our early conversations: "Are you saying that the geek way is the right way for *all* companies? Are there any situations where it wouldn't work, or would be a bad idea?" I had to think about that one for a while. Here's my answer: the geek way is the right way for *modern* companies, because modern companies have to move faster and innovate more than their predecessors did.

There are a few big reasons for this acceleration, including globalization and increased competition. I believe, though, the most fundamental reason is that companies today have a *lot* more digital technology than they used to, and the extraordinary rate of change and innovation in all these technologies means that the overall pace of business is quicker than it used to be, in every industry and every region. As venture capitalist Vinod Khosla put it to me, "There's always been a lot of technology-based disruption in high-tech industries. Starting about fifteen years ago it became technology disruption in every area of GDP."

Former Google CEO Eric Schmidt explained to me one of the biggest consequences of this shift: "In the classic corporate model, everything is run in a hierarchical way, the offices get bigger over time, and bureaucracies abound. Companies like this were actually successful for a long time because they have some strengths: they're predictable and they serve their customers well, as long as customers keep needing the same thing. The reason that culture doesn't work very well in the information age is that the customers need changes, and you have to be able to change more quickly than, you know, every five years."

The geek way is a set of solutions for thriving in this faster-moving world. They're cultural solutions, not technological ones. As much as the business geeks love technology they don't think that any particular suite of technologies holds the key to building a great modern company. There's no killer app for business success. What there is instead is what there have always been: people, groups, and the challenge of getting them to work well together in pursuit of goals. After thinking long and hard about this challenge, the business geeks have figured out some powerful and unconventional ways to tackle it. They've taken the standard corporate culture of the industrial era and given it an upgrade.

There's one big surprise in this upgrade, and one non-surprise. The non-surprise is what kind of organizational cultures the business geeks have come up with. They're what you'd expect to get if you put a bunch of smart, debate-loving, data-driven, contrarian problem-solvers who really, truly don't like being told what to do in charge of reimagining how a company should be run. As we'll see, the geek way leans into arguments and loathes bureaucracy. It favors iteration over planning, shuns coordination, and tolerates some chaos. Its practitioners are vocal and egalitarian, and they're not afraid to fail, challenge the boss, or be proven wrong. Instead of respecting hierarchy and credentials, they respect helpfulness and chops. In short, the cultures of geek companies are, well, geek-like.

The big surprise is how well these cultures work. Instead of collapsing into anarchy or acrimony, geek companies have demonstrated that they can scale and last. And as we'll see, they deliver extraordinary amounts of value to customers and investors while also being desirable places to work. We'll spend a lot of time in the pages ahead understanding how they accomplish this.

The most senior business geeks I've talked with—people like Eric Schmidt and former Autodesk CEO Carl Bass—tell me that aspects of the geek way were in place at Northern California's hardware and software companies well before the turn of the twenty-first century. Journalist Don Hoefler wrote an article in 1971 describing one area that was particularly rich in chipmaking companies as "Silicon Valley, USA." The name stuck, the Valley soon became home to the world's greatest concentration of business-minded geeks. They iterated and experimented their way forward over the following decades.

A clear statement of many aspects of the geek way appeared in 2009, when Netflix's CEO, Reed Hastings, and his chief talent officer, Patty McCord, uploaded a long PowerPoint presentation, titled "Netflix Culture: Freedom & Responsibility," to SlideShare, an online service that does exactly what its name implies. The Netflix culture deck became both blueprint and affirmation for many people trying to build companies, and it spread like a rumor (it's been viewed more than 17 million times). Those of us who write business books don't love the idea that what "may well be the most important document ever to come out of [Silicon] Valley" is a PowerPoint presentation. But that's what Facebook COO Sheryl Sandberg said about the Netflix culture deck. Hastings's ideas about how to build and sustain a culture of freedom and responsibility so impressed Sandberg and her colleagues that they asked Hastings to join Facebook's board of directors in 2011.

Over the years I kept seeing how much attention the geeks were paying to culture. In 2014, for example, Jeff Bezos said in an interview with journalist Henry Blodget, "My main job today: I work hard at helping to maintain the culture." In 2018, shortly after the cloud storage company Dropbox went public, I interviewed its founder and CEO, Drew Houston, onstage at

MIT. I asked him to share some of the most important things he learned along his entrepreneurial journey. He responded: "When the company was just starting I sat down with some of the people in tech I admired most and just asked for advice. I was expecting to hear about dealing with VCs and boards, or how to build a viral product, or things like that. Instead, they all said the same thing: they advised me to work hard from the start on getting the culture right, and never stop working on that."

These examples and many others were somewhere in my thoughts as I was babbling at Rafe. What his guidance and questioning unlocked was not just a label, but a window on the heart of the phenomenon: a loose band of obsessive mavericks converging on a set of practices that enable companies to perform better while, not at all coincidentally, providing healthy and desirable work environments.

A Problem-Solver Like Maria

So what are these practices? What makes geek companies and their cultures radically different from the mainstream of the industrial era? I'm going to spend most of this book answering those questions. Let me preview all my answers by describing a great gift my parents gave me. At an early age I became part of an organization founded by the patron saint of geeks. I'm not talking about Nikolai Tesla or Thomas Edison or Steve Jobs. I'm talking about Maria Montessori.

In 2004 journalist Barbara Walters interviewed Google cofounders Larry Page and Sergey Brin. Both of them had parents who were professors and scientists, and Walters asked if this family background was an important part of their success. But both Brin and Page highlighted something else. As Page put it, "We both went to Montessori school, and I think it was part of that training of not following rules and orders, and being self-motivated, questioning what's going on in the world, doing things a little bit differently."

I'll vouch for that. My initiation into geekdom happened long before I quizzed my mom about punchcards and computers. It came when my parents enrolled me in a Montessori school at the age of three.

For those unfamiliar with Montessori, here's a quick explanation. Montessori classrooms are designed to be self-directed learning labs for children. I remember my first one as a large, light-filled room, parts of which were dedicated to different activities. In one area there were beads strung together on wires to form lines, squares, and cubes (which turns out to be a great way to convey the difference between x, x^2, and x^3). Another space had cloth letters I could play with to ease me into the concept of reading. Other areas had polygons to trace, 3D shapes to play with, simple abacuses, pens and pencils and paper, and so on.

The gear in the classrooms was great, but what I really loved about my Montessori school was the freedom. There were a few scheduled activities each day—lunch, recess, "circle time," when teachers and students sat on the floor in a circle and talked about stuff—but most of the time I could do what I wanted. And what I and my classmates wanted wasn't to break things, run around yelling, or terrorize each other. Instead, we wanted to sit quietly and learn.

One of Montessori's most radical insights was that even young children are capable of concentration and deep study in the right environment. They're not inherently wild creatures that have to be penned. Instead, they're inherent learners. They have reserves of self-discipline that are activated when they're curious about something. Montessori wrote that "a child who has become master of his acts, . . . and who has been encouraged by the pleasant and interesting activities in which he has been engaged, is a child filled with health and joy and remarkable for his calmness and discipline." Jeff Bezos had a great deal of this discipline. Like Brin and Page, Bezos was also a Montessori kid as a toddler; according to his mother, he'd get so engrossed in what he was doing in the classroom that his teachers would have to physically pick him up and move him when it was time for a change.

I remember many times as a young child when I experienced that kind of flow state in the classroom. But those experiences came to a halt after third grade, which was as far as my Montessori school went. After that, public school was the only viable option in the Indiana town where I grew up.

I spent the first day of fourth grade in the public elementary school wondering if I'd angered my parents somehow and was being punished. No other explanation made sense. Sitting at the same desk all day? Rotating through subjects according to the clock on the wall, rather than my interests? Covering concepts that I'd mastered years earlier? Doing mind-numbing drills and worksheets? This school didn't feel like an educational institution; it felt like a reeducation camp designed to break my spirit.

The deepest mystery was why my autonomy and freedom had been replaced with so much pointless hierarchy and structure. It didn't make any sense. I eventually learned to get along and go along at my new school. But I never learned to like it, or to see the point.

Neither did Maria Montessori. Her schools, the first of which opened its doors in Rome in 1906, did away with daily schedules, teacher-led instruction, grids of desks, grades, and many other standard elements of primary education in the industrialized world. The mainstream view, in her era and our own, has been that these elements are necessary to ensure that children learn necessary skills. The thinking is that letting kids do what they want throughout the school day might make them happy, and might even make them creative, but it won't make them good at reading, writing, and arithmetic.

Montessori kept proving how wrong that view is. Early in the twentieth century, she demonstrated that disadvantaged children — even those traumatized by World War I — could, through her methods, make remarkable progress in acquiring all the basic skills they needed. Almost a hundred years later, in 2006, a study published in *Science* by psychologists Angeline Lillard and Nicole Else-Quest found that kids from low- and middle-income families in Milwaukee who were enrolled in Montessori schools did better than their peers in several of the cognitive and social domains evaluated, and worse in none of them.

Montessori is a hero to today's business geeks for three reasons. First, she was a true geek herself. She immersed herself in a tough and important problem — how do children learn best? — devised unconventional solutions, and then advocated tirelessly for them. Second, her educational methods foster the kinds of innovation and creativity that contribute to success in the business world. After surveying more than five hundred creative professionals, management researchers Hal Gregerson and Jeff Dyer were surprised at how many started off in Montessori schools. This research revealed the importance of curiosity and asking lots of questions. As Gregerson put it,

> If you look at 4-year-olds, they are constantly asking questions and wondering how things work. But by the time they are 6½ years old they stop asking questions because they quickly learn that teachers value the right answers more than provocative questions...We believe that the most innovative entrepreneurs were very lucky to have been raised in an atmosphere where inquisitiveness was encouraged...A number of [them] went to Montessori schools, where they learned to follow their curiosity.

Third, and most important, Maria Montessori showed us something joyous: *This can be better.* We don't have to keep educating young children the same way. We can improve on the educational status quo a lot, and those improvements will *not* come with a lot of downsides. If we give schoolchildren great autonomy we won't be sacrificing their ability to master basic skills or perform well on standardized tests. They don't need to be told what, when, and how to study in order to make progress; they do just fine on their own.

It's hard to overstate how radical Montessori's approaches were. The pioneers of universal childhood education in the US and elsewhere were heavily influenced by the Prussian primary school system of the mid-nineteenth century.* And the Prussian educators were in turn influenced by the philosopher Johann Gottlieb Fichte, who was clear that schooling really should be about breaking children's spirits. He wrote in 1807:

---

* Prussia was early in making state-funded education mandatory and universal, and in teaching practical skills. In 1843 the American educational reformer Horace Mann traveled there to study and learn. When he returned he helped convince Massachusetts, New York, and other states to follow the Prussian model.

Education should aim at destroying free will so that after pupils are thus schooled they will be incapable throughout the rest of their lives of thinking or acting otherwise than as their schoolmasters would have wished.

Montessori's worldview was as far from Fichte's as one could imagine. And yet her methods educate children as well as, or better than, the free will–destroying methods advocated by Fichte. Montessori demonstrated that the standard educational environment of her time (and, sadly, of ours as well) can be improved simultaneously across every important dimension, and that doing so doesn't require heroic teachers or massive additional spending. It just requires letting go of some incorrect assumptions and going about things in a different way, even if that way is far from the mainstream. It requires a geek's radical mindset.

A bunch of geeks are now doing for companies what Maria Montessori did for schools. They're reimagining them, improving them, and exposing false assumptions. A large and growing cohort of business leaders are now building very different companies—and, not coincidentally, very success-ful ones.

It's also not a coincidence that, as we'll see, the organizations they're creating are a lot less hierarchical, less rigid, less rules-based, and less top-down than those they're outpacing. Montessori showed that children can excel without these constraints; today's business geeks are showing that com-panies can as well. We overbuilt both classrooms and corporations during the industrial era. The geeks are showing us how much better things work when we remove the excess overhead and structure from both.

A New View of Me and You

Why does the geek way work so well? For an answer to this key question we're going to draw on a body of research that considers all kinds of human cultures—not just corporate ones—and looks at how they accumulate knowledge and know-how over time. This research starts from first principles. It's based on the theory of evolution, which is about as solid a foundation as there is in all of science.*

Now, looking to evolution is not the dominant approach within business studies. It doesn't even qualify as a minority approach. Even calling it "fringe" is probably too generous. As psychologist Gad Saad puts it, "The great majority of business scholars are unaware of, and at times are hostile to," the idea that studying evolution might provide insights into human organizational behavior.

My experience supports Saad's contention. In my nearly three decades at business schools, I've participated in countless conferences, seminars, research group meetings, and so on. I can remember only a couple times when someone seriously suggested that we look to the science of evolution.

It's time to change that, for the simple reason that, as the biologist Theodosius Dobzhansky put it in 1973, "nothing in biology makes sense except in the light of evolution." This insight applies to minds as well as bodies. The psychologist Anne Campbell puts it beautifully: "Evolution didn't stop at the neck." If we examine many aspects of our thinking and behavior in light of evolution, they'll make more sense. And this is what we're finally starting to do.

Over the past couple decades, research by a multidisciplinary band of social scientists has coalesced into a field of study called cultural evolution. This field gets at the classic *Why do we humans do what we do?* question by starting with an observation: we're not the only species on the planet that forms cultures, but we *are* the only species with cultures capable of launching spaceships and doing other insanely difficult and complicated things. This observation quickly leads to a bunch of questions:

How do human cultures get smarter over time? What accelerates that accumulation of knowledge, or slows it down? Why are some cultures more successful

---

* As philosopher Daniel Dennett wrote in his 1995 book, *Darwin's Dangerous Idea,* "If I were to give an award for the single best idea anyone ever had, I'd give it to Darwin, ahead of even Newton or Einstein and everyone else. In a single stroke, the idea of evolution by natural selection unifies the realm of life, meaning, and purpose with the realm of space and time, cause and effect, mechanism and physical law."

than others? When cultures clash, which ones win? What are the most common ways for cultures to decay? How do individuals acquire, generate, and pass on knowledge? How do we balance our individual interests with those of the group? When individuals misbehave, how do their cultures bring them back in line?

As we'll see, the field of cultural evolution has been investigating these questions for a while now and has come up with solid, stress-tested answers. The great news is that the answers apply to corporate cultures just as well as they do to all the other kinds of cultures we humans create. To see how helpful cultural evolution's answers are, let's reword the above questions just a bit:

How does innovation happen? What accelerates it, or slows it down? Why are some businesses more innovative and successful than others? When businesses compete, which ones win? What are the most common ways for businesses to become uncompetitive over time? What makes individuals productive? What makes teams work well together? How can we best align people's desire to get ahead with the goals of the organization? What kinds of bad behavior should we expect within an organization, and how can we minimize them?

The field of cultural evolution has given us a new way to approach questions like these, and has given us some new answers. This is great news, because they're such obviously important questions. For those of us who want to get ahead of the competition there's even better news: cultural evolution's insights haven't yet spread to the business world. So there's a huge opportunity to be at the forefront of applying them.

I can't recall ever hearing any manager, geek or not, talk about many of the key concepts we'll cover in the pages ahead: ultrasociality, prestige versus dominance, ultimate versus proximate questions, the press secretary module, and so on. I've also not come across any of these concepts in a business book written for a general audience (as opposed to an academic one). And while some concepts we'll explore in these pages are more familiar, like plausible deniability, observability, norms, common knowledge, Nash equilibria, and the prisoner's dilemma, they still aren't given enough emphasis given how important they turn out to be. In short, the new science of cultural evolution hasn't yet been transferred from university seminar rooms to corporate boardrooms and meeting rooms. It's not what they teach you at Harvard Business School* (trust me, I was there for fifteen years). The really exciting opportunity for me as the author of this book—and (I hope) for you as its reader—is to create a new understanding of some key business issues by bringing together theory and practice. Or, to be more specific, some new theory from the field of cultural evolution and some new practices from geek companies.

It's a fascinating coincidence that both the practices that make up the geek way and the theory that explains why the geek way works as well as it does are products of the twenty-first century. As we'll see, some of the early seminal geek business events—the first A/B test, the genesis of Agile programming—happened right around the turn of the century.

The roots of cultural evolution go back a bit further than that, but the field has really started to flourish in recent years. Many of the books I've relied on most heavily were published within the last decade or so. These include *Blueprint* (2019), *The Goodness Paradox* (2019), *Social* (2013), *The Ape That Understood the Universe* (2018), *The Folly of Fools* (2011), *Everybody Lies* (2017), *Why Everybody Else Is a Hypocrite* (2010), *The Elephant in the Brain* (2017), *The Enigma of Reason* (2017), *The Secret of Our Success* (2015), *Not Born Yesterday* (2020), *The WEIRDest People in the World* (2020), *Catching Fire* (2009), *The Social Instinct* (2021), and *Hidden Games* (2022). These cover a lot of different topics; what they all have in common is that they tell how evolution shaped us to be a uniquely culture-y† species.

The pioneering business geeks and the pioneers in the field of cultural evolution have both been doing fascinating and important work, but they've been working on parallel tracks that have not meaningfully intersected. It's high time to change that, hence this book.

---

* Or, for that matter, any other business school.
† Not a technical term.

Why We Should Care About the Why

We'll get two big benefits from bringing together theory and practice as we explore the geek way. The first and most obvious is that we'll make faster progress. When practical tinkerers interact with theory-minded scientists, the two sides learn from each other and we all benefit.

The tinkerers want to get something to work better. That something could be a sea kayak, poison made from a frog's skin, a steam engine, or a company. These folk rely mainly on their intelligence, experience, and intuition to guide their efforts. Their guiding question is "How can I improve this?" The scientists are more theoretical. Their guiding question is "Why does this work the way it does?" Why is one sea kayak faster than another? Why is poison prepared one particular way more potent? Why is this steam engine, or that company, more efficient?

"How...?" questions and "Why...?" questions go back and forth and improve the state of the world. The tinkerers often start the dialogue by making an improvement that gets the scientists curious. For example, scientists' questions about why James Watt's steam engine worked so much better than its predecessors helped create the discipline of thermodynamics. The scientists then deepen the tinkerers' understanding and give them better tools. The formulation of the famous three laws of thermodynamics has helped countless designers and engineers build better engines. The interplay between how and why happens in all fields. Antonio Stradivari worked for decades on how to make string instruments sound better. Since his death in 1737, we've learned a great deal about why his creations sound so wonderful, and we can now make violins that sound even better than a Stradivarius. Farmers were experimenting with crop rotation for centuries before George Washington Carver used chemistry to show why it was such a good idea. He got planters in the American South to improve their yields by alternating nitrogen-depleting cotton with nitrogen-providing peanuts or soybeans.

We're at a fascinating point in time right now. A critical mass of both kinds of curious people—how-asking tinkerers and why-asking scientists—have formed around questions of organizations, culture, and learning. This book is based on the premise that by bringing these two camps together we'll make faster progress on these things called companies.

What's more, these improvements will stick. The second major benefit of combining theory and practice is that we do a better job of sticking to new practices once we have a theory about why they work better—once we understand the first principles at work. Clay Christensen, the late, great management scholar and a mentor of mine, was adamant that "managers are voracious consumers of theory." I think this applies not just to managers, but to all of us. We don't just want to know *that* something works; we also want to know *why* it works.

Things that make sense within our theories about how the world works are easy for us to take on board. Things that don't make sense with our existing theories, on the other hand, are easy to reject. Far too easy sometimes, as the tragic story of a nineteenth-century doctor who was just a little ahead of his time makes clear. I want to tell his story as we begin our explanation of the geek way because it highlights the critical importance of not only being right, but also being able to convincingly explain *why* you're right. The difference between the two states can be the difference between changing the world and losing your mind.

The Germ of an Idea

In 1846 Ignaz Semmelweis, who was working as what we'd now call a chief medical resident at Vienna General Hospital, noticed that one of its two birth clinics was much more deadly than the other. About 10 percent of the women in the First Clinic died within days of giving birth, from what had long been called childbed fever.* In the Second Clinic, meanwhile, death rates were two and a half times lower, at around 4 percent. Word got around

---

* The dainty name *childbed fever* obscures the horrors of the disease, which brings fever, bleeding, headaches, and incapacitating pain to new mothers, even if it doesn't kill them. It's now called puerperal fever or maternal sepsis.

about this enormous difference, and women begged not to have to go to the First Clinic. Some even preferred to give birth in the street.

None of Semmelweis's colleagues seemed to find this discrepancy interesting, or to care much about reducing the appalling death rates in the First Clinic. As he wrote, "The disrespect displayed by the employees toward the [patients] of the First Clinic made me so miserable that life seemed worthless...Everything seemed inexplicable, everything was doubtful. Only the large number of deaths was an unquestionable reality." So in best geek fashion, he set out to study and solve the problem.

He began by documenting all the differences between the two clinics. Expectant mothers were assigned randomly between the clinics, so it wasn't that the two were seeing different types of patients.* The biggest difference Semmelweis found was that the First Clinic was staffed by medical students, while the Second Clinic was staffed by midwives in training. He investigated the daily routines of the two groups and learned that the medical students often came to their clinic right after performing autopsies. The midwives didn't, since autopsies were not part of their education.

Semmelweis hypothesized that the medical students left the autopsy room with some kind of "cadaverous particles" on their hands, which they transferred to women while assisting in their deliveries. It was these particles that made the mothers sick and caused so many deaths. He experimented with ways to stop the transfer using the only test available to him: what would make the students' hands stop smelling like putrid corpses? He found that a solution of chlorinated lime worked best, and in May of 1847 Semmelweis instituted mandatory handwashing for medical students before they entered the First Clinic.† In April, the maternal mortality rate had been 18.3 percent; in June it was 2.2 percent, and in July 1.2 percent. The benefits

---

* All mothers admitted on one day went to the First Clinic, then all mothers admitted the next day went to the Second.

† Yes, you read that right. As recently as the 1840s, physicians in the richest and most technologically sophisticated countries in the world didn't wash their hands between autopsies and deliveries.

of handwashing were so large that they seemed miraculous. In 1848, there were two months in which no women died in the First Clinic.

The story of the fight to protect women against childbed fever has a happy ending. Unfortunately, though, this medical triumph is not due to Semmelweis. His ideas about how to protect mothers giving birth were repeatedly rejected, even though the improvements in his clinics were undeniable.

Why were Semmelweis's advances ignored? Because he failed to change the mindset of his fellow physicians. In the middle of the nineteenth century, the dominant view was that many diseases were spread by *miasmas,* or foul-smelling air emanating from rotting matter. This theory was based on a logical and intuitive chain of reasoning: smells spread through the air, and after a rotting smell appears, people often start getting sick. Therefore (the reasoning goes) it's the air itself that spreads the sickness. Semmelweis's ideas about cadaverous particles made no sense to a medical establishment brought up on miasma theory. Neither did his recommendation of handwashing, so it was disparaged and ignored.

His inability to convince his peers and stop all the needless suffering and death drove Semmelweis insane. He became belligerent, depressed, and erratic. In 1865, he was committed to a Viennese asylum where, after two weeks, he died from gangrene.* His death was hardly noticed by the medical community. The director who took over from Semmelweis at his last clinic stopped the practice of handwashing. Maternal mortality rates immediately jumped sixfold.

The virtual elimination of childbed fever happened not because of Semmelweis's contributions, but instead thanks to Louis Pasteur's. Why? Because Pasteur changed not just a procedure, but an entire science. In the 1860s, he conducted a set of experiments that demonstrated to physicians not only that Semmelweis had been right, but *why* he had been right.

Pasteur showed conclusively that many diseases were caused not by

---

* Semmelweis's treatments in the asylum included being soaked in cold water and force-fed laxatives. The gangrene that killed him likely started in a wound he received during a severe beating from the guards.

foul-smelling atmospheric miasmas, but instead by very small organisms called germs.* Semmelweis's "cadaverous particles" were in fact microorganisms that were responsible for more than just contagious illnesses — Pasteur showed that they also caused bread to rise, cheese to ripen, beer and wine to ferment, and so on.†

He founded the science of microbiology, which has vastly improved our understanding of the world. Once we understood microbiology we started pasteurizing milk, developing vaccines, and washing our hands before conducting medical procedures. It's hard to fully wrap our minds around all the benefits we've gained from this understanding, but here's one statistic relevant to our story: the *global* average maternal mortality rate is now around 0.2 percent (in Austria, the rate is 0.004 percent). Pasteur became a living legend in France, where a major research institute was founded in his name. When he died, in 1895, he was given a state funeral and buried in the Cathedral of Notre Dame.‡

The difference between the careers of Pasteur and Semmelweis could hardly be more stark. One changed the world. The other was driven mad because he couldn't get people to see what he saw. Semmelweis failed to effect the change he was so passionate about in large part because this change made no sense within the system of established beliefs and attitudes — the mindset — of his medical peers. They were lost in a miasma of incorrect beliefs. As a result, Semmelweis's ideas were repeatedly mocked,

---

* In one of his most famous experiments Pasteur made use of a glass flask that had an unusual shape: its long neck went up from the base of the flask, then bent down 180 degrees, then bent back up 180 degrees. The upward bend served to trap all the dust and other particles as outside air moved into the flask. Pasteur put a nutrient-rich broth in the base of this "swan neck" flask and boiled it until both flask and broth were sterilized. He then opened the end of the long neck, exposing the broth to outside air. If air really did carry disease, then the broth would putrefy. But it didn't because all the germs (which were attached to particles) got trapped in the upward bend and never came into contact with the broth. The swan neck flask experiments were instrumental in convincing people that the miasma theory of disease was incorrect, and the germ theory correct.

† Can you tell that Pasteur was French?

‡ His body was later moved to the Pasteur Institute.

ignored, and rejected. But as soon as biologists and doctors saw Pasteur's proof they became ready, willing, and able to change not only what they believed, but also how they behaved. Over the last quarter of the nineteenth century medical practitioners in Europe turned away from the idea of miasmas, took up the germ theory of disease, and worked hard to avoid accidentally exposing patients to these microorganisms. As the germ theory and its practical implications spread around the world, the spread of disease slowed. (Can you imagine what would happen today to an obstetrician who refused to wash their hands before assisting in a delivery?)

Those of us who want better companies are better off than poor Ignaz Semmelweis, because the equivalents of Pasteur's demonstrations have recently taken place. As we'll see, many puzzles have been resolved around the important topic of how we humans create our cultures. We understand ourselves better now, which means that we're less likely to keep making the mistakes of the past. I'm confident that the geek way will endure and spread not just because it works better, but because we now understand why it works so well. In the pages ahead I'll spend a lot of time explaining how the business geeks run their companies. But I'll spend at least as much time explaining why these approaches work as well as they do. With that understanding, any company that wants to can quickly get geekier.

Chapter Summary

We've paid a lot of attention to the computer revolution kicked off by the geeks. But I think we've been misunderstanding the other revolution they initiated: a still-unfolding revolution in the company itself. The business geeks have taken the standard corporate culture of the industrial era and given it an upgrade.

The geek way is a set of solutions for thriving in a faster-moving business world. They're cultural solutions, not technological ones.

The geek way leans into arguments and loathes bureaucracy. It favors iteration over planning, shuns coordination, and tolerates some chaos. Its practitioners are vocal and egalitarian, and they're not afraid to fail, challenge the boss, or be proven wrong. Instead of respecting hierarchy and credentials, they respect helpfulness and chops.

To understand why the geek way works so well, we're going to draw on research from the young field of cultural evolution. Cultural evolution's insights haven't yet spread to the business world. So there's a huge opportunity to be at the forefront of applying them.

I'll spend a lot of time explaining how the business geeks run their companies. But I'll spend at least as much time explaining why these approaches work as well as they do. With that understanding, any company that wants to can quickly get geekier.

CHAPTER 1

The Fourfold Path to Geekdom

The minute that you understand that you can poke life and...that you can change it, you can mold it. That's maybe the most important thing...

Once you learn it, you'll want to change life and make it better, cause it's kind of messed up, in a lot of ways. Once you learn that, you'll never be the same again. *—Steve Jobs*

Geek companies have looser dress codes, better snacks, and more dogs and foosball tables in the office than their industrial-era counterparts, but these aren't the important differences. I hope no one believes that they'll be able to adopt the geek way by embracing hoodies and huskies in the workplace. So what *are* the key differences that separate geek from nongeek organizations? My answer is that there are four. Let me illustrate them with four short case studies about walking away from the established practices of the industrial era and embracing the geek way.

Unusual Activity in Area 51

Like a lot of people, Will Marshall wondered if a smartphone would work in outer space. Unlike most people, Marshall was in a position to find out, since he was an actual rocket scientist.

From the time he started working at NASA, in 2006, Marshall got invaluable training and experience in the discipline of systems engineering, which is concerned with creating not just a single product but rather an interdependent set of components. Systems engineering is inherently complex, and it requires a lot of planning before components are built, integrated, and tested. As Marshall explained to me,

> NASA teaches you to undertake complicated systems-level challenges. In software, you can take an approach of "Let's just put something out there and see if it works." But you can't put up a satellite and then go "Oh shit, we haven't built the software yet," or "Actually that radio doesn't work with that solar panel. Let's take it down and fix it." Well, you can't, because it's in space.

Over time, though, Marshall grew frustrated at how long it took NASA to complete projects, especially lower-risk ones where there were no lives at stake. He also saw how much up-front planning took place before anything got tested or built. He came to believe that it would be possible to get better results by moving faster and learning by doing, even in the inherently complicated domains of systems engineering and space exploration. By taking a different approach, one centered around fast cycles of iteration and experimentation and a different risk model (of redundancy and low cost rather than removing all failure modes), he thought that it would be possible to land a craft on the moon for less than $100 million. Few of his colleagues or superiors agreed. Marshall recalled, "We were told in no uncertain terms that you cannot do it for under $1 billion, so go away."

But he didn't. Instead, he and his colleagues got permission (and protection) from director Pete Worden at the agency to try their approach. In a small building christened Area 51 at NASA's Ames Research Center in Northern California, they built and tested descent and landing systems for a lunar vehicle. They used off-the-shelf components instead of "space-grade" ones and got a prototype system working for about $300,000. As Marshall tells it,

> We brought the NASA brass round and they were like, "Oh shit, you've done the hardest bit." And they said, "We still don't believe

you, but here's $80 million, have a go." ... We sent it to the moon and we succeeded in doing that mission for $79 million. And that was about an order of magnitude lower cost [than the status quo], and the lowest-cost lunar mission that NASA had ever sent.

That mission, LCROSS, won a Breakthrough Award from *Popular Mechanics*, in part because its spacecraft "was outfitted with commercial off-the-shelf instruments, ... saving the team time and the costly development of custom instruments." It also found water on the Moon — a significant scientific discovery.

Marshall and his colleagues then decided to launch some smartphones into space and see if the devices could send pictures back to Earth. After all, they reasoned, modern phones had everything they needed to take and transmit photos. Pete Klupar, a director at NASA Ames under Worden and a mentor of Marshall's, often held up a smartphone saying, "Why are we making spacecraft so expensive? This has most of what we need." As Marshall put it, "If you look at what a communications satellite has and what a smartphone has, it's 90 percent overlapping." So, after nearly being denied permission to do so and nearly getting himself fired, Marshall and his team sent some phones into space and had them take some photos, which, as he told me,

> we got down with the help of amateur radio enthusiasts who got packets of the data from the phone's radio. Then they emailed us those packets and we stitched them into an image that was taken from space with a smartphone. And we were like, well, that phone cost $500. Most NASA spacecraft cost $500 million. *What are those extra six zeros doing for us?*

The idea that it was possible to knock some zeroes off the cost of building useful satellites led Marshall to found Planet Labs with fellow former NASA scientists Chris Boshuizen and Robbie Schingler, in late 2010. Planet now scans the Earth every day with a network of more than two hundred satellites of its own design and sells the data and imagery it collects to governments and industry. Marshall estimates that Planet has something like a thousandfold cost advantage over other providers of space imagery.

This advantage comes from three main sources. The first two are Planet's willingness to use cheap, commercially available components, and its tolerance for failure. As Marshall told me, "We've said we'll take the latest tech from things like smartphones, stuff them into our satellite, and fly a few more than we need. And if only 80 or 90 percent of them work, we'll be great with that." The third is Planet's preference for working fast, iterating quickly, and learning from each cycle. Marshall says that "on average, every three months for the last five years we've had a new rocket that goes up and launches about twenty of our satellites. Each launch also includes the next-generation tech that we're testing — the next radio or camera or whatever. And then if that tech works, the next whole fleet of satellites will include it. So we have an iteration time scale that's measured in months while NASA's is measured in a decade or two."

Marshall summarized to me the differences between Planet and his previous employer: "At NASA I was part of five spacecraft missions in six years. And that was considered prolific; most people do one or two in their NASA career. Subsequently, in the ten years of Planet, we've launched five hundred spacecraft on thirty-five rockets, with eighteen design/build iterations of the spacecraft concept. It's a different pace of innovation."

The Hardest Button to Push

Ardine Williams didn't know how to get her work done. After being at Amazon for almost three months she'd made good progress on a project but couldn't figure out how to complete it.

Williams was part of a small team working to bring Amazon into compliance with federal hiring regulations. She thought she had a solution and wanted to get it implemented, but she couldn't figure out how to take the final step: making a change on the Amazon.jobs website. The problem was that she hadn't learned yet who was responsible for these kinds of changes. In fact, it was starting to feel to her like *no one* was.

Williams came out of retirement to join Amazon. She had worked in a variety of roles at Hewlett-Packard and Intel, where she had ended her career (she thought) as a vice president in charge of human resource services like staffing, payroll, and benefits delivery. Then, as she tells it, she got a call from a corporate recruiter in the fall of 2014.

> I'm sitting on the patio, drinking a martini, looking at the mountains. I said to the headhunter, "I'm happy to talk to you, but I'm not going back to work." And she said, "Before you say no to me, let me tell you about the opportunity; it's with Amazon." I was like, "Amazon, okay. I order books." And she said, "It's not that part of Amazon. It's Amazon Web Services."
>
> And I sat down my glass because I knew that cloud computing was changing business. It was reducing the up-front investment needed to build a technology infrastructure and allowing companies to instead put money into things that mattered to customers. I thought, "Hey, you know what? This could be fun."

Amazon Web Services (AWS) employed only a few thousand people when the recruiter reached out to Williams, but its sales were growing at about 40 percent per year. It was clear that cloud computing had a chance to be a big part of Amazon's future, and that to realize its potential AWS needed executives who knew how to help an organization find and retain the right people. Williams joined Amazon in the fall of 2014 as a vice president focused on staffing for AWS.

She quickly learned that Amazon didn't operate like the other big tech firms she was familiar with. For one thing, the technology to support back-office functions like staffing wasn't as mature. As she recalls,

> I got in there and I was like, how the hell does this place run? I was responsible for a monthly report on our progress in hiring all the people we needed at AWS. And it would take me like three days to do that in four different systems and a whiteboard with yellow

stickies on it. So the infrastructure just wasn't there. But what they did have was a boatload of smart people. I was really fortunate—I inherited people who understood how Amazon worked, so we were able to do some pretty cool things.

Then one day Williams got something that was very much *not* cool: a phone call from a lawyer. It was one of Amazon's own lawyers, calling about a potential problem. As Williams recalls:

Amazon had recently secured a number of federal government con-tracts for data centers and other support. And once you become a federal contractor, you have to comply with a statute which basically says that if I'm interviewing you for a job and you work for the gov-ernment or have worked for the government, I have to ask you, "Have you spoken with your ethics officer? Does your ethics officer know that you are interviewing and has she or he approved your pursuing this process?" Our problem was that we weren't asking that question to people who applied via the Amazon.jobs website.

After talking about it for a while, the attorney said, "Hey, could we self-certify? What if we showed language to *all* applicants saying, 'If you are a current or former government employee, you acknowledge by your application that you have spoken with your ethics officer'?" And we agreed that yeah, we can probably do that. So he crafted the language. I went to a web developer who did the programming work to include that language on the site. He got it done.

Then this quick project got bogged down because, as Williams tells it,

I started looking for who had to approve it. This was in my first ninety days at the company, and I felt like I'd landed on Mars. It felt sort of like a free-for-all. I couldn't understand how you could run like a startup with more than a hundred thousand employees, but it really had that vibe. I couldn't see much formal process or structure for things like dealing with compliance issues or making changes to the website.

Williams asked for advice from a senior colleague who had been at Amazon a long time:

> I said, "I can't find out who can approve this." He said, "What are you talking about?" And I said, "I'm getting ready to change the Amazon.jobs website. There's gotta be some kind of management review committee. Somebody has to look at this." He said, "Somebody already did—*you*. You're telling me that we've got legal approval. We also have business approval; that's you. So why don't you push the button and make the change?"
>
> And I honestly couldn't answer the question. I just couldn't answer the question. So he asked me, "What happens if this change you're proposing is a mess?" And I said, "Well, we turn it off." He said, "How long will that take?" And I said, "Less than twenty-four hours." He said, "I'm back to where I started, Ardine. Push the button. Bringing more people along with you in the decision is *not* going to change the outcome."
>
> And I've got to tell you, calling the developer and saying, "Okay, push the button," was probably one of the hardest things I've done in my career personally, because it was just so contrary to how I had grown up.

Like most knowledge workers, Williams had grown up professionally in environments full of established ways of doing things. A change as important as a modification to the website in order to comply with federal regulation would go before a management review committee. There would be a process for proposing changes, submitting required documentation and justifications, and so on. This committee would be staffed by people from many parts of the company, including human resources, information systems, communications, and the legal department. There might well be a subcommittee that determined which changes were significant enough to go before the full committee. When the full committee met, it would approve some changes, deny some, and request additional information before making final decisions on others. When I asked Williams how long it would have taken one of her previous employers to make the website change she proposed, she answered, "About three months."

But at Amazon, when projects were done people just pushed buttons.

Making HiPPOs an Endangered Species

By the spring of 2009 Google's visual design head, Doug Bowman, had had enough and quit his job. He liked his "incredibly smart and talented" colleagues, learned a great deal, and would miss the "free food,...occasional massage, [and] the authors, politicians, and celebrities that come to speak or perform." But what he didn't like and wouldn't miss was having to justify all of his decisions with data.

Rather than accepting the judgments of experienced design professionals like Bowman, Google instead followed a process he described in mechanical terms: "Reduce each decision to a simple logic problem. Remove all subjectivity and just look at the data. Data in your favor? OK, launch it. Data shows negative effects? Back to the drawing board."

Like many others in his field, Bowman thought that this approach was fundamentally misguided. Coming up with a good design for a web page or anything else was in his view an inherently subjective and creative process — one that relied much more on the arts than on science. As the legendary designer Paul Rand put it, "The roots of good design lie in aesthetics: painting, drawing, and architecture, while those of business and market research are in demographics and statistics; aesthetics and business are traditionally incompatible disciplines." Bowman gave a couple examples of how statistics intruded on aesthetics at Google: "A team...couldn't decide between two blues, so they're testing forty-one shades between each blue to see which one performs better. I had a recent debate over whether a border should be three, four, or five pixels wide, and was asked to prove my case. I can't operate in an environment like that."

That environment was born on February 27, 2000, when a team at Google showed one version of a search results page to a randomly chosen group of visitors to the site, and a different version to a parallel group. This was the first known A/B test in the history of the World Wide Web. There have been countless millions since.

As the twenty-first century progressed, a culture of testing and following the data came to permeate decision-making at Google, even for decisions in allegedly subjective areas like design. Hal Varian, the company's chief economist, stressed that "we don't want high-level executives discussing whether a blue background or a yellow background will lead to more ad clicks…Why debate this point, since we can simply run an experiment to find out?" In 2014, Google estimated that getting the shade of blue right via the kind of testing that Bowman disparaged had led to an additional $200 million per year in ad revenue.

A/B testing developed passionate advocates because it showed that experts' intuition about users' preferences were often inaccurate, and sometimes just plain wrong. Experiments revealed that even experienced design professionals didn't know how people actually wanted websites to look or feel. Supporters of heavy testing came up with a dismissive acronym for relying on such people: it was decision-making by HiPPO, or "highest-paid person's opinion." As Avinash Kaushik, a digital marketing evangelist for Google and one of the creators of the acronym, succinctly put it, "Most websites suck because HiPPOs create them."

Google still employs professional designers—thousands of them. But instead of taking their judgments about what users want as the final word on the topic, the company instead tests their judgments before rolling them out widely. Google trusts that its designers have good intuition and deep expertise. That trust, however, isn't the end of the company's design process. As its heavy reliance on A/B testing and other types of experimentation shows, Google follows the advice of the old Russian proverb *Doveryai, no proveryai:* Trust, but verify.

A CEO, a Professor, and a New Hire Walk into a Meeting

In the summer of 2006 Brian Halligan sat down in my office at Harvard Business School and started asking me questions about an article I'd recently published. He had just finished the MIT Sloan Fellows program, a twelve-month MBA, and was about to launch a company with classmate Dharmesh Shah. The article that had caught his eye was about using tools like blogs and wikis (the software that's at the heart of Wikipedia) within companies, and he wanted to explore the topic more deeply. In our initial conversation, we learned that we were both excited about technology's potential for making businesses work better, and that we were both Boston Red Sox fans. We formed a geeky bond, and stayed in touch.

By 2009, HubSpot, the marketing software company he and Shah founded, was growing quickly. Halligan was the CEO, and he came back to my office to talk about putting together in-house education programs for his employees. He wanted to give HubSpotters the chance to pick up new skills via evening classes. This isn't unusual; most companies offer training. But Halligan went about it in a novel way.

I'd been teaching in business schools for a decade and had been part of many executive education programs. Company-specific programs typically occur because a top manager wants to, say, prepare her division for the Internet economy and so reaches out to a business school. The manager and the school settle on a curriculum, and the program becomes reality.

Halligan took a different approach. After he and I brainstormed for a bit, he said, "Okay, come into the office; let's present this idea to the Hub-Spotters and see what they think." So we did. I found it one of the more eye-opening meetings of my career because of how Halligan interacted with his employees.

After he introduced me to the assembled group of about twenty people, I talked about the curriculum we'd been brainstorming. Then he talked about the skills he wanted HubSpotters to have. He finished with "So what do you think?" and sat down. In my experience, this was a cue for employees to tell their CEO that what they'd just heard from him was great, really the right idea at the right time, and they only had a couple suggestions—building on what they'd just heard—to make it even better.

Instead, the first person to speak, who looked too young to have been anything except a recent hire, opened with "There are a couple things that I don't like" and continued on. I felt a little bit sorry for the kid. Flatly contradicting your CEO in public might not be a career-ender, but it would at least serve as a teachable moment for him and the rest of the people in the room. Of course, Halligan wouldn't respond with anything as obvious as "Watch yourself, youngster," but would he take the usual approach of making a self-deprecating comment that everyone in the room would implicitly interpret as a warning? Would the other attendees rush in with "What I think you mean to say...," or "I hear a lot of agreement here!," or any of the other standard lines intended to restore all-important harmony?

What actually happened was that Halligan said, "Yeah—good point. I hadn't thought of that," and continued from there. His body language didn't change, the tension in the room didn't rise, and no one except me looked the least bit surprised. When he and I met afterward to discuss what we'd heard, he didn't mention the incident at all. To him, it was business as usual. He didn't want the group to rubber-stamp his ideas or celebrate his munificence; he wanted an honest and egalitarian exchange of views on a topic. Which was what he got.

Halligan's and Shah's efforts to build a strong culture at HubSpot paid off over the years. In 2014, the workplace review site Glassdoor started publishing a list of the top small and medium-sized companies to work for in America, based on what the companies' own employees said about them. HubSpot was number 12 on the list. Two years later, the company had grown so much that it moved into Glassdoor's large-company list, where it took the number 4 spot. In 2020, Glassdoor named HubSpot the best large company to work for in America.

The Norms Geeks Form

As these four examples show, the geek way is not about a suite of technologies (like machine learning or robotics) or a style of strategic thinking.

Instead, it's about *norms:* behaviors that a group's members expect of each other. Norms are extraordinarily important for any organization because they're a kind of community policing: if you don't follow them, your peers will let you know it and work to bring you back in line. Norms aren't maintained solely by the bosses, and they aren't all written down in the employee handbook. But even though they can seem nebulous, they're powerful; they shape people's behavior in deep ways.

We'll see plenty of examples of norms in the pages ahead. Here's a quick one to clarify the concept. In the spring of 1995, Barbara Ley Toffler arrived at the Chicago office of the accounting firm Arthur Andersen for a first job interview. As she put it, "[I] found myself bobbing along in a sea of golf shirts. The Firm didn't have casual dress—ties were de rigueur—but the day had been devoted to a series of workshops, so the dress code had been relaxed. The funny thing about the casual outfit was that everyone wore the exact same thing…This was, I immediately sensed, a place with a distinct culture." Toffler was insightful about two things: that norms are a key part of any organization's culture, and that Andersen had distinct ones. The firm had a strong norm of conformity, which Toffler learned more about after she started working there. This norm was communicated and reinforced to her in all kinds of ways beyond the way "Androids" dressed. In one of her initial training sessions, more-senior colleagues acted out a comedy sketch about "career-limiting moves." The skit was intended to be humorous, but it got its point across. The first of the moves was "overcustomizing your office."

In chapter 7 we'll see how Andersen's stultifying norms contributed to the firm's sad decline and fall. Modern business geeks want something very different: they want norms that contribute to success and vitality. They've settled on four of them.

The first great geek norm, which is epitomized by Will Marshall's journey from NASA to Planet, is *speed:* a preference for achieving results by iterating rapidly instead of planning extensively. Ardine Williams's experience early in her time at Amazon illustrates the second norm, which is *ownership.* Compared to industrial-era organizations, geek companies have higher levels of personal autonomy, empowerment, and responsibility; fewer cross-functional processes; and less coordination.

Doug Bowman left Google because that company decided to make design decisions based not on judgment or expertise, but instead on the norm of *science:* conducting experiments, generating data, and debating how to interpret evidence. In the interaction I witnessed with his employees, Brian Halligan demonstrated the fourth and final great geek norm, which is *openness.* Halligan convened an open discussion of his proposal, was open to being challenged by a subordinate, and (most critically, I think) was open to the idea that he might not be right and might need to change his mind.

The geek way, then, is about speed, ownership, science, and openness. So is this book. As the previous stories show, the geek way can be followed in many circumstances: in industries as diverse as space exploration, cloud computing, software, and advertising, and in departments ranging from research and development to human resources to design. The stories also show that the geek way isn't just practiced by computer scientists and other STEM professionals. Instead, it permeates companies and extends from founder CEOs to managers to individual contributors.

Now that we have an idea of what the four great geek norms are, let's take a look at how all four are practiced within a single company, and the roles that leaders play in shaping and maintaining them. Let's also look at another company in the same industry that went about things in a decidedly nongeek way. Here are the stories of two startups that wanted to shake up the entertainment industry. One of them seemed ideally positioned to succeed. The other didn't look like it stood a chance.

A New Venture Quickly Bites the Dust

As 2020 drew near, if you had to place a bet on someone to understand, shape, and profit from the future of filmed entertainment, you might well have picked Jeffrey Katzenberg. After all, that's what he'd been doing throughout his entire career. Although he wasn't as well known to the public as the most famous actors and directors, Katzenberg was a Hollywood legend—someone who had demonstrated uncanny instincts, decade after decade, about how people wanted to be entertained and how the entertainment business was changing.

His entire professional life was spent developing those instincts. Before he was twenty-five he was working for Barry Diller, who was then the chairman of Paramount Pictures. Before Katzenberg was thirty, Diller added him to a team charged with somehow reviving *Star Trek*, a TV series with a cult following that had gone off the air almost a decade earlier, in 1969. Katzenberg flew across the country to convince Leonard Nimoy, the last holdout from the cast of the original show, to join *Star Trek: The Motion Picture*, which was a huge success when it was released in 1979. From that point on, the *Star Trek* franchise kept boldly going where no one had gone before. So did Katzenberg's career.

In 1984, he moved to the Walt Disney Company and was put in charge of its motion picture unit, which at the time had the lowest box-office receipts of any major studio. Within three years, it had climbed to number 1, thanks to hits like *Three Men and a Baby, Down and Out in Beverly Hills,* and *Good Morning, Vietnam.* Katzenberg was also responsible for the long-running TV shows *Golden Girls* and *Home Improvement.* But his biggest successes at Disney were the animated films he oversaw: *Who Framed Roger Rabbit, The Little Mermaid, Aladdin, The Lion King,* and *Beauty and the Beast*—the first animated film to be nominated for the Oscar for Best Picture. Katzenberg's successes spanned multiple genres, from science fiction to comedy to drama to animation, and they touched audiences of all kinds.

Hollywood respects making good deals at least as much as making good entertainment, and here too Katzenberg excelled. He was instrumental in Disney's acquisition of Miramax Studios, and in establishing Disney's partnership with Pixar. In 1994, he decided it was time for a partnership of his own. Along with Steven Spielberg and David Geffen, he launched the studio Dreamworks SKG. Ten years later, he spun off Dreamworks Animation as a separate company. In 2016, it was acquired by NBCUniversal (part of Comcast) for $3.8 billion.

Katzenberg was the consummate industry insider: a brilliant hit-maker, dealmaker, career-maker for many creative professionals, and, of course, moneymaker. He knew how showbiz worked, and he knew all of the major players. He was also a workaholic and endlessly ambitious. So, in 2018, when he announced his new venture to create streaming videos—the entertainment industry's potent new fusion of content and distribution—it seemed like he couldn't miss.

It also appeared likely that once again he'd seen more clearly than others the future of entertainment. It wasn't sitting in front of the TV in your living room at night, watching shows and movies that were anywhere from thirty minutes to more than two hours long. Instead, it was catching quick bites of compelling streamed content on your phone's screen throughout the day while you were on the go or taking a break.

This idea of quick bites led to the company Quibi, which Katzenberg unveiled in October of 2018. It was an extremely well-capitalized startup, with $1.75 billion in funding from investors including Disney, 20th Century Fox, and many other studios; Goldman Sachs; JPMorgan Chase; and China's Alibaba Group. Katzenberg had also inked production deals with such Hollywood A-listers as actors Idris Elba, Anna Kendrik, and Liam Helmsworth; directors Guillermo del Toro and Ridley Scott; and the Kardashians. And Quibi had a CEO as well known in high tech as Katzenberg was in entertainment. He had persuaded Meg Whitman to partner up with him after she retired from Hewlett-Packard, which she had led for seven years. Prior to that, she had been eBay's CEO for almost a decade.

The Quibi app and streaming service launched on April 6, 2020. From the start, people inside the company and out kept a close eye on how many times the app was downloaded. The initial numbers looked good: number 3 in the Apple app store on day one, and 1.7 million downloads in the first week.

But enthusiasm tapered off quickly. Initial reviews of the shows Katzenberg had approved and nurtured were scathing. For example, the pop culture website *Vulture* titled an April 2020 judgment of the service's offerings "Yep, Quibi Is Bad." Author Kathryn VanArendonk rendered a verdict that would dismay anyone trying to sell subscriptions based on a promise of must-see entertainment: "But its badness doesn't explain why everything I watched was also incomprehensibly unmemorable."

Quibi fell out of the top 50 list of free iPhone app downloads a week after its launch, and was sitting at number 125 on May 11. In a *New York Times* interview published that day Katzenberg said, "I attribute everything that has gone wrong to coronavirus. Everything." Others weren't so sure. They pointed out that smartphone use had soared during the pandemic, as had the popularity of TikTok, YouTube, and other apps that featured short videos. TikTok, for example, saw its monthly active users climb from 40 million in late 2019 to more than 100 million by August of 2020.

Observers also pointed out the Quibi app had some puzzling shortcomings. For one thing, it didn't let users share snippets of content they particularly liked on Facebook, Instagram, and other popular social networks. In many cases, in fact, the contracts Quibi had signed with content creators explicitly forbade this kind of sharing, even though by 2020 it was important viral marketing for many shows. Subscribers also couldn't watch on any device except their phone; at home, they couldn't switch over to their TVs.

To try to mount a comeback in the face of disappointing growth, Quibi changed its app to allow casting to TVs and sharing of screenshots. To conserve cash, it also slashed budgets for marketing and content creation. Whitman took a 10 percent pay cut in late spring, and encouraged other executives to follow suit. But nothing seemed to get more people to download the app or use the service. By June of 2020, the service was projected to have 2 million subscribers after its first year, which was well below the company's target of 7.4 million.

The summer months brought no improvement and by September the *Wall Street Journal* reported that Quibi was "exploring several strategic options including a possible sale." The option it chose was to cease operations altogether. On October 21, Katzenberg and Whitman confirmed that the

Quibi experiment was ending. The company had raised nearly $2 billion, yet announced its shutdown fewer than two hundred days after its launch.*

The Autopsy of an Attacking Ewok

Quibi's surprisingly rapid decline and demise was a juicy story, and entertainment industry journalists pounced. As I read the many accounts of what happened, one thought kept occurring to me: *This is not at all a geek company.*

Quibi positioned itself as an Internet-era startup, but it was structured and run like a twentieth-century Hollywood studio. The company was led by an experienced industry insider who made all the most important decisions. At Quibi there were two of these leaders: Katzenberg, who made decisions about content and user experience, and Whitman, who oversaw marketing the service.

Companies that are set up that way rise or fall based on how good their leaders' judgments and intuitions are. At Quibi, they were often bad. This is easiest to see in Katzenberg's case. He seemed out of touch and out of date in the new environment he was trying to dominate, and made decisions that had observers scratching their heads and paying customers staying away in droves. Yet he very rarely showed any openness to changing course or changing his mind.

Most of the accounts and analyses I've read of Quibi's short life stress how confident Katzenberg was in his judgments about how to make the platform successful, and how he wasn't open to listening to others. A postmortem in the *Wall Street Journal* reported that from the start, Quibi advisors and executives recommended that subscribers should have the ability to watch shows on their TVs and share snippets with their social networks. It's

---

* After announcing its shutdown, the company returned most remaining cash—about $350 million—to investors. On December 1, the Quibi app stopped streaming content. The company retained rights to distribute more than seventy-five shows; these rights were sold to the streaming company Roku in January of 2021 for "significantly less" than $100 million.

a safe bet that Katzenberg was responsible for refusing to include these features. When asked about streaming to TVs, he said in an interview, "Nobody has made [premium] content that was native to, and only for, the phone. We want to do one thing which no one else is doing and see if we can do it really great." The original Quibi app went so far as to disable smartphones' standard ability to cast content to nearby TVs. A Quibi spokesperson declined to comment on the record about the genesis of this odd feature, but it fit in with Katzenberg's insistence that Quibi was for phones, full stop.

Katzenberg's lack of openness to other ideas, or to the notion that he might be wrong, was spoken of by others with something like awe. One creator who went to the company's lavish headquarters to propose a show said, "I can honestly say I've never been in such a cocky pitch environment." A producer who worked with Quibi said that Katzenberg's certainty was core to the "Quibi story: 'Everyone else is fucking wrong; I'm just going to do it.'" A former employee remembers that "there was an incredible lack of knowledge of the audience and dismissiveness of the audience. A thing Jeffrey always says is, 'I'm not a child or mother, but I made movies children and mothers loved. I know millennials better than millennials.'"

The geek norm of science, based on producing and evaluating evidence, seemed alien to Katzenberg. Whitman observed in an interview that his ideas didn't need to be supported by a lot of evidence: "I say, 'Where's your data?' He says, 'There is none. You just have to go with your gut.'" In another interview, an unnamed "high-level Quibi colleague who is actually several years younger than Katzenberg" commented further on his evidence-free confidence. As this person put it, "I don't pretend to know what kids are going to like anymore. But Jeffrey is, like many entrepreneurs, a true believer in [his] own underlying ideas." (Whitman is several years younger than Katzenberg.)

The only case I've been able to find where Katzenberg was convinced *not* to go with his gut on an important decision had to do with naming the company. It's perhaps a sign that he had lost touch with mainstream American taste that his preferred name for the startup was Omakase, the term for a tasting menu at a sushi restaurant. Whitman talked him out of that name, but the one they settled on didn't strike everyone as a winner. An unnamed insider opined that "Quibi" sounded like a "quinoa-based doggy snack" or "the cry of an attacking Ewok."

What about speed? In some ways, Quibi was very fast. Starting from scratch, it built up a large library of new content and a complete technology infrastructure in a year and a half. But this is not the kind of speed that matters to business geeks. In the geek way, speed doesn't mean velocity; it instead means the cadence at which a company can iterate. Speed refers to how quickly a team can build something, get it in front of a customer or otherwise test it in real-world conditions, get feedback, and fold that feedback into the next version. As we saw earlier in this chapter, one of Planet's advantages over incumbents like NASA is its ability to iterate with a cycle time of months instead of years.

By this definition of speed, Quibi was running in place. It didn't widely release alpha or beta versions of its app to get users' feedback before launch. Instead, the company raced to execute Katzenberg's vision of a streaming service that didn't let members watch content on their TVs or share snippets on social media. Quibi didn't iterate to determine if this was a vision that would succeed in the marketplace; it just charged ahead with it. Katzenberg mentioned a beta *after* Quibi had publicly launched, when he said in June of 2020 that the service's anemic start had "actually given us the opportunity to have almost a beta…We have actually now seen so many aspects of the content, about what is working for them, what is most appealing to them, where our weaknesses are. All of that is being retooled as we talk here right now." Followers of the geek way would wonder why that retooling started so late.

Technology analyst Benedict Evans summarized the geek's view of Quibi's approach to iteration and feedback with a tweet on April 6, 2020, the day the service launched:

> General [Silicon Valley] view of Quibi in the last 12 months:
> - that's a vast amount of money to raise and spend before contact with the customer tells you what works
> - this is an entertainment company, not a tech company
> - skepticism, but who knows?

Evans's skepticism proved to be well-founded, in part because Quibi didn't embrace the geek norm of speed.

The last of the four great geek norms is ownership, or giving people throughout the organization authority to take action and responsibility for results. Ownership is closely related to autonomy, empowerment, and devolution. None of these come naturally to micromanagers, and Katzenberg was a famous micromanager. At Quibi, he was deeply involved with many of the venture's shows, providing notes on "everything from casting to wardrobe to graphic design." However, his points of comparison were programs such as *America's Funniest Home Videos* (which debuted in 1989), the movie reviewers Siskel and Ebert (1982), and Jane Fonda's workout videos (1982). This heavy reliance on decades-old examples at a time when the landscape of entertainment was rapidly expanding felt out of touch to younger content creators. One of them dismissed Quibi as: "Take the worst parts of Hollywood, bake it into a phone, and that's what you got." Whitman's expensive marketing plan also seemed outdated: though the service was aimed primarily at younger people, Quibi placed a TV spot during the Oscars, where the average viewer is more than fifty-five years old.

Let's give the final word about ownership at Quibi, and about the overall experience of working at the company, to "a person with firsthand knowledge" (most likely an employee). This person gave a brilliant summary of what it feels like to be part of a culture where the geek norms are absent, and where the leaders are entirely sure of themselves, don't listen to others, and don't devolve authority and responsibility: "Unless you agree with [Katzenberg and Whitman], you're a troublemaker. Meg believes she's a marketing genius; Jeffrey believes he's a content genius. So you end up in shitty jobs where you're there to execute their vision, which no one else there believes in." Because that vision was so far from anything customers actually wanted, those jobs didn't last long.

Now let's look at an entertainment industry startup that *did* follow the geek way, and actually helped popularize it.

Hollywood Ending

As the year 2000 drew near, if you had to place a bet on someone to under-stand, shape, and profit from the future of filmed entertainment, you prob-ably wouldn't have picked Reed Hastings. He had no experience whatsoever in the sector, and nothing in his career up to that point suggested that he had any interest in becoming part of Hollywood, let alone transforming it. Instead, he appeared to be a classic example of a successful computer geek.

Hastings was a math major who taught in Swaziland as a Peace Corps volunteer, then earned a master's degree in computer science from Stanford in 1988. After working as a software debugger for a couple years, he launched Pure Software, which built debugging tools. Pure went public in 1995, merged with Atria Software in 1996, and was acquired by Rational Software in 1997. At that time, Hastings hadn't distinguished himself as a great builder of companies. By his own estimation he did a "mediocre job" at Pure, leading it into becoming bureaucratic and slow-moving. The market agreed that it was an underwhelming business; when the acquisition by Rational was announced, both companies' stock prices fell by about 40 percent.

Hollywood first appeared on Hastings's professional radar when he was in his late thirties because of an insight about technological change and... postage rates. The tech change was the advent in the late 1990s of not only e-commerce websites but also digital video discs (DVDs), which were much smaller, slimmer, and lighter than the videocassettes they replaced. This meant that the discs could be mailed around America as (cheap) first-class letters instead of (expensive) packages. To test how well this would work, Hastings and his colleague Marc Randolph mailed DVDs to their own houses. When the discs arrived unbroken, unscratched, and perfectly watch-able, the pair concluded that they had a business opportunity. They launched Netflix in 1997 as an online DVD rental-by-mail company.

Netflix grew rapidly and went public in 2002. In the following years, the company prepared for another technological shift: not just renting mov-ies over the Internet, but also watching them that way. Hastings saw that this would become feasible as more households got a fast Internet connection, and he wanted his company to lead the charge toward delivering entertainment online and on demand. Streaming on Netflix started in 2007 with a thousand movies that could be watched via Internet Explorer on PCs. As we all know, it's expanded a lot since then. By 2019, Netflix streaming accounted for more than 12.5 percent of all the downstream Internet traffic in the world, and more than 20 percent of the world's online video traffic.

The company's most recent shift, and its most consequential one, has been to not just stream other studios' content, but to also produce its own shows and movies. The Hollywood establishment did not initially find any cause for concern. As Time Warner CEO Jeff Bewkes put it in 2010, when discussing Netflix's likely impact on the entertainment industry, "It's a little bit like, is the Albanian army going to take over the world? I don't think so." Hastings got a set of Albanian army dog tags to wear around his neck for motivation and got to work to try to beat the studios at their own game.

In 2013, Netflix debuted its first original content, the hit series *House of Cards*. Since then, the company has become the entertainment industry's most successful producer of filmed content for home viewing. By 2019, Netflix was second only to HBO in both Emmy nominations and wins. In 2020, Netflix took the lead in nominations, but still finished second in wins. In 2021, it was number 1 in both. That year, it tied a nearly fifty-year-old record for the most wins by a single platform. It now produces hundreds of shows and movies around the world, in languages from Arabic to Yiddish, and many foreign productions have captivated American audiences. This is a particularly impressive accomplishment, given how hard it has been to overcome "the one-inch-tall barrier of subtitles" (as Korean director Bong Joon Ho put it) and get Americans to watch entertainment in other languages. But Netflix showed that this barrier was not insurmountable. The Korean dystopian drama *Squid Game* became the platform's most popular show in America (and almost a hundred other countries) after it debuted in September 2021.

How much has Netflix upended the industry? In August 2020, the *New*

York Times published an article by media columnist Ben Smith about the streaming revolution pioneered by Hastings and his company. "The Week Old Hollywood Finally, Actually Died" was an in-the-moment case study of what former Quibi executive Janice Min described as "the brutal final scenes of Hollywood as people here knew it, as streaming investment and infrastructure take precedence. Politesse and production deal kiss-offs for those at the top, and, more importantly, the financial fire hose to float a bureaucracy, seem to be disappearing. It's like a club...running out of dues to feed all its members."

That club had been particularly hospitable to its most senior members. Studio heads like Katzenberg were typically given great power and deference, and lavish perks that often lasted longer than their jobs. As Smith put it, "For decades, the best thing about being a Hollywood executive, really, was how you got fired. Studio executives would be gradually, gently, even lovingly nudged aside, given months to shape their own narratives and find new work, or even promoted." The *Times* article was prompted by an unmistakable sign that times had changed: the mass firing, done with little advance warning and sometimes by video call, of hundreds of executives—including the chairman of the entertainment division—at one of America's oldest and most storied studios.

It's a bit of real-world poetic justice that this studio was WarnerMedia, whose CEO, Jeff Bewkes, had said a decade earlier that having Netflix disrupt Hollywood would be like having the Albanian army take over the world. Yet that disruption did in fact happen. Barry Diller, who had helped launch Katzenberg's career decades earlier, used a sports metaphor instead of a military one to describe its impact. The changes spearheaded by Netflix, he said, made most of the entertainment industry's former leaders "caddies on a golf course they'll never play."*

---

* WarnerMedia continued to have tough times after the layoffs. In 2022, its parent company, AT&T, combined it with Discovery, another of its entertainment holdings, and spun them out into a separate company. The *New York Times* estimated that the spin-off represented a $47 billion loss for the shareholders of AT&T, which owned WarnerMedia for about four years.

Recently, however, Netflix has encountered a run of bad business results and souring investor sentiment. After soaring during the pandemic, the company's share price began a steep descent in late 2021. From a high of nearly $700 in late October, it shrank by about 75 percent over the course of six months. Other entertainment companies also saw their share prices suffer as competition in streaming intensified (Disney, for example, saw its share price decline by over 45 percent), but Netflix was particularly hard hit as it lost subscribers for the first time in a decade and faced criticism for spending too much on content and not producing enough hits.

As I write in early 2023, the company faces real headwinds, yet it's also still a strong business and a tough rival. It has a dominant market share in the US, is expanding rapidly around the world, and has a solid balance sheet and many of the most sought-after shows globally. Even at its lowest share price, the company was valued at around $85 billion. Shonda Rhimes, the creator of several hit shows for Netflix and others, summarized its prospects in May of 2022: "I live in this space and I wouldn't bet against Netflix."

Excellent Results, SOSO Culture

As Netflix continued to grow and upend the entertainment industry it became one of the companies most widely studied and admired by organization geeks. The culture deck and Hastings's 2020 book, *No Rules Rules,* which he wrote with management scholar Erin Meyer, make clear that Netflix practices all four of the great geek norms: science, openness, speed, and ownership. Of these, the company's heavy use of science has received the most attention. Within the entertainment industry, Netflix pioneered the use of data and algorithms for making decisions: first about buying DVDs, and then about developing original programming. Ted Sarandos, Netflix's chief of content since 2000 and co-CEO since 2020, estimated in 2015 that programming decisions at the company were "probably a seventy-thirty mix...Seventy is the data, and thirty is judgment. But the thirty needs to be on top, if that makes sense." In other words, the company leads with the data, but always interprets and asks questions about it. As we'll see in chapter 4, this interplay between cold, hard evidence and warm-blooded human beings is the heart of the scientific method.

Speed—the geek habit of iterating rapidly to get feedback and incorporate it—has also long been standard practice at Netflix. As early as 2006, the company was rolling out a new version of its website every two weeks. As designer Joshua Porter put it after a visit that year, "The designers of Netflix .com have a smashing success on their hands, but we didn't find them resting on their laurels. They want to get even better, and for them that means iterate, iterate, iterate."

Science and speed are both important elements of Netflix's culture, but what most clearly marks it as a geek company is its fidelity to the other two great geek norms: openness and ownership. Hastings and his colleagues spent years working to put them in place, and refused to give up on them even when they proved elusive.

Hastings had long believed that openness was essential for making good decisions. The culture deck, for example, addresses an ideal colleague and says "You say what you think even if it's controversial" and "You are known for candor and directness." Such colleagues, however, were in short supply just a couple years after the culture deck was published. In 2011 Hastings had an idea as bad as any hatched at Quibi. (In an ominous bit of foreshadowing, this idea too started with a *Q.*) Hastings became convinced of the need to split his company into two distinct entities: Netflix, which would handle streaming, and one named Qwikster by Hastings, which would continue the legacy business of mailing out DVDs. The change was announced on July 12.

It was poorly received for several reasons. For one, it meant that subscribers who wanted to keep both services would have to sign into two websites and manage two separate accounts. For another, they'd have to pay about 60 percent more. Online commenters started calling the Netflix CEO "Greed" Hastings. And then there was the name. No one liked it. One columnist opined, "Qwikster sounds like a lot of things—a super cool startup from 1998 that's going to be totally rad and revolutionize the way you 'surf' the 'web'; something a cop in a 1930s talkie picture might call an elusive criminal...but a DVD-by-mail service in 2011 it does not." It turned out that the @Qwikster Twitter handle was already taken. The name associated with the account was Jason Castillo; the associated image was of Elmo smoking a joint.*

In September, Hastings responded to the mounting criticism by having Netflix post an odd, amateurish video that simultaneously defended the change and sort of apologized for it. In a sure sign that things were going off track in a public way, the video was parodied on *Saturday Night Live*. By October, the entire Qwikster plan was dropped. Netflix's stock had dropped by more than 75 percent while it was under consideration and Hastings, who had been *Fortune*'s Businessperson of the Year in 2010, saw his reputation badly tarnished. As one obituary for the service put it, "Qwikster was a dumb idea. Dumb, dumb, dumb. It should certainly be a first ballot entrant into the Bad Decision Hall of Fame, enshrined next to New Coke, Prohibition, and that time Garth Brooks dyed his hair black and played rock music under the name Chris Gaines. Better choices have been made at 24/7 Las Vegas chapels after too many Limoncello shots."

In the wake of all this Hastings wondered why he didn't get more internal opposition to Qwikster before it launched. It was a dumb idea after all (dumb, dumb, dumb), and he had worked to build a culture in which it was okay, even expected, for colleagues to give negative feedback when warranted, even to those higher up on the org chart—when, for example, an executive came up with a dumb idea. So he asked around to find out what had happened. Why had the culture of openness failed, despite what the culture deck said?

He learned that people within the company had hesitated to tell him what they thought about Qwikster because he was so passionate about the idea and so sure of himself. As one of his colleagues told him, "I knew it was

---

* As it became clear that @Qwikster was a valuable piece of online real estate, its owner tweeted out strategy: "Man so much to plan so much deal so much negotiation n I want a plan when I still have part of it n stiL be making bank" (since deleted from Twitter).

going to be a disaster, but I thought, 'Reed is always right,' so I kept quiet."
And in a pattern we see over and over with people, no one spoke up because,
well, no one was speaking up. As one Netflixer recalled, "We thought it was
crazy…But everyone else seemed to be going along with the idea, so we
did too."

After the Qwikster debacle, Hastings realized that all the work done up
to that point to make Netflix a place where open and honest feedback flowed
still wasn't enough. So he reinforced the norm of openness by putting in
place a policy—one of the few formal policies ever instituted at Netflix—
that required executives to "farm for dissent" before launching anything
big. Well before a launch, the responsible executive writes a memo about the
idea and invites a group of colleagues to critique it. In some cases, the executive takes a poll asking people to rate the idea on a scale from 1 (truly terrible) to 10 (truly great). It might not be a coincidence that Netflix hasn't
experienced another Qwikster-level fiasco since farming for dissent became
mandatory.

A milder version of farming for dissent at Netflix is called "socializing"
an idea by presenting it to multiple colleagues and collecting their feedback.
As Hastings writes in *No Rules Rules,* "Socializing is a type of farming for
dissent with less emphasis on the dissent and more on the farming." It's a
practice that caused him to change his mind about investing heavily in kids'
programming. Hastings thought this was not a good use of Netflix's
funds—as he put it, "I was convinced adults choose Netflix because they
love our content. Their kids will just watch whatever we have available"—
but at a senior management meeting in 2016, he decided to socialize the idea
by having an open discussion about it. In a sign of how much things had
changed since the time of Qwikster, he found no shortage of people willing
to disagree with him.

His colleagues told him that Netflix's curated environment made them
feel safer letting their kids browse through it than on YouTube, that their
children were the main Netflix customers in their households, and that these
young consumers were vocal about their preferences. Hastings realized that
his assumptions had been wrong, and the company began to invest heavily

in kids' content. By the time *No Rules Rules* was published, Netflix had won more than a dozen Daytime Emmys for children's programming.

One last example shows how successful Netflix became at fostering candor and disagreement, and at building a culture that embodies the final great geek norm of ownership. In 2015, Hastings was convinced that it would not be a good use of engineering resources to build into the Netflix app the capability to download shows so that they could be watched later. As he wrote in a company-wide document,

> We are focused on streaming, and as the Internet expands (planes, etc.) the consumer desire for downloading will go away. Our competitors will be stuck with supporting a shrinking downloading use case for years. We'll end up far ahead on brand quality sentiment on this issue…The [user experience] complexities of downloading are material for a 1 percent use case, so we are avoiding this approach. It's our judgment call for utility against complexity.

At a lot of companies (including, one gets the strong impression, Quibi), this would have been the end of the discussion. But not at Netflix. Even though Hastings and Neil Hunt, who was at the time the chief product officer, were against downloading, Todd Yellin, the vice president of product (who worked for Hunt), still thought it might be a good idea. He took ownership of investigating the issue and asked senior user experience researcher Zach Schendel to conduct interviews about downloading with users of streaming services in the US, Germany, and India.

It can be uncomfortable for a lower-level employee to take on an assignment that might reveal that their CEO is wrong. As Schendel put it, "I thought, 'Neil and Reed are against this idea. Is it okay to test it out?' At any of my past employers, that would not have been a good move. But the lore at Netflix is all about lower-level employees accomplishing amazing things in the face of hierarchical opposition. With that in mind I went ahead."

The interviews revealed that in all three countries people frequently used the download feature on all streaming services that included it. In fact, the lowest percentage of downloaders Schendel encountered in his interviews wasn't anywhere near Hastings's estimate of 1 percent; instead, it was 15 percent. When Hastings and Hunt saw the results of this research they realized that they had been wrong, and changed course. Netflix now includes a download feature.*

Schendel gave a self-deprecating summary of his experience. "Let me be clear…I'm just some researcher. Yet I was able to push back against a strong and publicly stated opinion from the top leadership to rally excitement for this feature. This is what Netflix is all about." For a quick summary of the benefits of the geek way, compare Schendel's view with that of the anonymous Quibi insider who described "shitty jobs where you're there to execute their vision, which no one else there believes in."

The New Radicals

The geek way is new. It was incubated around the start of the twenty-first century, and as the examples we've seen indicate it really started to come together around 2010. It's still very much a work in progress. The business geeks continue to work through important issues, such as how to balance A/B testing and other scientific approaches with leaps of human creativity. The geek way will never be fully defined and complete, any more than the microchip or theory of evolution will. All of them will be changed and improved as knowledge accumulates.

One thing to point out at the start of our exploration of the geek way is that it's simultaneously rigorous and unstructured. Geek companies are like Google in that they take a rigorous, data-driven approach to many decisions, but also like HubSpot in that they strive for egalitarian, nonhierarchical interactions. In many circumstances, in fact, the geeks are rigorous about being unstructured. Ardine Williams's mentor made clear to her that even though Amazon was a company of more than a hundred thousand people in 2014, it was still a place where leaders were expected to take ownership and

---

* Which I use heavily.

"push the button" instead of coordinating their work, following well-defined processes, and seeking approval. Similarly, even though Planet came out of the slow-moving, fault-intolerant culture of NASA, Will Marshall and his colleagues were adamant that they were *not* going to plan everything out in advance, and were instead going to embrace speed and iteration and accept some failed spacecraft.

Reed Hastings was also adamant. In *No Rules Rules,* he wrote that "at Netflix we have pockets of the company where safety and error prevention are our primary goals and there we fence off an area to build a little symphony orchestra that plays pitch-perfect rules-and-process." But these pockets, Hastings advised, should be the exception, not the rule: "For those of you who are operating…where innovation, speed, and flexibility are the keys to success, consider throwing out the orchestra and focusing instead on making a different kind of music."

In the pages ahead we'll explore why the geek way — this "different kind of music" — works as well as it does: why being rigorous about being unstructured helps the geeks avoid many of the chronic dysfunctions that plague industrial-era companies. There's a wealth of insights from recent research that show why the geek way works so well.

As we'll see over and over, geeks are obsessed about getting to the fundamental nature of things — to the heart of what's going on. Will Marshall and Chris Boshuizen wondered why, to Klupar's provocation, spacecraft cost $500 million when smartphones only cost $500. It seems obvious that we should listen to highly trained and experienced (and paid) experts in domains like website design, but engineers at Google wondered if they could build better sites via extensive testing instead of listening to HiPPOs. Brian Halligan spent much of his time as CEO of HubSpot thinking about what makes a company a great place to work. Reed Hastings spent a lot of time thinking about how he had led Pure Software into sclerosis and decline, and which of his beliefs about running a company he had to walk away from in order to do better at Netflix.

The business geeks questioned many of the basic assumptions that got built up during the industrial era: assumptions about how to build a company, how to make good decisions, how to organize a big project, how people should interact, how information should be shared, and so on. The geeks have concluded that a lot of those assumptions are bad. Sometimes they're bad because they're outdated. Relying on expert judgment, for example, made more sense when digital data was scarce and computers weren't available to run algorithms. But some bad ideas have simply always been bad. Deferring to experts without allowing others to stress-test their ideas is just a lousy idea, regardless of the state of technology.

Modern business geeks are pulling away from the competition because they're doing the radical work of questioning assumptions (including their own) about how to run a company, discarding what doesn't work and replacing it with something better. In short, the geeks are upgrading the company. This upgrade is universally applicable and available. To install it at your own organization you don't need venture capital funding, a workforce full of young computer science PhDs, or a headquarters in Silicon Valley. You just need to be willing to do some things differently. The challenge is that these are fundamental things: organizing major efforts, making decisions, executing and coordinating work, interacting with colleagues, and — maybe most importantly — deciding which behaviors get rewarded and which ones get discouraged.

The companies that have upgraded themselves and embraced the geek way are far from identical, but they do have some striking similarities. They share norms of science, ownership, speed, and openness. As a result, their cultures are more freewheeling, fast-moving, evidence-driven, egalitarian, argumentative, and autonomous than those of the typical industrial-era corporation.

These cultures fuel impressive performance. The successes of Amazon and Google speak for themselves. Planet has huge cost and performance advantages over NASA and other space agencies, and is democratizing access to information about our planet. While Halligan was leading HubSpot from its founding through years of rapid growth and a successful

IPO, the company was repeatedly named one of the best places to work in the country.

These aren't isolated examples. Instead, they're indications that the business geeks' radical mindset has yielded a new and improved way to run a company. It's high time to give geek companies the attention they're due, for a lot of reasons. One is their excellent performance. Another is that they've accomplished something that my community of business academics has been talking about for a long time: creating and sustaining environments that empower people and give them autonomy. "Empowerment" and "autonomy" are two of the most common buzzwords in business writing. But they've been a lot easier to find in articles and books than in actual companies. That's finally changing. As we'll see, employees at geek companies report high levels of both. It's no coincidence that they also report that their organizations excel simultaneously at innovation, execution, and agility. Nor is it a coincidence that these organizations are among the most sought-after and attractive places to work.

In the pages ahead I'm going to use the word *geek* as both a noun and an adjective: a noun to describe the innovators themselves (that is, the "business geeks" or "organization geeks") and an adjective to describe the organizations they've built. This book is about how those organizations work, which I'm calling the geek way. The geek way challenges us to rethink our notions of what is possible, and to reorient our thinking about what a company can—and should—be. The geek way largely originated in the tech sector, but because it works so well it's going to spread far beyond it. As a result even industries that seem far away from Silicon Valley are going to be transformed, whether they like it or not.

Let me state my main argument as clearly as I can: A bunch of geeks have figured out a better way to run a company. As a result, they're taking over the economy. And they're just getting started.

Chapter Summary

The geek way consists of four *norms:* behaviors that a group's members expect of each other.

The first is *speed:* a preference for achieving results by iterating rapidly instead of planning extensively. The second norm is *ownership.* Compared to industrial-era organizations, geek companies have higher levels of personal autonomy, empowerment, and responsibility, fewer cross-functional processes, and less coordination. Third is the norm of *science:* conducting experiments, generating data, and debating how to interpret evidence. The fourth and final great geek norm is *openness:* sharing information and being receptive to arguments, reevaluations, and changes in direction.

Because of these norms, geek companies' cultures are more freewheeling, fast-moving, evidence-driven, egalitarian, argumentative, and autonomous than those of the typical industrial-era corporation.

These cultures fuel impressive performance, and they empower people and give them autonomy.

A bunch of geeks have figured out a better way to run a company. As a result, they're taking over the economy.

CHAPTER 2

Dialed In

The Performance and Culture of Geek Companies

> What's terrible is to pretend that the second-rate is the
> first-rate... or you like your work when you know
> quite well you're capable of better.
>
> *—Doris Lessing*

I'm claiming that a bunch of business geeks, many of them working in what we loosely call the tech space, have come up with a better way to run a company. It's better in two ways. First, it leads to excellent performance. Second, it creates a work environment that features high levels of autonomy and empowerment. Those are pretty strong claims. What's the evidence for them?

To address that important question, imagine that we have a geek norm detector that works like a Geiger counter does. A Geiger counter emits its distinctive click whenever it encounters ionizing radiation like alpha particles, beta particles, or gamma rays. Our imaginary norm detector is a little bit different. It emits its clicks based on the density of geek norms in the area—what percentage of all the norms around it are norms of science, ownership, speed, or openness. In a bureaucratic, sclerotic company where the bosses don't tolerate any back talk or dissent from underlings, and decisions are made based on the judgments of HiPPOs, the detector would be pretty silent. I think, for example, that it would not have been making a lot of noise if we walked through the hallways of Quibi with it.

At Netflix, on the other hand, our geek norm detector would be pretty loud. And if we left that company's headquarters in Los Gatos, California, and traveled through nearby towns, the detector would continue to click a lot. The heart of Silicon Valley is often held to be the garage in Palo Alto where Bill Hewlett and David Packard conducted experiments before founding Hewlett-Packard in 1939. If we draw a circle around that garage with a radius of thirty miles (big enough to include San Francisco) the headquarters of Netflix would fall inside it, as would Planet and Google, not to mention Apple, PayPal, Zoom, eBay, Cisco, LinkedIn, Dropbox, Adobe, and Intel.

None of those companies follow all of the great geek norms all the time—no company does—but my guess is that the detector would be clicking away at many of them. I say that based on personal experience, and also because those companies are close to Netflix. Geographically close, yes, but also close in how heavily they use digital technologies and where they get their talent from. This latter point is especially important. People moving among Northern California's companies over the course of their careers pick up good ideas, add to them, and pass them on. As we'll see in the pages ahead, this kind of learning is one of our species' superpowers. A/B testing and the Netflix culture deck both originated within our Silicon Valley circle. So have lots of other innovations in how companies run themselves—innovations related to science, ownership, speed, and openness.

Of course, they've also spread outside the circle. In chapter 1, we learned that Amazon, which is headquartered in Seattle, Washington, has a strong culture of ownership. We'll see that it's also adamant about the other great geek norms; our detector would get loud inside Amazon's offices. These days it would also be noisy at Microsoft, which is based east of Seattle in Redmond, Washington. In chapter 5, we'll see how embracing the great geek norms helped Microsoft accomplish one of the most impressive comebacks in corporate history. Cambridge, Massachusetts, is about as far from Northern California or Seattle as it's possible to be while remaining in the Lower 48 but HubSpot, which is headquartered in Cambridge, hasn't let this distance keep it from putting in place openness and the other great geek norms. Our detector, in short, could start clicking anywhere.

The Westward Expansion

Let's look at my first claim, that geek companies are excellent performers. One way to test that claim is to see if the regions with the highest concentrations of geek companies also have the most high-performing companies. This test isn't perfect—it could be the nongeek companies in those regions that are the high performers—but it does tell us if we're on the right track.

For public companies, a prime measure of performance is market capitalization—how much they're worth in the eyes of investors. If the geeks really are building better companies, then the market should be valuing them highly. Share prices tend to fluctuate as investors react (and sometimes overreact) to new information, but over the longer term, share prices generally reflect the actual ability of companies to succeed. As Warren Buffett famously put it (paraphrasing his mentor Benjamin Graham), "In the short run, [the market] is a voting machine; in the long run, it's a weighing machine."

Here's how the US stock market has weighed its largest companies' prospects at two points in time twenty years apart. Below is a visualization of the one hundred most valuable publicly traded companies in the country at the end of 2002. Each company is represented by a bubble, the size of which is proportional to its market capitalization. The bubbles are separated into two bunches based on the location of the company's headquarters (at the time it became publicly traded). The bunch on the left contains West Coast companies, most of which are headquartered in Northern California. The bunch on the right contains companies headquartered anywhere else in the US. Bubbles are shaded based on how old they are, with the youngest companies having the darkest shading. Bubbles with black borders represent companies in "tech" industries.

This visualization shows that by the end of 2002 the West Coast was home to a cluster of large tech companies that were comparatively young. However, most big companies were elsewhere. Eighty-four of the one hundred largest companies were outside the West Coast, as was more than 80 percent of the total stock market value of this group. America's large-company landscape was dominated by names that had been around for a while: Citigroup, J.P. Morgan, and the American International Group (AIG) in financial services; Merck, Pfizer, and Johnson & Johnson in life sciences; IBM in information technology; and the General Electric conglomerate.

100 Most Valuable US Companies Grouped by Headquarters Location

2002 year end

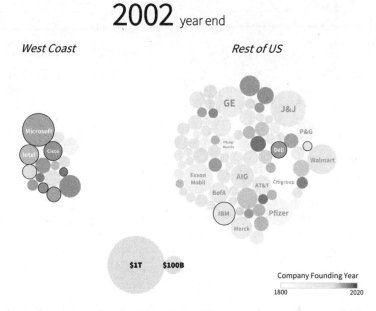

Black border indicates a technology company. These are companies classified by FactSet as primarily doing business in one of the following industries: Interactive Media & Services; Internet & Direct Marketing Retail; Semiconductors & Semiconductor Equipment; Software; Technology Hardware Storage & Peripherals. **Headquarters location assessed at time of IPO.** Source: FactSet.

Now let's look at the same map at the end of 2022, which was a brutal year for lots of companies that would make the geek norm detector noisy. The tech-heavy Nasdaq index dropped by almost a third in 2022 (its worst performance in more than two decades), and companies including Amazon, Tesla, and Netflix lost 50 percent or more of their market capitalization. So how did our map look at the end of 2022?

100 Most Valuable US Companies Grouped by Headquarters Location

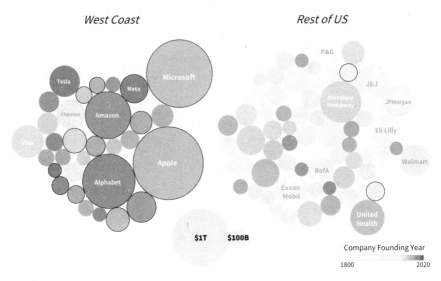

Black border indicates a technology company. These are companies classified by FactSet as primarily doing business in one of the following industries: Interactive Media & Services; Internet & Direct Marketing Retail; Semiconductors & Semiconductor Equipment; Software; Technology Hardware Storage & Peripherals. **Headquarters location assessed at time of IPO.** Source: FactSet.

Even after tech's brutal 2022, at the end of the year our Northern California circle (which contains less than 0.1 percent of America's land) was still by far the hottest spot in the country for highly valuable companies. Thanks to Amazon and Microsoft, the Seattle area also stood out. Meanwhile, the rest of the country hadn't demonstrated much of an ability to grow large tech companies, or large young companies. In fact, most of the bubbles in the right-hand bunch didn't grow much at all from 2002 to 2022, after taking inflation into account. By the end of 2022, the West Coast bunch contained almost as much large-company stock market value (47 percent) as did the entire rest of the country (53 percent).

If we look across the Atlantic Ocean to the continent that was the birthplace of the Industrial Revolution, the comparison is even more stark. At the end of 2022, the market capitalization of all public companies in our Northern California circle was more than half as big as the stock market value of the EU and UK combined, a rich region of over 500 million people. Asia's landmass and population are both enormous, yet the market cap of all its public companies is less than four times larger than the market cap of companies in our circle. The towns of Silicon Valley feel like sleepy suburbs, but they've become the world's epicenter of capitalist value creation.

Companies founded there, in the part of the world where the geek norm detector would be noisiest, have disrupted industries ranging from advertising to media and entertainment to consumer electronics to automobile making. They've come up with world-changing innovations like search engines and smartphones, and the market anticipates that they'll continue to innovate and grow. (Remember, the market capitalization of a company doesn't reflect its history; it's instead investors' estimate of the company's *future* financial prospects.)* Some of these companies have become so large and powerful that they're now attracting antitrust scrutiny in America and elsewhere.

The standard explanation for this remarkable performance is that Silicon Valley is the center of the US tech industry, which profited greatly as the business world digitalized. There's some truth to this explanation, but as we've seen, "tech" is no longer a meaningful way to categorize companies. So I'm telling a different story about the creation of all that value inside our circle. Instead of focusing on the growth of an industry called tech, my story is about the rise of a corporate culture called geek.

My story isn't about strategy, but that's not because strategy is irrelevant. It's critical, and the companies represented by those big 2022 bubbles have made all sorts of smart strategic moves. As the saying goes, though, "Culture eats strategy for breakfast." Some companies can successfully execute the strategies they come up with. Some can't. The differences between these two types are largely cultural.

---

* The first premise of corporate valuation is that at any point in time, a company is worth the present value of its future free cash flow. If "free cash flow" isn't a familiar concept to you, just mentally substitute "profits." But don't tell an accounting professor that's what you're doing, unless you're really in the mood for a lecture.

Insider Grading

The big problem with making claims about corporate cultures and their ties to performance is that such claims have been hard to support with data. Up until recently, there hasn't been much good, systematic evidence about corporate cultures. They're notoriously difficult to measure. How can we accurately assess how much a given company has a culture of openness, or speed, or anything else? Should we interview the CEO? Read the annual report? It's pretty clear we won't get objective answers that way. How about surveying employees? That would likely yield more reliable conclusions, but people don't like filling out long surveys, companies don't like sharing the results of the internal ones they've conducted, and it's hard to administer such a survey from the outside. As a result, we haven't had many solid, data-rich ways to compare companies' cultures.

The good news is that the situation is starting to change. Our ignorance about companies' cultures is giving way to insight. This shift is happening because of two recent developments. The first is the appearance of lots of reviews of companies, left online by their own employees. Just like people review the books they've read and hotels they've stayed at, they now review their workplaces.* Sites including Glassdoor collect these reviews anonymously and take steps to protect reviewers from being identified and retaliated against by their employers.

The second helpful development is the wide availability of powerful machine learning (ML) software. The most common variant of ML, called supervised learning, starts with a set of labeled training data. For analyzing Glassdoor data, the training data could be a set of employee reviews that have been labeled by people along two dimensions: the aspect of culture that is being discussed, and the employee's feeling about that aspect (for example,

---

* My favorite review of our book *The Second Machine Age* was just five words: "Too much based on evidences."

"This is a *highly favorable* review about *agility* at the company"). After the ML software is trained with enough labeled data, it can go through all the Glassdoor reviews for a large group of companies and classify them automatically. This process yields a consistent analysis of culture across companies, and so allows comparisons and rankings.

Business researchers Don and Charlie Sull have done this for more than five hundred companies, most of them based in the US, that have enough Glassdoor reviews to enable meaningful analysis. As far as I know, their Culture 500 project is the first large-scale quantitative analysis of corporate cultures that uses employees' views. The results are revealing.

The Sulls investigated what they call the Big Nine cultural values, or the ones most cited by companies in their official values statements. They are (in alphabetical order) agility, collaboration, customer, diversity, execution, innovation, integrity, performance, and respect. Every company in the Culture 500 is ranked on each value, based on the results of the ML analysis. So it's possible to see, for example, where Netflix ranks on agility.* Is it at the 50th percentile? The 75th? It's at the 99th percentile. No wonder the culture deck was so popular.

The Culture 500 research didn't directly investigate the great geek norms of science, ownership, speed, and openness, but it did focus on related concepts like agility, execution, and innovation. We can therefore use the Culture 500 data to see if there's support for my arguments about the geek way. The Sulls created groups of companies and placed Netflix in two of them: Tech Giants and Internet. Let's combine those two and call the resulting set the Likely Suspects for having geek cultures. These are the companies where I'd expect our geek norm detector to be making the most noise. The table below lists the thirty-three Likely Suspects, 60 percent of which were founded within our Northern California circle.

---

* To be a bit more precise, it's possible to see where Netflix's employees' aggregate view of the company's agility compares to the parallel views at all other Culture 500 companies.

Airbnb*	HubSpot	Twitter*
Akamai	IBM	Uber*
Alphabet*	Intel*	Wayfair
Amazon	LinkedIn*	Workday*
Apple*	Lyft*	Yahoo*
Cisco Systems*	Microsoft	Yelp*
DoorDash*	Netflix*	Zillow
eBay*	Oracle*	
Expedia	PayPal*	
Facebook (Meta)*	Postmates*	
GoDaddy	Salesforce*	
Groupon	Stitch Fix*	
Grubhub	Support.com*	
*Founded in Northern California		

I calculated the average across the Likely Suspects of each of the Culture 500's Big Nine values, and compared this group average to Netflix's scores on each of the Big Nine. The graph below shows the results.

Comparison of Netflix vs. "Tech Giant and Internet" Companies Across Culture 500 Big Nine Values

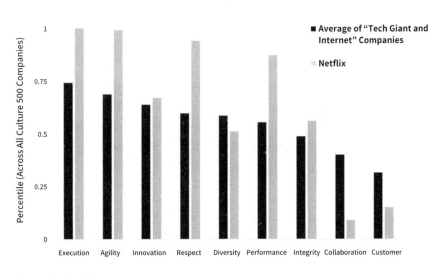

Source: CultureX

The Likely Suspects are, as a group, pretty similar to Netflix. All are in the top half of the Culture 500 for six of the nine values: execution, agility, innovation, respect, diversity, and performance.

Geek companies' relatively high diversity ranking is surprising, given the tech industry's reputation as a monoculture. And to be clear, this reputation is in important ways justified. Women make up only a third of the workforce at the five largest tech companies, for example, and the percentage of technical employees at Microsoft and Google who are either Black or Hispanic improved by only one percentage point between 2014 and 2019. A 2021 analysis by Bloomberg found that the professional and managerial ranks at tech companies contained significantly fewer women, Blacks, and Hispanics than did other large companies. So geek companies' high diversity score could be at least partly due to the fact that the largely white, male majority in these companies believes that there's no problem with diversity, and that the views of this majority drown out those who feel differently. On a topic as important as this, more research is clearly necessary.

Like Netflix, the Likely Suspects are also ranked well below average in two areas of corporate culture: collaboration and customer. The low collaboration ranking is neither surprising nor concerning. As we'll see, geek companies that adopt norms of ownership and high autonomy tend to place much lower on extensive collaboration, and actually often work hard to minimize it. The low customer scores could, as Don Sull pointed out to me, be due to the fact that most employees at tech companies don't interact directly with customers, and that platforms tend to have more than one customer group.

Corporate Culture Club

Let's concentrate on the tall columns on the left side of the graph. As a group, our Likely Suspects rank highest exactly where Netflix does: on execution (where Netflix anchors the 100th percentile) and agility (the 99th). The Sulls define execution as the extent to which "employees are empowered to act, have the resources they need, adhere to process discipline, and are held accountable for results," and agility as the ability to "respond quickly and effectively to changes in the marketplace and seize new opportunities." The Likely Suspects' third-highest score is for innovation, a measure of the degree to which "the company pioneers novel products, services, technologies, or ways of working." If you polled my community of business academics about the drivers of corporate performance, the trio of agility, execution, and innovation would all be right at the top of the list of results. The Sulls' Culture 500 research shows us that according to their own employees, our Likely Suspects for having geek cultures are doing well at all three of these critical activities. This research also lets us compare our Likely Suspects to other industry groups, so we can see if the geeks have any real competition here. As the graph below shows, they don't; it's not even close.

Average Culture 500 Agility, Execution, and Innovation Scores by Industry Group

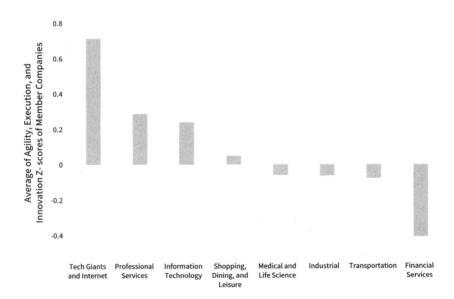

Source: CultureX

The average combined score for agility + execution + innovation in the Likely Suspects group of companies is more than twice as high as in any other industry group. Professional services firms and IT companies do pretty well across these three activities (again, according to their own employees). And that's about it. Most of the other industry groups hover around a score of zero; finance stands out for its low averages on agility, execution, and innovation.

The more I look at this graph, the more surprising I find it. Over the decades I've spent in business academia I've heard countless discussions about the importance of empowerment, autonomy, and embrace of novelty, and about how the healthiest corporate cultures are the ones with the highest levels of freedom, trust, responsibility, and accountability. If all of the books and articles written about the power of such cultures were collected in one place, the pile would be sky-high. Very few documents in that pile predicted that a bunch of Internet geeks would be the ones to build these cultures. Yet according to the best evidence we have, that's what has happened.

This is a shock. It's as if a group of inexperienced flight enthusiasts learned how to build excellent airplanes while the mainstream aviation industry couldn't keep its machines from falling out of the sky. And it's not just that the companies in the Likely Suspects set are comparatively young, and so haven't had time to build up bureaucracy and other problems. They *are* young, but they score significantly higher on agility, execution, and innovation than equally young companies in other industries. The Culture 500 research supports a core element of my argument: not only that there is a distinct geek corporate culture, but also that it's characterized by high levels of empowerment and autonomy and is highly supportive of innovation, agility, and execution.

Another intriguing piece of evidence that the business geeks have built desirable cultures comes from the professional social network LinkedIn, which in 2016 revealed its Top Attractors. These were the companies that were most interesting to LinkedIn's members as determined not by their opinions, but instead solely by their actions: job applications, views of employee and corporate pages, and the length of time that new hires stayed with companies. LinkedIn summarized its Top Attractors list as "the first ranking of its kind to be based entirely on actions of users."*

The actions of users revealed that our Likely Suspects were extremely attractive. In the US, ten of the top eleven spots on the Top Attractors list were occupied by Likely Suspects, and all except Microsoft were headquartered in Northern California (the eleventh was Tesla, a very geeky company in important ways, as we'll see in chapter 6). Globally the situation was much the same, with the top spots going to seven of the same companies. Journalist Suzy Welch highlighted just how skewed the Top Attractors were, and how much of the industrial era was absent from the list:

Tech comprises less than 10% of the American GDP, but every single one of the top 10 companies on the Top Attractors list is in the tech space. And, looking at all 40 companies on the U.S. list, tech's 45% of the total . . .

By contrast, companies in the energy space and retail space, which together comprise 7.5% of the GDP and 25% of the top 40 companies in the *Fortune* 500, show up not at all. (I repeat, not at all.) Of note as well: traditional manufacturing . . . still comprises 12% of the American economy and a full 10% of the *Fortune* 500's top 40 companies. On LinkedIn's Top Attractors list, however, the only company that comes close to being in that category is Tesla, showing up at No. 8, but it's about as much a traditional manufacturing company as, well, a tech company that makes electric cars.

It could be that the Likely Suspects are so attractive because they pay so well, but that view is hard to square with the fact that finance, which also pays quite well, made a poor showing of only four firms on the Top Attractors list (Visa, at number 13; Blackrock, at number 19; Goldman Sachs, at

---

* In later years LinkedIn replaced its Top Attractors list with "Top Companies" and expanded the criteria for inclusion beyond the actions of users: "The LinkedIn [Top Company] rankings are based on seven pillars: ability to advance, skills growth, company stability, external opportunities, company affinity, gender diversity, and educational background."

number 27; and Morgan Stanley, at number 40). Psychologist Adam Grant has a better explanation for why the Top Attractors list is dominated by our Likely Suspects: "Tech companies have raised the bar on what it means to be a great place to work: not just free food and ping pong tables, but a chance to do creative work on important problems, collaborate with highly motivated, talented colleagues, learn from world-class experts, and have a real voice." Welch, Grant, and many others continue to use an industry label—"tech"—to describe the Likely Suspects. But I think the cultural label of "geek" is more appropriate. Grant's description of a great place to work, for example, is all about culture, not industry.

I'm not saying that geek companies are perfect. Of course they're not. They have failed at important tasks like achieving enough female and minority representation in their workforces, minimizing bias in the offerings they release, protecting the health of their frontline workers, and preventing foreign meddling in elections and the spread of false news and hate speech on their social media platforms. In the pages ahead, we'll see plenty of examples of mistakes made by business geeks. I'm also not making the case in this book that geek companies' hearts are in the right place, or that they're morally correct, or that they should be left alone and not regulated. My goal here isn't to get you to like geek companies, or trust them.

My goal is narrower and simpler: to show that many geek companies are excellent performers, in large part because of the cultures they've created. They've demonstrated the ability to do the main thing that companies exist to do: profitably turn out offerings that customers value, and keep doing so over long periods of time. If you're passionate about stakeholder capitalism; the environment; social and governance criteria; corporate social responsibility; diversity, equity, and inclusion; or any of the other movements seeking to reshape the business world, sustained, excellent performance will help you accomplish your aims.

If you don't like the power and influence of today's largest geek companies I think you should study them particularly closely. Sports teams scout and study their archrivals, after all, and the US military and intelligence services spend a great deal of time trying to understand the capabilities of

China, Russia, and North Korea. This is not because America thinks these countries are worthy of admiration; it's because they are worthy adversaries—competitors that should be taken seriously.

In short, whether you're a fan or foe or competitor of geek companies, it's valuable to spend time understanding how they got so big. My argument is simple: the cultures they've created are critical enablers of their growth.

Let's Not Go There

As I visited tech's alpha geeks and their companies over the years, I realized something striking: they rarely talk about the corporate cultures or practices of the industrial era in favorable terms. In fact, they rarely talk about them at all. When they do, it's usually to illustrate what they want to avoid. Among the business geeks, the customs of the industrial era are much more honored in the breach than the observance.

If images work better for you than Shakespearean figures of speech, try this: every company faces the same small set of fundamental trade-offs—giving people autonomy versus establishing structure and standardized processes; placing faith in data, experiments, and algorithms versus relying on intuition, experience, and judgment; moving fast versus being methodical; embracing argument and disagreement versus valuing collegiality and consensus; utilizing flat versus hierarchical structures, and loosely versus tightly integrated ones. If each of these trade-offs is like a dial, the people who design and run companies adjust the dials until they find a configuration that seems right for their circumstances.

As we'll see in the chapters ahead the geeks take all these dials and twist them as far as possible in the same direction—the one that fosters norms of science, ownership, speed, and openness, and that creates a fast-moving, freewheeling, egalitarian, evidence-driven, argumentative, autonomous corporate culture. According to the conventional wisdom of the industrial era, this isn't a good idea. A culture like that might be appropriate for a young startup, or a homogeneous group of tech bros, or a Skunk Works (a small division set up within a big company to work on secret projects). But at some point, the standard business advice goes, you have to grow up. You have to move the dials toward the center as a company grows and matures, as it has to execute with high reliability instead of just innovating, and as its workforce grows and becomes more dispersed and diverse.

The geeks appear to be immune to this advice. In fact, they have an almost existential objection to it. To paraphrase guidance often attributed to the writer Dorothy Parker, they believe that moving the dials toward the center is not an idea to be lightly tossed aside. Rather, it should be thrown away with great force.

Why do they believe this? In part because they're unimpressed with the results generated by this advice—with the kinds of companies and outcomes it yields. If that sounds like an overly harsh judgment, consider the following:

- In a 2017 *Harvard Business Review* survey, nearly two-thirds of respondents reported that their companies had moderate to severe bureaucracy, and only 1 percent felt bureaucracy-free.
- In 2018, nearly three hundred corporate leaders were asked about the biggest barriers to innovation in their companies. The two top responses, each cited by around half the respondents, were "politics/ turf wars" and the perennial favorite, "cultural issues."
- Most large projects are finished late and over budget (if they're finished at all), and many, from construction to consumer electronics to software development, suffer from the "90 percent syndrome": everything appears to be on track and on time until the project is 80 to 90 percent finished, at which point progress suddenly slows to a crawl.
- A 2020 study of over five hundred large US companies found essentially no correlation between stated corporate values and actual culture as assessed by employees.
- Surveys in the twenty-first century have consistently found that no more than half of employees, and sometimes less than 10 percent, know what's expected of them on the job, or how their work aligns with their companies' goals and strategies.

The geeks asked, *Can't we do better?* Why should we tolerate corporate cultures that are the biggest barriers to innovation instead of the biggest supporters and nurturers of this critical activity? Why should we accept that important efforts are just about always going to be late, or that high levels of bureaucracy and hypocrisy are to be expected? Why should so few employees actually know why they're doing what they're doing?

The business geeks looked at the typical company of the early twenty-first century and came to the same conclusion that Maria Montessori did after studying Italian schools in the early twentieth: *We can do better along every dimension that matters.* The geeks believed that they could build companies that move faster, execute better, and innovate more, while giving their people a better sense of belonging and empowerment.

Building these kinds of companies isn't just important because they'll turn out better goods and services. It's also important because they'll be better places to work, and work is a central part of the lives of most people. In the United States full-time workers spend, on average, just about as much time each week at work—forty-seven hours—as they do asleep. During their prime working years, they spend about as much time with their coworkers as with their partners, and only a bit less than with their children. And they're not putting in all this time for the paycheck alone. As we all know (and we'll explore in the pages ahead), our work provides us with opportunities to do things that are of the highest importance to human beings: to feel part of a community, to have a sense of purpose, to learn and teach, to gain status, and so on.

The image of zombified workers punching the clock at dead-end jobs is a common setup for both comedy and tragedy, but it's not accurate. The General Social Survey asked American workers in 2016, "If you were to get enough money to live as comfortably as you would like for the rest of your life, would you continue to work or would you stop working?" Fully 70 percent said they would keep working, and that percentage was actually highest among the least educated workers and those who held the least prestigious jobs. The misery comes not when you have a job, but when you're afraid you might lose it. Social scientist Arthur Brooks found that

American adults who reported that they were "very" or "fairly" likely to lose their job in 2018 were more than three times more likely to say they were "not too happy" with their life than people who felt they were "not likely" to be let go...In 2014, economists found that a one-percentage-point increase in unemployment lowers national well-being by more than five times as much as a one-point increase in the inflation rate.

Companies are going to have rich cultures. It's almost impossible for them not to, given how much of our days and our identities are occupied by work. But "rich" doesn't always mean "healthy." Nor does it mean "planned." Lots of business leaders don't spend much time on their companies' cultures. Instead, they let them evolve largely on their own. As a team of organizational researchers put it in a 2018 *Harvard Business Review* article, "In our experience it is...common for leaders seeking to build high-performing organizations to be confounded by culture. Indeed, many either let it go unmanaged or relegate it to the HR function, where it becomes a secondary concern for the business. They may lay out detailed, thoughtful plans for strategy and execution, but because they don't understand culture's power and dynamics, their plans go off the rails." This is an enormous missed opportunity. It's like running a supermarket and paying no attention to which products go on which shelves.

Any such store would quickly become an uncompetitive mess. As I look at the evidence about industrial-era companies' cultures, and at how those companies are doing in their battles with culture-obsessed geeks, "uncompetitive mess" often seems like an appropriate phrase. There's no reason to perpetuate the mess. People want to work in healthy environments, and we now know how to create them, thanks to two very different communities: a new cohort of geek business founders and leaders, and scientists asking and answering different kinds of questions about human behavior.

As we've seen in this chapter, there's good evidence that the business geeks are succeeding in their attempts to build something better. They're following the advice of HubSpot cofounder Dharmesh Shah, who says, "You're going to have a culture anyways—might as well build one you love."

Chapter Summary

The towns of Silicon Valley feel like sleepy suburbs, but in the twenty-first century they've become the world's epicenter of capitalist value creation. The Valley has more fast-growing, innovative, world-changing companies than anyplace else.

The standard explanation for this remarkable performance is that Silicon Valley is the center of the US tech industry, but instead of focusing on the growth of an industry called tech, my story is about the rise of a corporate culture called geek.

Recent research indicates that there's a distinct geek corporate culture with high levels of empowerment and autonomy; it fosters innovation, agility, and execution.

Whether you're a fan or foe or competitor of geek companies, it's valuable to spend time understanding how they became so dominant. My argument is simple: the cultures they've created are critical enablers of their success.

People want to work in healthy environments, and we now know how to create them, thanks to two very different communities: a new cohort of geek business founders and leaders, and scientists asking and answering questions about human behavior and cultural evolution.

CHAPTER 3

Ultra and Ultimate

A New Way to Think About Us

> We are the miracle of force and matter making itself
> over into imagination and will. Incredible. The Life
> Force experimenting with forms. You for one. Me for
> another. The Universe has shouted itself alive. We are
> one of the shouts.
>
> — *Ray Bradbury*

W e're in a league of our own, we human beings. There's nothing else like us on the planet—not even close. But what truly sets us apart isn't what most people think.

Most people think that what distinguishes us from our fellow creatures is our intelligence. That view is so widespread and long-standing that it's reflected in the scientific name for our species: the *sapiens* part of *Homo sapiens* means "wise." And it's true that we are much smarter in many ways than our closest relatives. By the age of two and a half, human children already reason as well about space, quantities, and causality as adult chimps and orangutans (and of course our intelligence in these domains increases for a long time after our toddler years).

A Better Name for Our Species

However, there are a couple problems with the "we're so much smarter" view of human uniqueness. One of them is that we're actually worse than our closest evolutionary relatives at some important kinds of reasoning. Spatial memory and information processing speed are closely related to other types of intelligence in humans, so it seems likely that adults would outperform chimps in these areas.* Primatologists Sana Inoue and Tetsuro Matsuzawa tested if this was the case by pitting a group of (human) university students against a group of chimps at a task: the experimenters briefly showed their subjects a string of consecutive numbers distributed around a computer screen (for example, "1" was at the bottom left of the screen, "2" was near the middle, "3" was in the upper left, and so on), then covered all the numbers with blank rectangles. The subject had to demonstrate their spatial memory by tapping the rectangles in numerical sequence (that is, first the rectangle that was covering up the "1," then the "2," . . .) as quickly as possible without making any mistakes.

If a subject succeeded at correctly remembering the sequence of hidden numbers on a screen that contained, say, six rectangles, the next screen they saw contained seven. The most crowded screen contained nine numbers. In addition to varying how many numbers were on the screen, the experimenters also varied how long they were visible until they were covered by rectangles; the longest time was 0.65 seconds, the shortest 0.2 seconds. To measure information processing speed, the experiment tracked how long it took subjects to start tapping the rectangles after they appeared.

The overall champ at spatial memory was a five-year-old chimp named Ayumu, who showed admirable sangfroid by performing the same no matter how quickly the numbers disappeared (all the rest of the subjects, human and chimp, saw their performance deteriorate). The humans beat the other chimps at the spatial memory task, but all humans lost to all chimps in the domain of information processing speed. The chimps started tapping rectangles faster than any of the humans, and, unlike the humans, didn't do worse if they started tapping more quickly.

Our performance against the chimps in these tests lets a bit of air out

---

* The better your spatial memory and information processing speed, the more likely you are to also be good at problem-solving and reasoning.

of the "we're so much smarter" view of ourselves. But what really punctures that view is the fact that we *Homo* (alleged) *sapiens* aren't wise enough to keep ourselves alive on our own, even when we're given everything you'd think we'd need to survive. Individually we're not even smart enough to keep existing.

To see what I mean, consider an unsettling thought experiment: Take a group of human children soon after they're weaned from their mothers' milk and put them in the most hospitable possible environment: no predators, pathogens, poisons, or enemies; warm, mild weather, day and night; plenty of shelter, bedding, and clothing; abundant fresh water; and easy access to endless fruit, vegetables, nuts, grains, and even fridges full of fresh raw meat, poultry, and fish. The only things this Eden lacks are elders and fire.

If you did this experiment with any other mammal, the main problem would be eventual overpopulation. The human kids, though, would face the opposite problem. Without anyone around to teach them how to make fire and cook food, they'd eventually starve.*

This extraordinary situation came about because long ago our ancestors started to cook at least some of their food.† Cooked food is denser in nutrition and easier to chew and digest. These benefits are so great that they changed our species. As the practice of cooking food became universal across human societies, evolution took over, shrinking our stomachs and intestinal tracts (since cooked food required less time and energy to digest) and weakening our jaw muscles (since we didn't need to chew as much). As a result of

---

* In 1978, the Robertsons, a Scottish family, survived on a boat in the Pacific Ocean for thirty-eight days. After their prepared foods ran out, they survived on raw meat from fish and turtles that they caught. However, as primatologist Richard Wrangham writes in his 2009 book *Catching Fire*, "their experience shows that with abundant food, people can survive well on a raw animal-based diet for at least a month. But people sometimes survive with no food at all for a month, provided they have water. The lack of any evidence for longer-term survival on raw wild food suggests that even in extremis, people need their food cooked."

† There's debate about when humans started to cook their food. Richard Wrangham believes that the transition happened about 1.8 million years ago, when the species *Homo erectus* appeared. Others believe that the transition is much more recent, occurring within the past few hundred thousand years.

these and other adaptations, modern humans can't exist on a diet of raw, unprepared foods.* We have an "obligate dependence" on fire. Charles Darwin realized that harnessing fire was a fundamental development for our species. As he put it, fire was "probably the greatest ever [discovery] by man, excepting language."

If evolution made us dependent on fire, it's logical to expect that evolution would have also given us the wherewithal to create it. But it didn't. Virtually none of us can figure out by ourselves how to start a fire. We have to be taught this skill; we're not intelligent enough to acquire it on our own. A long, long time ago the ancestors of everyone alive today figured out at least one method for making fire (by striking the right kinds of rocks against each other to create sparks, for example, or rubbing two pieces of wood against each other so quickly that they get hot enough to cause tinder to burst into flame).† These folk then taught this method to their peers, who taught it (perhaps with some improvements) to their children, and so on. Within human groups each generation teaches the one after it how to create and maintain fire, and how to use it to cook food and do other essential things.

And it's not just making fire. We humans have to be taught by others how to hunt, detoxify food, make clothing and tools, build shelter, and do many other things that are essential to our survival. Humans have learned how to live in deserts, rainforests, and just about every ecosystem in between, but that learning doesn't happen anew for each individual. Instead, it's accumulated by many people and groups over many lifetimes and passed down through generations.

We humans have struck a fascinating evolutionary bargain. We've

---

* "Raw vegan" diets involve extensive food preparation with blenders and other modern tools. The energy and physique of rock star Lenny Kravitz, who is in his mid-fifties and "primarily raw," strongly suggest that these diets might be the way to go.

† One exception here might be the isolated and rarely contacted people of North Sentinel Island in the Bay of Bengal. Anthropologist Triloknath Pandit is one of few outsiders to have contact with the Sentinelese. He observed that they don't know how to create fire themselves. Instead, they take burning wood from trees that were struck by lightning back to their huts and keep these fires alive over time.

accepted individual helplessness as the price of fantastic group strength. Our intelligence alone can't keep us alive, but our social groups can, and do. Our groups hold the knowledge and know-how we need. Without them, we're goners. Within them, we get smart enough to build spaceships.

Launching a spaceship is an impressive accomplishment, and one that's unique to our species. Chimps haven't put anything into orbit, and I think it's safe to say that they're not going to anytime soon. But why not? As we've seen, they're pretty smart in important ways. They also learn from each other. Chimpanzees have cultures: customs and social learning that vary across groups and carry on for generations. Chimp cultures differ from each other in lots of ways, including how members build sleeping nests, use tools to get honey out of logs, and court their mates. Other nonhuman primates also have cultures, as do many cetaceans—whales, dolphins, and porpoises.

The list of culture-possessing animals might actually be long, but psychologist Steve Stewart-Williams drives home the key difference between all of them and us: "Ten thousand years ago, the pinnacle of chimpanzee culture was using twigs to extract termites from termite mounds. Today, the pinnacle of chimpanzee culture is... using twigs to extract termites from termite mounds." Chimpanzee innovations like tool use are real and important, and they spread from peer to peer and from parent to child, but they don't build on each other over time.* Human innovations, meanwhile, clearly do; we've advanced from using twigs to throwing spears to launching spaceships.

We need a definition of our cultures that captures what's unique about them. I'll use anthropologist Joe Henrich's: "By 'culture' I mean the large body of practices, techniques, heuristics, tools, motivations, values, and beliefs that we all acquire while growing up, mostly by learning from other people." That "learning from other people" bit captures much of what sets us humans apart from chimps and every other species. We learn more types of

---

* Some primates can apparently learn from humans. In 2008, a picture was taken in Borneo of an orangutan exhibiting a previously unknown behavior: using a long stick like a spear to try to catch fish in the Gohong River. The ape presumably saw people fishing this way, and copied them. (It also copied many humans in that it didn't catch anything.)

things from more different individuals than does any other creature on Earth. And as we'll see, we also synthesize what we learn from others, effortlessly creating a blend of the best examples we see.

In addition to learning, the other thing that makes humans stand out is how well we work together. We're the only species that cooperates intensely in large groups of unrelated individuals. Ants, bees, and a few other social insects do well at the "cooperate intensely" part—they communicate, coordinate, and specialize as they get food, fight invaders, and raise their young—but they do it all as members of one big family; they're all genetically related. Some other animals cooperate, but not nearly as deeply as the social insects do. As psychologist Michael Tomasello says about the species that's our closest relative: "It is inconceivable that you would ever see two chimpanzees carrying a log together."

Now look at we humans. We routinely cooperate intensely and in large numbers with nonkin. There were 70 million combatants in World War II—70 million individuals, almost all unrelated, who were willing to stake their lives to defend an abstract notion like "country." And we get together with huge numbers of strangers even when we don't want to kill each other. We send spaceships out into the cosmos; create economies and link them together via trade; invent and distribute vaccines in response to a global pandemic; and create smartphones, worldwide communications networks, and translation software that get us close to the point of finally all being able to talk to each other.

All of these cultural accomplishments require a lot of learning and knowledge accumulation. We humans alone achieve them, and we achieve them with remarkable speed. Nothing in the prior history of life on Earth suggested that a species could master this kind of rapid cultural evolution. The only analogy to it I can come up with comes from science fiction.

Lots of sci-fi incorporates faster-than-light travel. It's a way to get around the fact that the vastness of interstellar space doesn't lend itself to snappy plots,* and also an excuse to show cool visual effects as spaceships activate

---

* The fastest human-built object ever to travel through space would require about nineteen thousand years to reach Proxima Centauri, the star closest to our sun.

their warp drive, then wind up moments later in a galaxy far, far away, in flagrant violation of the laws of physics.* The reason we humans have become so successful and dominant on Earth is that we have our own warp drive: a type of evolution possessed by no other species. In addition to biological evolution (which every living thing has), we also have cultural evolution, which is much, much, much faster. If biological evolution is like travel that's limited by the speed of light, then cultural evolution is humanity's warp speed.

To see just how fast cultural evolution is, let's look at the development of spaceships. After spending millennia dreaming of flight, humans finally left the Earth's surface in 1783 in a balloon built in France by the Montgolfier brothers. A bit more than a century later, in 1903, one of the Wright brothers made the first airplane flight in Kitty Hawk, North Carolina. After that, the milestones started being counted in decades. Sputnik orbited the Earth in 1957, and Neil Armstrong walked on the moon in 1969. We landed a spacecraft on Mars in 1976, and flew another one past Pluto less than forty years later. In 2021, we started the whole cycle over again on another planet; the *Ingenuity* helicopter made a short flight from the deck of the *Perseverance* rover, which was on Mars at the time. The physicist and philosopher David Deutsch has a brilliant summary of the cumulative impact of all this work: "Earth is or will soon be the only object in the known universe that could repel an object instead of attracting it," because of our ability to build a planetary asteroid defense system.

And it's not just technology; other fundamental elements of our cultures also change with disorienting speed. In 1980, more than 80 percent of China's population lived in villages. By 2019, 60 percent of the country's people lived in cities. In 1970, 10 percent of all births in the United States occurred outside of marriage; by 2018, that percentage had quadrupled. In 1945, a bit over 11 percent of the world's people lived in a democracy; in 2015, more than 55 percent did.

---

* If you didn't like that sentence because I mixed technology from *Star Trek* with a phrase from *Star Wars,* you have just identified yourself as a science fiction geek.

I'm not labeling these changes as "good" or "bad"; I'm just labeling them as *fast*. Most people would agree that their communities' lifestyles, mating and child-rearing practices, and forms of government are all important and perhaps shouldn't be changed willy-nilly. Yet we make massive changes in how we live not over hundreds or thousands of generations, but within one or two. Biological evolution can't do this. Cultural evolution accomplishes it easily.

The voraciousness of our learning, the extent of our cooperation, and the fast evolution of our cultures are all aspects of human sociality (just like the dance that tells the rest of the hive where the flowers are is an aspect of bee sociality). The more I learn about human sociality, the more extraordinary and unique it seems. I'm not the only one who feels this way. Many scientists who study the history of living things believe that because of our spaceship-generating sociality the appearance of human beings was one of the "major evolutionary transitions" in life on Earth. There have been only a handful of these transitions, and they are indeed major. They include the development of chromosomes (around 4 billion years ago); the appearance of cells with nuclei (2.7 billion years); the dawn of multicellular organisms (1.5 billion years); and the emergence of social insects like bees and ants (130 million years).*

Not to get too self-congratulatory, but it's a pretty big deal for us humans to get a place on the list of major evolutionary transitions. It's a short list, after all, and we're the first new entry in more than 100 million years. We're also the only entry that consists of a single genus—*Homo*. We earned our place because as far as we can tell we're the only living things in the Earth's history that cooperate intensely with huge numbers of nonkin and

---

* Just like us ultrasocial human beings, the social insects have in evolutionary terms been "fantastically successful," as one review put it. Ants, bees, social wasps, and termites are found all over the world in vast numbers. In one tropical ecosystem, for example, they made up 80 percent of the biomass of all insects. And as far as we can tell from the fossil record, none of the major lineages of these animals have gone extinct.

experience rapid cultural evolution. Along with our place on the list, we get our own label: we're the planet's only *ultrasocial* creatures.*

Note that we did *not* earn our place on the list of major evolutionary transitions because of our intelligence. So maybe *Homo sapiens* isn't the best name for our species. I think a better name — one that really highlights what makes us unique and what has made us so successful — is *Homo ultrasocialis*. It's hard for me to keep thinking of our species as exceptionally wise when we can't figure out on our own how to set a pile of twigs on fire if our life depended on it. But it makes a ton of sense to me to consider myself a member of a species that's evolved into ultrasociality and accepted individual helplessness (at firemaking and lots of other things) as the price of unbounded group strength.

A lot of human behaviors are like our inability to make fire: they seem odd or even inexplicable when we think about humans as wise individuals, but make a lot of sense once we shift perspective and think of ourselves first and foremost as ultrasocial creatures. To see what I mean, let's revisit one of the most famous experiments in all of social psychology. It took place at a seminary in New Jersey over the course of a few days in December 1970.

What We Learned at Princeton

At the Princeton Theological Seminary, founded in 1812 as a training ground for Presbyterian ministers, students were recruited to participate in an experiment. Psychologists John Darley and Daniel Batson wanted to explore what makes people behave more or less altruistically. Is it a matter of personality — are some people just more giving and helpful than others? Or is it about mindfulness — are people more likely to help others when they are in the midst of thinking about altruism and helpfulness?

---

* There is debate about whether we humans belong on the list of major evolutionary transitions, and what terminology we should use to describe our sociality. I follow complexity scientist Peter Turchin and others in saying that we do belong on the list, and that "ultrasocial" is the right word to describe us.

To find out how important personality is for altruistic behavior Darley and Batson gave all of their seminarian subjects tests designed to assess the nature of their religiosity (was religion a means to an end, for example, or an end in itself?). To test how important mindfulness is, the researchers divided their subjects into two groups and manipulated the members of one group so that helpfulness and altruism were at the top of their minds. They did this by asking all the seminarians to prepare and deliver a short talk, but not the same talk; half got the assignment to speak about careers for seminary graduates, while the other half were asked to speak about the biblical parable of the Good Samaritan.

The researchers could be confident that members of the latter group had altruism at the top of their minds as they walked across campus to deliver their talk. The parable of the Good Samaritan is perhaps the most famous story told by Jesus in the Bible. In it, a man is beaten by robbers and left by the side of the road. A rabbi and a Levite (a religious functionary) cross the road to avoid the wounded man, but a Samaritan stops and aids him greatly. Samaritans and Jews were traditional enemies, so Jesus's followers heard in his parable a clear message: virtue comes from being helpful to those in need, not from practicing the right religion. The parable ends with Jesus bidding his disciples to "go and do likewise."

Darley and Batson gave their subjects a chance to do likewise. The route all the seminarians followed to the room where they would deliver their talk took them down an alley where they encountered one person: a man "sitting slumped in a doorway, head down, eyes closed, not moving." He coughed twice and groaned as the seminarians passed him. But he wasn't actually sick or hurt. He was a confederate in the experiment, placed there to see which of the subjects would stop and offer to help him.

Were seminarians with a particular personality type more likely to stop and help? No. No personality type was more likely to be altruistic than others in the experiment. What's far more surprising is that seminarians who were on their way to give a talk about the parable of the Good Samaritan were not more likely to stop and offer help to the slumped man than were seminarians on their way to give a talk about careers. In other words, people who had the story of the Good Samaritan at the top of their minds were not significantly more likely to be Good Samaritans themselves. In the experiment, making people mindful about helpfulness didn't affect their helpfulness.

The only thing that *did* have an effect was whether or not the subjects in the experiment believed that they were violating a norm. Darley and Batson included one more manipulation in the Princeton experiment: they varied how much time pressure the seminarians felt as they neared the slumped man. A third of them felt no rush, because at the office where they checked in, they were told they had a few extra minutes to get to "Professor Steiner's laboratory," where they would deliver their talk. Another third were more hurried; they were told, "The assistant is ready for you, so please go right over." The final third were made to feel rushed. They were told, "Oh, you're late. They were expecting you a few minutes ago. We'd better get moving. The assistant should be waiting for you, so you'd better hurry."

That manipulation was all it took to significantly change the amount of help offered. Just 10 percent of students who had been told "you're late" helped the slumped man. Among those who were told to "go right over," 45 percent offered help. Only when explicitly told that they had a few extra minutes did a majority of seminarians (63 percent) act like Good Samaritans on their own campus.

The results of the Princeton Seminary experiment are stunning. Seminary students are on campus because they want to understand and spread Christ's teachings. And the parable of the Good Samaritan—a lesson from Jesus about the importance of helpfulness—might be the clearest and most straightforward to apply of all these teachings. Yet a majority of seminarians who were under a bit of time pressure walked right past someone who apparently needed help, even though they were thinking about helpfulness. As Darley and Batson note with barely contained glee, "On several occasions, a seminary student going to give his talk on the parable of the Good Samaritan literally stepped over the victim as he hurried on his way!"

Why did the time pressure matter so much? Well, being late to an appointment is rarely considered excellent behavior (you're making someone else wait, after all), but Presbyterians seem to really value being on time. As an 1864 article in *Reformed Presbyterian* magazine put it,

What a striking example of punctuality God gives us, and how worthy of being imitated! His sun rises and sets at his appointed time. The moon infallibly observes her season. The stars make their appearance at the very moment when we are taught to look for them. Even the erratic comet, that wanders far into immensity, returns with unvarying Precision... Punctuality is a source of pleasure to those by whom it is cultivated; it ensures confidence and respect from others.

Darley and Batson picked a campus community that had a strong norm of punctuality. Then they manipulated their experiment's subjects to feel like they were violating this norm to varying degrees. The bigger the violation, the less willing the subjects were to stop and see if someone needed help, even if they had helpfulness and altruism right at the top of their mind.

When I think about us humans as wise individuals, the results of the Princeton Seminary experiment are puzzling. But when I think about us as members of *Homo ultrasocialis,* a species whose members can't even survive unless they're part of a group, everything falls into place. Of course members of that species have a strong innate tendency to follow their group's norms. Not following them is a bad strategy for, you know, staying alive.

Our norm psychology is deeper than bone-deep. It's gene-deep. As we'll see, so are many other aspects of our behavior within groups. We adjust our behavior in all kinds of ways, in response to all kinds of cues, in order to maintain or improve our position within the group. And when the group-level environment shifts, we shift right along with it. Sometimes the resulting behavior changes are so big that it seems as if they could only have come about by swapping out the people involved.

In the pages ahead, we'll see Microsoft change from being a fast-moving, innovative company to one paralyzed by bureaucracy and sclerosis. We'll see

Arthur Andersen, a firm with a decades-long reputation for excellent ethics, driven out of business in just a few years because of the sleazy practices it adopted. We'll see projects full of people blithely lying to each other and their bosses, and offices full of people deceiving and defrauding their customers. In none of these cases can the bad behavior be traced to personnel changes—to good people leaving or bad people showing up (Andersen, in fact, hired its first professional ethicist just a few years before the federal conviction that drove it out of business). Instead, we'll see that these dysfunctions arose from changes to the group-level environment.

We'll also see plenty of positive examples. We'll look at how Microsoft accomplished its spectacular recent comeback. We'll see how, early in its history, Amazon reversed course and became much less bureaucratic and top-heavy. We'll examine how Salesforce keeps its more than seventy thousand employees aligned and working toward the company's goals, how the venture capital firm Andreessen Horowitz decides how to place big bets in a highly uncertain environment, and how a cast of geek characters including frustrated programmers and a fighter pilot changed not only the way that software is written but also how major efforts—from product launches to military campaigns—are managed around the world.

None of these success stories rely on large-scale personnel changes—on getting rid of the bad people who were messing things up and replacing them with good people. Instead, these companies all rely on the same small set of group-level tools, techniques, and approaches, which we'll explore in the pages ahead. A good way to start exploring this toolkit is to look at an intervention that's like the Princeton experiment, but in reverse: it harnesses our ultrasociality to boost altruistic behavior instead of causing it to wither away in an alley.

Normalizing Altruism

In 2017, economist Erez Yoeli realized that a little ultrasocial intervention and norm creation might be just the thing to get people to take all of their tuberculosis (TB) medicine. The word "all" in that last sentence is the tricky one. Antibiotics work to quickly relieve to relieve the fever, chest pain, fatigue, coughing (which can be constant and severe enough to cause internal bleeding), and other symptoms of TB, a debilitating and sometimes fatal disease. And because TB is so contagious, people suffering from it are often shunned or ostracized, which makes patients all the more eager to be cured—preferably before anyone around them even realizes they're sick. They're often willing to start taking a daily antibiotic strong enough to cause nausea and dizziness, and to miss work and travel to a clinic when they need more pills.

Once the disease's symptoms vanish, however, continuing to obtain and take the pills for several more months can seem like much more trouble than it's worth. But it's not; the antibiotic needs all that time to reach the last of the bacteria hiding deep in the patient's lungs and joints. If the disease isn't completely wiped out it can evolve into an antibiotic-resistant strain that's much more difficult and expensive to treat.

The first phase of treating TB is relatively easy because the benefit to the patient (feeling better) is often perceived as greater than the costs they bear (dizziness, nausea, inconvenience, time away from work). The latter phases are much more difficult because the costs continue, but the direct and obvious individual benefit has already been received. So patients need to be altruistic in order for their communities to avoid the scourge of antibiotic-resistant TB.

For a TB treatment program in Kenya, Yoeli and his colleagues came up with two ways to use human ultrasociality to elicit this altruism and get people to finish their entire course of medication. The first was similar to what Darley and Batson did at Princeton: have someone make the subject aware that they were behind schedule on an obligation. Patients in the Kenyan program received daily automatic messages on their phones asking them if they'd taken their medicine. If they didn't respond, two automated follow-up messages were sent. If they still didn't respond, they were contacted via messages and phone calls by a person who had successfully gone through the program. If *that* didn't work, someone from the clinic dispensing the medicine tried to contact the patient.

One reason for the human contact was to see if the patient had any questions or problems that could be resolved. But another reason was simply to make sure that patients felt that other people—in this case, a peer who had been through the same experience, and then, if necessary, a medical professional—were aware of what they were doing and had expectations that they'd stay on track. In other words, all the contacts reinforced to patients that there was a norm: finish all of your TB medication.

The other way the researchers tapped into patients' ultrasociality was to remind them that they were members of a human community—in which they wanted to remain members in good standing. However, this community absolutely could *not* be the patients' neighbors. TB carries a strong stigma because of its contagiousness, so neighbors couldn't be enlisted or notified (in fact, it could be dangerous for women if even their husbands found out that they had the disease). So instead the researchers created online groups consisting of the patients themselves. Members in these communities could encourage each other, see where they ranked on a leaderboard of reported adherence, and earn entry into a "winners' circle" if they reported that they took their medication on at least 90 percent of days.

These interventions may sound lightweight, but they made a big positive difference (like simply having someone tell the Princeton seminarians they were late led to a big negative difference). In a trial of more than a thousand patients served by seventeen clinics in and around Nairobi, the intervention reduced the number of patients who failed to complete the whole course of treatment by about two-thirds.

Two aspects of this intervention deserve special attention. The first is *observability,* or making important aspects of a situation widely visible. We ultrasocial humans are always watching what's going on around us in order to figure out (among other things) how we should behave, where we rank, and—let's be honest—what we can get away with. The TB patients' online communities and leaderboards showed who was taking their medication regularly, and who was not. Those who were got positive feedback and recognition. Those who weren't got the feeling that they were falling behind in the eyes of other members of the group. This lousy feeling encouraged people to take their medicine.

A useful rule of thumb is that observability increases adherence to norms. This rule held true in the Princeton Seminary experiment. Subjects who were told they would be late knew that their tardiness would be observable once they got to their destination, so they hurried. They also believed, even if they didn't consciously admit it to themselves, that if they walked past the slumped man (or, indeed, "literally stepped over" him), this act would *not* be seen, since it took place in what they thought was an otherwise deserted alley. Most of the seminarians behaved as if they were reacting to what was observable, not what was "right" or "moral" or "Christian."

The second aspect of the two experiments I want to highlight is close to the opposite of observability; it's *plausible deniability*. Can a person make a claim like "that wasn't me" or "that's not what happened" or "I didn't know / see / hear / do that" and have any hope of being believed? Just like it's a great idea to increase observability when establishing a new norm among a group of us ultrasocial human beings, it's also smart to reduce plausible deniability (and, if possible, eliminate it). In the Kenyan experiment, TB patients had a hard time claiming to themselves or anyone else that they didn't know that they were supposed to keep taking their medication every day for the entire course of treatment. The escalating sequence of daily messages and phone calls removed plausible deniability about that and helped ensure compliance. The Princeton seminarians, on the other hand, could plausibly claim all kinds of things about what did or didn't happen during what they thought was an unobserved encounter with the slumped man in the alley. "Yes, I passed by someone, but he didn't seem to be in any distress." "No, he wasn't coughing or anything." "No, I didn't notice anyone at all." As we'll see in the next chapter, we humans effortlessly come up with statements like these — statements intended to make us look good to other people. We very often even believe them ourselves.

Increasing observability and decreasing plausible deniability are core to the geek way, even if the business geeks themselves don't typically use those terms. They're two essential tools in the geek toolkit for building and maintaining healthy norms. We'll explore this toolkit more deeply in the pages ahead.

An Ultimate Way to Think

As we begin this exploration, I want to encourage you to think not only about *Homo sapiens,* but also about *Homo ultrasocialis.* In other words, in addition to thinking about people as intelligent individuals (which we are!) I also want you to think about people as members of a uniquely group-y species. Doing so helps us understand the results of the Princeton Seminary and Kenyan tuberculosis experiments. In both cases, the results are well explained by *Homo ultrasocialis's* innate tendency to follow norms, especially when observability is high and plausible deniability low. Thinking about wise *Homo sapiens,* meanwhile, doesn't much help us understand the Princeton seminarians' general lack of helpfulness even when they had helpfulness right at the top of their minds. The boxer Mike Tyson (whom we'll encounter again later in these pages) famously said that "everybody has plans until they get hit for the first time." I think it's equally true that everyone has a mindset until they encounter a norm. In those encounters, the norm usually dominates.

The *Homo ultrasocialis* view has been brewing for a while and has gained momentum in recent years. We can trace its origin to a famous 1963 paper titled "On Aims and Methods of Ethology," by the Nobel Prize–winning biologist Nikolaas Tinbergen.* Ethology is the study of animal behavior—everything from humans speaking to each other to peacocks showing off their amazing tails. Tinbergen proposed four kinds of questions to guide our study of such behaviors. Two of these questions are labeled *proximate,* because they're concerned with the here and now. Proximate questions are about *mechanism* ("How do humans produce speech?") and *ontogeny,* or development over a lifetime ("When do babies begin saying words? When do they start speaking in complete sentences?").

The other two kinds of questions are called *ultimate,* not because they're more profound, but because they take a longer view. Tinbergen's ultimate

---

* Nikolaas was not the only member of his family to win the Nobel Prize. In 1969, his brother Jan received the first Nobel Memorial Prize in Economic Sciences ever awarded. Nikolaas got his, in the Physiology or Medicine category, in 1973.

questions have to do with *function* ("Why do peacocks have such elaborate tails? What purpose do they serve?") and *phylogeny,* or evolutionary development ("When did the peacock's ancestors start developing big tails?").

You can forget about ontogeny and phylogeny now if you want to; they're not important for our purposes.* But it's critical to keep Tinbergen's other two categories in mind: proximate questions about how a behavior is accomplished—what its *mechanism* is—and ultimate questions about why it's there in the first place—what its *function* is.

It's critical because we learn a lot from answering both types of questions about our behaviors. Take overconfidence, for example. Within the *Homo sapiens* perspective, it's usually seen as a flaw in our generally excellent reasoning abilities. A lot of proximate research has investigated just how overconfident we are, and how this common cognitive bias can be elicited. This is valuable work. But it's also valuable to ask, Why does overconfidence exist? What's the function of overconfidence? Why, in other words, would evolution have designed humans to be overconfident?

The *Homo sapiens* perspective doesn't have many answers to these questions; it's not great at explaining why a wise creature would also be so unwise. But the *Homo ultrasocialis* perspective immediately points to an answer. Why are we so often overconfident? Because appearing confident—even more confident than is warranted—must provide some benefit to members of our ultra group-y species. As we'll see in the next chapter, there's a lot of

---

* However, there are two reasons to keep ontogeny and phylogeny in mind. The first is that you'll know what someone means when they try to sound deep by saying "ontogeny recapitulates phylogeny." This is a statement of the "biogenetic law," formulated in the nineteenth century, which holds that as an embryo develops, it successively takes the form of all its species' evolutionary ancestors (for example, human beings evolved from marine creatures, so human embryos pass through a stage where they look like fish). This "law" is nonsense, and you should be wary of the scientific credentials of anyone who repeats the "recapitulates" phrase. The second reason is that if you keep phylogeny in mind, you'll definitely know which came first, the chicken or the egg. Hard-shelled eggs first appeared hundreds of millions of years ago, whereas chickens as a species are less than sixty thousand years old. So there's a clear ultimate answer to that age-old riddle: the egg came first.

evidence that it does. Overconfident people generally do well, so we've been shaped by evolution to be overconfident.

As with overconfidence, so too with a lot of our other behaviors. The *Homo ultrasocialis* perspective suggests answers to ultimate questions. Why, for example, is "myside" bias so prevalent—why are we more likely to believe things we've heard from members of our own religion or political party? Because it's important for us ultrasocial human beings to be members in good standing of our group, going along with its beliefs and not questioning them too much. Why do so many societies stress deference to elders? Because elders are storehouses of important knowledge and know-how—of the products of the group's cultural evolution—and for most of our history as a species, we didn't have Wikipedia, libraries, or other ways to access this knowledge.*

Speaking of Wikipedia, by early 2022 its "List of Cognitive Biases" contained about two hundred entries. These departures from rationality are fascinating, and we've been investigating them within organizational scholarship for about half a century. Much of this work was sparked by the landmark paper "Judgment Under Uncertainty: Heuristics and Biases," published in *Science* in 1974 by psychologists Amos Tversky and Daniel Kahneman.

Their work was instrumental in launching the field of behavioral decision-making, which is still going strong. It's a field that has led to Nobel Prizes (for Kahneman and others), MacArthur "genius grants" (for Tversky and others), and countless important insights into how our minds work. It's also helped us improve everything from making parole decisions to helping people save for retirement. I have trouble thinking of other fields in the postwar social sciences that have made greater contributions.

However, most of the research in behavioral decision-making has been proximate. It asks questions like "How big is this bias? How much does it distort our decisions? How is it elicited?" If it asks the ultimate question "Why does this bias exist?," the answer is usually something like "It's a

---

* Also, the mere fact that elders have lived a long time in a challenging environment indicates that they know what they're doing, and should be listened to.

heuristic (that is, a rule of thumb) that lets us economize on difficult thinking and get to a good-enough answer quickly. In other words, it's a time- and laborsaving device." But many entries in the Wikipedia list aren't considered to be heuristics. The proximate view is that they're simply biases: flaws in human cognition, bugs in our mental hardware and software.

From a *Homo ultrasocialis* perspective, however, the Wikipedia list looks very different. It's not primarily a list of bugs. Instead, it's in large part a list of *features*—of human behaviors that are there for a reason. The challenge for ultimate researchers is to figure out what those reasons are: why a behavior exists, and what its function is.

The challenge for entrepreneurs, executives, and managers is to build healthy, fast-learning companies. From the *Homo sapiens* perspective, cognitive biases look like flaws that could hurt a company. Overconfident people, for example, could launch a product that flops in the marketplace, or disappoint investors by overestimating how fast growth will be. Flaws like overconfidence need to be fixed, and the way to fix them is to point them out to people who, being wise, will recognize them for what they are and try to fix them. I certainly want to be less overconfident, less tribal in my thinking, and so on. And there are great books and other resources out there to help with that work. There are plenty of ways to get wiser and cultivate better habits of mind.

If you adopt the *Homo ultrasocialis* perspective, you won't throw away those books or stop trying to cultivate better habits of mind, but you will start doing something else. You'll work on creating better habits of groupmind—better norms. In addition to helping people become less overconfident, for example, you'll also take it for granted that some level of overconfidence will always be with us (that it's just part of human nature) and think about how to put it to good use. As we'll see in the next chapter, that's exactly what the great geek norm of science does, and it works astonishingly well.

There are plenty of other ways to put the *Homo ultrasocialis* perspective to use. For example, this perspective causes leaders to ask different questions about the critical topic of ethics. In addition to asking, "What kind of ethics training should we have for our people?," they'll also ask, "What are ethical behaviors we want to encourage? How can we turn these behaviors into norms? How can we increase observability that these norms are being followed, and reduce plausible deniability that they're not?" As this example shows, taking the *Homo ultrasocialis* perspective focuses us on group-level interventions, while the *Homo sapiens* perspective often focuses on individuals.

The more I learn, the more skeptical I get about the ability of individual-level training and education to make a lasting difference at an organization. I agree with the psychologist Jonathan Haidt, who says, "Nobody is ever going to invent an ethics class that makes people behave ethically after they step out of the classroom" and go back to work. But as we saw with the Kenyan TB medicine study, changes at the level of the group can make a huge positive difference in prosocial behaviors.

Thanks to a lot of excellent ultimate research, we're much better at designing group-level interventions now than we were just a couple decades ago. As we'll see, this research asks some version of the ultimate question "Why do we humans behave the way we do?" Very often the answers center around some combination of ultrasociality, norms, learning, and cultural evolution.

We're going to put those answers to work in the pages ahead. This is an ultimate business book — one that starts from ultimate questions about why we weird and wonderful human beings behave the way we do. Immersing myself in those questions has led me to adopt a *Homo ultrasocialis* view of my fellow humans, as well as a *Homo sapiens* view. I hope the following pages will encourage you to do the same.

The Great Geek Ground Rule

Business geeks and scientists who study evolution have independently come to the same conclusion: that humanity's superpower is at the level of the group, not the individual, so it makes sense to focus on the group. Evolutionary scientists think that our fast-learning groups, rather than our big brains, have brought us to where we are. Business geeks who want to build fast-learning companies—innovative, agile, responsive, productive ones, in other words—likewise focus their efforts on improving groups rather than individuals. The geeks think of our species more as *Homo ultrasocialis* than *Homo sapiens*.

We've already seen several examples of the geek focus on groups over individuals. Recall from chapter 1 what happened after Reed Hastings almost sank Netflix with his disastrous Qwikster idea. In *No Rules Rules* he doesn't reveal that he made a solemn vow to himself to make fewer bone-headed decisions. Or read lots of self-help books about how to reason more effectively or sharpen his judgment. Or (ahem) sign up for an executive education course on strategy at an elite business school. In short, he didn't try to make himself a better individual decision maker. Instead, he made sure that important decisions at Netflix were put before a group of *Homo ultrasocialis*. Farming for dissent, socializing ideas, enabling junior employees to gather evidence and challenge executives with it—these are all group-level activities.

In the wake of his bad decision on Qwikster, Hastings's approach was not to try to equip himself with better habits of mind. Instead, it was to work to equip his company with better habits of groupmind. That's a savvy approach, because habits of groupmind—norms, in other words—are so important to our ultrasocial species. A company with the wrong norms generates bureaucracy, sclerosis, delays, hypocrisy, cultures full of undiscussable topics, and lousy jobs. A company with the right ones generates excellent performance and a healthy work environment. What most clearly separates the Quibis of the business world from the Netflixes isn't the individual brilliance of their leaders; it's the emphasis that their leaders place on creating and maintaining the right culture. Another way to say the same thing is that "geek" isn't a state of mind possessed by an individual. Instead, it's a particular state of groupmind possessed by a collection of ultrasocial, culture-producing humans.

As we saw from the companies featured in chapter 1, the geek state of groupmind emphasizes science, ownership, speed, and openness. The next four chapters will explore each of these four great geek norms in turn. We'll see why they work so well, and how geek leaders go about establishing and maintaining them. All of their efforts follow a single ground rule, which we can state using some of the terminology we've picked up so far.

Are you ready for it? Here it is. Here's the ultimate geek ground rule: *Shape the ultrasociality of group members so that the group's cultural evolution is as rapid as possible in the desired direction.* That ground rule might not have made a lot of sense before you started reading this book, but I hope it makes some sense now. At a high level, shaping the group's ultrasociality means putting in place the norms of science, ownership, speed, and openness. At a lower level, it means increasing observability, decreasing plausible deniability, and doing other things that we'll explore in the pages ahead. Making cultural evolution as rapid as possible means compressing the time it takes you to launch your spaceships, or whatever you're launching. Innovate more. Improve faster. Become more nimble. Make your customers happier. Operate with greater efficiency and reliability. Get higher productivity growth (or, for you noneconomists, get better at converting all your inputs into outputs). All of these are business versions of cultural evolution. In recent decades, we've learned a lot about how cultural evolution happens. As a result, we know how to speed it up.

We also know how easily it can go off track. We need "in the desired direction" at the end of the ground rule because a culture can evolve in undesired directions: toward bureaucracy, sclerosis, infighting, unethical behavior, harassment and abuse, and other woes. The business geeks are keenly aware of this possibility, and keen to avoid it. As we'll see, the great geek norms help companies avoid devolving into dysfunction.

Chapter Summary

Maybe *Homo sapiens* isn't the best name for our species. I think a better name—one that really highlights what makes us unique and what has made us so successful—is *Homo ultrasocialis*. Humans cooperate more intensely and evolve their cultures faster than any other animals. We're the planet's only *ultrasocial* creatures.

Our intelligence alone can't keep us alive, but our social groups can and do. Our groups hold the knowledge and know-how we need. Without them, we're goners. Within them, we build spaceships.

Because evolution has shaped us to be so social, we adjust our behavior in all kinds of ways, in response to all kinds of cues, in order to maintain or improve our position within the group. And when the social environment shifts, we shift right along with it.

Increasing observability and decreasing plausible deniability are core to the geek way. They're two essential tools in the geek toolkit for building and maintaining healthy norms.

Business geeks and scientists who study evolution have independently come to the same conclusion: that humanity's superpower is at the level of the group, not the individual, so it makes sense to focus on the group.

Here's the ultimate geek ground rule: *Shape the ultrasociality of group members so that the group's cultural evolution is as rapid as possible in the desired direction.*

CHAPTER 4

Science

The Press Secretary Versus the Iron Rule

It does not make any difference how beautiful your guess is. It does not make any difference how smart you are, who made the guess, or what his name is—if it disagrees with experiment it is wrong. That is all there is to it.

—*Richard Feynman*

M anagement scholar Margaret Neale has what every public speaker wants: a foolproof live demonstration.

That's almost an oxymoron. Anything that can go wrong in front of an audience usually does, and many demos flop or fail. But when Neale takes the stage carrying a glass bottle full of paper clips, she knows what's going to happen: she's going to reveal to the audience members how bad they are at a simple task, and how most of them are bad in the same odd way. Her demo helps us understand something fundamental: why it's so common for companies to make really bad decisions.

A 2007 Stanford podcast features a session in which Neale asks audience members to guess how many paper clips are in the bottle. She tells them that the bottle is about 80 percent full of standard paper clips, and that the actual number is between one and 1 million. She asks everyone to write down their best guess.

"What I want you to do now," Neale says, "is I want you to give me a 95 percent confidence interval. Now, what I mean by that is I want you to give me a range in which you are 95 percent certain that number actually falls."

After a few seconds Neale reveals that the bottle contains 488 paper clips. She asks how many people guessed that number exactly. No one did. Then she says, "How many of you got—and I want you to hold your hands up proudly—got 488 *in your range?*"

Neale narrates the surprising result:

Maybe half. You guys were half right… On average, 95 percent of you should have gotten it right. And about 50 percent did. You guys suck at paper clips.

Then Neale reveals the point of this exercise:

Now you're probably thinking, "But Maggie, *we don't care about paper clips.*" And I agree with you. I don't care if you can guess paper clips accurately. But what I *do* care about is that you know what you know and you know what you don't know.

Why did you miss my number 488 in your range? What was the characteristic of your range? *Too narrow.* What would a narrow range suggest? "I would be good at guessing paper clips." If you thought you were really *bad* at guessing paper clips, I was trying to help you. I said one to a million!

But no, you guys said, "I'm good at this stuff. I can guess those paper clips." You guys are *overconfident.*

As we saw in the previous chapter, the ultimate view of overconfidence is that it's a feature, not a bug. To say the same thing a different way, overconfidence isn't a flaw in the mental hardware of *Homo sapiens*. Instead, it actually has a function for us *Homo ultrasocialis;* it's there for a reason. That reason can be hard to discern, though, because overconfidence causes so many harms.

Textbook Cases of Cognitive Bias

As psychologist Scott Plous puts it, "Overconfidence has been called the most 'pervasive and potentially catastrophic' of all the cognitive biases to which human beings fall victim. It has been blamed for lawsuits, strikes, wars, and stock market bubbles and crashes." As we see with the examples of both Jeffrey Katzenberg at Quibi and Reed Hastings at Netflix, being an experienced and successful executive is no guarantee against overconfidence. Katzenberg launched the ill-conceived Quibi app without widely beta testing it. And Hastings, after being disastrously wrong about Qwikster, was still overconfident in his judgment about both kids' programming and the demand for downloading among Netflix subscribers (Hastings thought it was a "1 percent use case"; actual demand was at least 15 percent).

It gets worse: we like our overconfident judgments so much that we go around actively trying to confirm them instead of stress-testing them or subjecting them to real scrutiny. In other words, our overconfidence goes hand in hand with the *confirmation bias:* a tendency to favor information that supports or reinforces our existing beliefs, and to downplay or ignore information that contradicts them. As the cognitive scientists Hugo Mercier and Dan Sperber write, "The list [of examples of the confirmation bias] could go on for pages (indeed for chapters or books, even). Moreover,... it is not only ordinary participants who fall prey to the confirmation bias. Being gifted, focused, motivated, or open minded is no protection against the confirmation bias."

Neither is being a huge multinational corporation with a lot to lose from getting a big decision wrong. The story that follows, one of the oddest in modern corporate history, serves as a reminder that overconfidence and confirmation bias know no bounds.

On April 23, 1985, at a New York press conference, Coca-Cola CEO Roberto Goizueta announced the unthinkable: his company was changing its flagship product. As he confidently put it, "The best has been made even better... Simply stated, we have a new formula for Coke." The "New Coke" would be rolled out quickly around the world and the existing recipe, which had been in use since 1886, would be retired.* In response to a dumbfounded reporter's question, Goizueta called it "one of the easiest [decisions] we have ever made."

It was so easy because Goizueta and a few confidants had evidence that people liked New Coke better. In 1985 Coke was still the clear leader in carbonated beverages, but it had been steadily losing market share to Pepsi. One reason the gap was shrinking was a successful ad campaign based around a type of A/B test. This was the "Pepsi challenge," a blind side-by-side taste test in which a majority of people preferred the sweeter, less sharp taste of Pepsi over Coke after taking a sip of each.

Coke's internal tests showed the same thing as the Pepsi challenge, which convinced Goizueta of the need for change. He enlisted a few executives in a plan to strike back at Pepsi. They came up with a sweeter cola formulation that beat the existing recipe in secretly conducted taste tests, 55 percent to 45 percent. This formulation became New Coke, which quickly became a disaster.

After the press conference Coke drinkers immediately started calling the company to complain. By June, there were eight thousand such calls a day. Customers angry at the change formed protest groups with names like Old Cola Drinkers of America. They poured New Coke down sewers and complained that the people at the top of the company had "taken away my freedom of choice." At least one lawsuit was filed. To hold off the New Coke–only future for as long as possible, people stockpiled all the old-recipe inventory they could get their hands on. A Beverly Hills wine merchant started selling the vintage stuff for $50 per case, and soon sold out. A Hollywood producer rented a $1,200-per-month wine cellar to hold his stash. And Coca-Cola's powerful independent bottlers complained at least as loudly as consumers did. Even Fidel Castro weighed in, calling the decision to switch to New Coke a sign of American capitalism's decadence.

---

* Prior to New Coke there were two significant changes to the recipe for Coca-Cola. In 1980, sugar from beet and cane was replaced with high-fructose corn syrup. And in 1905, the extract of coca leaves (cocaine, in other words) was removed.

Goizueta soon realized that he'd made a huge mistake. On July 10, the company announced, "We want people to know that we are sorry for any discontent we have caused them. For almost three months we have hurt you and for that we are very sorry." Coca-Cola brought back the original recipe, rebranded it as Coke Classic, and sold it alongside New Coke. The furor died down, and New Coke eventually died out.* There's no more Coke Classic; it's once again just Coke.

Can anyone avoid succumbing to overconfidence and confirmation bias? We might think that the people most resistant to them would be scientists. After all, their whole business is the pursuit of objective truth. This pursuit could well attract those who are more rational and less prone to self-delusion. We might further think that the scientists who study our cognitive biases would be the least susceptible to them, and that the top scientists in the field would be the least prone to making fundamental errors due to over-confidence and confirmation bias.

We might think all that but we'd be wrong, as the story of an elite cognitive scientist trying to bring a product to market shows.

Psychologist Danny Kahneman is one of the foremost experts in how our minds work. His contributions to our understanding of ourselves are so important that they were recognized with the first Nobel Prize in Economics ever awarded to a noneconomist. In his landmark book *Thinking, Fast and Slow,* Kahneman tells the story of how he convinced the Israeli government of the need for a high school textbook on judgment and decision-making. The all-star team he assembled to create the book included Seymour Fox, an expert on curriculum design. Kahneman writes that "after meeting every Friday afternoon for about a year, we had constructed a detailed outline of the syllabus, had written a couple of chapters, and had run a few sample lessons in the classroom. We all felt that we had made good progress."

At that point, Kahneman had the smart idea to use a technique—one that would be included in the textbook—for surveying the members of a

---

* A limited supply of New Coke was released in 2019 as part of the promotional campaign for the Netflix series *Stranger Things,* which was set in the mid-1980s.

group. During a team meeting he asked everyone to write down how long they thought it would take to finish the book. (He hadn't discussed the topic with anyone else before the meeting.) These independent estimates ranged from one and a half to two and a half years, with an average right in the middle.

Kahneman then had another good idea. He tried to find out what the *base rate* was: how long did previous projects take to create a first textbook for a brand-new curriculum? He posed the question to Fox, the veteran on the project. As Kahneman relates,

> He fell silent. When he finally spoke, it seemed to me that he was blushing, embarrassed by his own answer: "You know, I never realized this before, but in fact not all the teams at a stage comparable to ours ever did complete their task. A substantial fraction of the teams ended up failing to finish the job."
>
> This was worrisome; we had never considered the possibility that we might fail. My anxiety rising, I asked how large he estimated that fraction was. "About 40 percent," he answered. By now, a pall of gloom was falling over the room. The next question was obvious: "Those who finished," I asked. "How long did it take them?" "I cannot think of any group that finished in less than seven years," he replied.

Under cross-examination by Kahneman, Fox acknowledged that the base rate he had just given might not apply to their team. But this was because the team was slightly *below* average in terms of their experience and resources. So it was likely that they would take more than seven years to finish, not less. Fox also acknowledged that his own original estimate for how long the project would take — the one he had written down just minutes earlier — had been as optimistic as his colleagues'.

After receiving all this highly relevant information, what did Kahneman and the rest of the team do with it? They ignored it. As Kahneman explains:

The statistics that Seymour provided were treated as base rates normally are—noted and promptly set aside…After a few minutes of desultory debate, we gathered ourselves together and carried on as if nothing had happened.

The textbook ended up taking eight years to finish, by which time the priorities of the Israeli Ministry of Education had changed. The book was never used in the country's classrooms. Kahneman's summary of the project is concise: "We should have quit [the] day [of that meeting]."

The Secretary of Our Interior

How could so many smart, experienced scientists ignore clear evidence—evidence about an important topic in their professional lives—that was right in front of them? It's not because Kahneman is worse than his peers at thinking clearly (I'm singling him out only because he was forthcoming enough to write about his own faulty reasoning). It turns out that overconfidence and confirmation bias seem to be as common among scientists as they are among people in other professions. In his 2020 book, *The Knowledge Machine,* philosopher Michael Strevens concludes that scientists are just as biased and mentally sloppy as the rest of us: "In their thinking about the connection between theory and data, scientists seem scarcely to follow any rules at all." Kahneman and his colleagues on the textbook project, in fact, followed a completely unscientific rule of "ignore data you don't like." What caused them to do this? And whatever it is, how can it possibly be a feature instead of a bug—how can it be useful for us to be so chronically biased in our thinking?

Dear reader, let me introduce you to your press secretary. It's a mental module responsible for giving you confidence by making you look good. To yourself.

This module was identified and named in a 2007 paper by psychologists Robert Kurzban and Athena Aktipis. They proposed that the press secretary—and overconfidence, in large part—exist because confidence is so important for us *Homo ultrasocialis.* Confident people have an easier time attracting allies, psyching out opponents, and attracting mates. Recent research finds that confidence is, in fact, sexy, even more so than prestige. Everyone from a Nobel Prize–winning French scientist (Marie Curie: "We must have perseverance and above all confidence in ourselves") to a Jamaican political activist (Marcus Garvey: "If you have no confidence in self you are twice defeated in the race of life. With confidence you have won even before you have started") to an American football quarterback (Joe Namath: "When you have confidence, you can have a lot of fun. And when you have fun, you can do amazing things") agrees on the power of confidence.

My favorite explanation of the ultimate importance of confidence is found in David Mamet's 1987 film, *House of Games.* In it, con man — *confidence* man — Mike Mancuso explains the social dynamic at the heart of his trade:

> It's called a confidence game. Why? Because you give me your confidence? No. *Because I give you mine.*

In 2016 Kahneman and I had a conversation about an especially talented player of this game. We were riding in a van from the airport to a conference, talking about — what else? — the upcoming American presidential election. It was still early in the campaign, but Donald Trump already had a huge amount of momentum. I asked Kahneman if he had an explanation for the Trump phenomenon, which I found puzzling given how inconsistent Trump's daily pronouncements were. Kahneman thought for a bit, then said (with a level of insight that I think is typical for him), "I think part of it is that he's *confidently* inconsistent. If he were inconsistently confident, on the other hand, he wouldn't be nearly as popular."

So how do we achieve consistent confidence? We could remind or train ourselves to appear confident all the time, but that takes constant work and vigilance. It would be much easier if we could just naturally and effortlessly *be* confident — more confident than is justified by events and evidence.

Biologist Robert Trivers argues that humans excel at exactly this state of being, which he labels self-deception. And we deceive ourselves not just about the quality of our ideas and judgment, but also about many other things: our generosity, our morals and ethics, our social status, our looks — any arena, in short, where it would be advantageous for us *Homo ultrasocialis* to be perceived favorably by others. As Trivers explains it,

> This entire counterintuitive arrangement [of deceiving ourselves] exists for the benefit of manipulating others. We hide reality from our conscious minds the better to hide it from onlookers.

Trivers and others have marshaled a lot of evidence that we're chronic self-deceivers:

- At one company studied, 40 percent of engineers said that they were among the best 5 percent.
- Fewer than 10 percent of college professors acknowledge that their own work is below average.
- Twenty-five percent of high school seniors believe that they're truly amazing "people people" — among the top 1 percent in ability to get along with others.
- Middle-aged adults appear to push memories of immoral actions a decade deeper into the past than memories of moral actions. This has the effect of making the immoral versions of themselves old news.
- For an experiment, researchers manipulated photos of participants to make them appear more or less attractive, then asked the participants which photos most closely resembled themselves. On average, people chose the 20 percent more attractive photos.
- In one particularly devilish study, participants were asked how often they engaged in a range of moral behaviors. Six weeks later, they were shown the averaged responses of all participants and asked how they compared. Most people rated themselves as well above average on most behaviors. However, the "averages" they were looking at were actually just *their own responses* from six weeks earlier. So participants unknowingly rated themselves as more moral than...themselves.

There might be a lot of evidence supporting the theory of self-deception, but it appears to rest on a shaky foundation: the idea that one part of our mind can hide information from another. This feels like a contradiction in terms, since we're used to thinking about our mind as a single entity. Most disciplines that consider the human mind share this view. From psychology to economics to philosophy, the mainstream view has long been that we humans have a unitary mind; there's a single "me," a single "you," and so on.

Modular, Machiavellian Minds

But in recent decades a different view has emerged. It argues that our minds are deeply modular—composed of many distinct regions, each of which is dedicated to one or more specialized tasks. Many of these modules don't need or "want" to interact with each other in order to accomplish their tasks. So they don't. Robert Kurzban gives an ultimate explanation for this arrangement:

> Because of the way evolution operates, the mind consists of many, many parts, and these parts have many different functions. Because they're designed to do different things, they don't always work in perfect harmony...An important consequence of this view is that it makes us think about the "self" in a way that is very different from how people usually understand it. In particular, it makes the very notion of a "self" something of a problem, and perhaps even quite a bit less useful than one might think.

Let me describe one especially convincing demonstration of our minds' modularity. It was part of a landmark series of experiments conducted by psychologist Michael Gazzaniga and neuroscientist Joseph LeDoux on split-brain patients.

In the 1960s a small number of patients with severe epilepsy had surgery that severed the corpus callosum, the region of the brain that links the two hemispheres.* The procedure alleviated their symptoms and left their cognitive capabilities intact, but gave them physically split brains; their right and left hemispheres couldn't share information with each other.

It was known at the time that most people have their entire speech center in the brain's left hemisphere. It was also known that each hemisphere of the human brain is "wired" to one half of the body; the left hemisphere controls the right arm, receives inputs from the right side of the visual field, and so on. This arrangement allowed the researchers to work with a split-brain patient and observe, via a clever experimental design, what happened when his speech center was asked to explain something that his nonspeech (right) side of the brain did (remember, there was no communication possible between the two sides of this patient's brain).

The results of these experiments were consistent and astonishing. The split-brain patient immediately and confidently offered an explanation that couldn't be correct. The researchers knew that it was incorrect because of the way that they had set up the experiment. They knew that the speech side of the patient's brain was sensing and responding exclusively to one set of information — call it S — while the nonspeech side was sensing and responding exclusively to a different set of information — call it N — which did not at all overlap with S. When the patient was asked to explain why the nonspeech side did what it did, his speech side came up with and verbally delivered an explanation that relied completely on S, but not at all on N.† That explanation couldn't be correct, because the nonspeech side was completely

---

* I'm simplifying the medical science of the split-brain patients a bit here in order to not get bogged down in details.

† If you're interested in the details of this experiment, here they are: The patient's visual field connected to the speech side was shown a chicken foot, while at the same time the visual field connected to the nonspeech side was shown a snowy scene. The patient was then asked to look at a group of images and point with each hand to an image that was related to what they'd just been looking at. As expected, his speech-side hand pointed to an image of a chicken (remember, the speech-side visual field had been looking at a chicken foot). Also as expected, his nonspeech hand pointed at an image of a snow shovel (since the nonspeech visual field had been looking at a snowy scene). (*continued on next page*)

ignorant about S when it acted. What's remarkable is that that ignorance didn't stop the speech center, or even slow it down, from offering a confident explanation based exclusively on S. The speech center didn't know what it didn't know. It didn't even know *that* it didn't know. It thought that it was in possession of all relevant information, and effortlessly offered an S-based explanation.

Kurzban poses a key question raised by this experiment, and one with an uncomfortable answer:

What did "the patient" think was going on? Here's the thing. There's no such thing as "the patient." There's no real answer to that question because "the patient" is two more or less disconnected hemispheres. You can only ask about what individual, distinct, and separated parts think. The question asking what "the patient" sees is bad, and the answer is meaningless... It's a mistake to pay attention only to what comes out of the mouth when we're trying to understand what's in the mind, because there are many, many parts of the mind that can't talk... There's nothing special about the bit of the brain that controls the vocal cords; it's just another piece of meat in your head.

The experimenters then asked the patient why his speech-side hand was pointing to a picture of a chicken. Since his speech-side visual field had been looking at a chicken foot just seconds earlier, he gave a perfectly reasonable answer: "The chicken goes with the chicken foot."

Now comes the really interesting part: the experimenters then asked the patient why his nonspeech hand was pointing to a picture of a shovel. What happened? The patient immediately and effortlessly explained why: it was because "you need a shovel to clean out the chicken shed."

Except that *that can't be why he pointed to the shovel*, because at the time of pointing his nonspeech side knew nothing about chickens. It only knew about the snowy scene it had been looking at. His speech side, meanwhile, was completely ignorant about what the nonspeech side saw, or why it directed its hand to point at anything. Remember, there was no communication possible between the two sides after the severing of the corpus callosum.

This ignorance, however, didn't bother the patient's speech module at all. In fact, it didn't even know that it was ignorant. It thought that it was in possession of all relevant information—pictures of a chicken foot, a chicken, and a shovel—and effortlessly told a story that linked those pieces of information together.

This view is alien and counterintuitive to most of us, since we're used to thinking about minds as essentially unitary entities instead of modular ones. We're also used to thinking of ourselves as self-aware people who are capable of accurate introspection; we believe that we can successfully query our own motives and reasoning and talk accurately about them. Most of us also believe that we know what we don't know—that we're aware when our introspection comes up short or draws a blank.

By and large, nope. The split-brain experiments and lots of other research challenge those beliefs, and challenge them deeply. This work presents a human mind like the one described by Kurzban: modular, not deeply interconnected, often not self-aware, and always happy to tell *and believe* stories that don't line up with reality as long as those stories make us look good.

The theory of self-deception advanced by Trivers, Kurzban, and others is an ultimate theory. It proposes that evolution has made use of the human brain's modularity for a particular function: to allow us to tell favorable stories about ourselves to ourselves, so that we can confidently and in all good conscience tell them to other members of our ultrasocial species. This is the press secretary in action. Its speciality is putting the best possible spin on everything about us: our performance, our accomplishments, our morals, our looks, our behavior, our progress toward goals, and so on.

The press secretary is always on call, takes on a wide variety of assignments, and works very quickly. About a decade ago a friend and I went from Boston to Manhattan for the weekend. We took her car, and I drove. As we approached New York City, the car suddenly started slowing down no matter how hard I stomped on the accelerator. A couple tense seconds of scanning the environment showed that the car was in fact out of gas.

The next few seconds were also tense. I had to find the car's hazard lights, turn them on, cross multiple lanes of traffic, and come to a stop on the shoulder of the highway. During that time I was working pretty hard. So was my press secretary. But it wasn't working on preserving our safety; it was working on preserving my self-image. It instantaneously composed and delivered a memo about how all the blame lay elsewhere. This memo highlighted that it wasn't my car; my friend hadn't put gas in it, or told me that it was low when we set off; the gas gauge was way off to the side of the dash-board, and didn't start blinking or chiming or anything when the tank got low. The memo stressed that *this is not my fault and I am an excellent driver.* As I look back on the incident, I still find it remarkable how quickly and naturally these thoughts occurred at a time when I would have expected my brain to be 100 percent focused on the emergency at hand. And my press secretary instantly delivered the memo to my speech center. I could have confidently explained to my companion and anyone else that *this is not my fault and I am an excellent driver.* All this despite the fact that it was clearly my fault that a car I was driving ran out of gas.*

The press secretary works on long-term projects as well as emergencies. When I was younger I played a lot of squash (which is kind of like racquet-ball played with long-handled rackets).† On most Saturday mornings, I'd go to my gym for a clinic led by a pro. We often did drills in which we'd work on particular shots.

Your ability to hit a good squash shot depends on two things: your own skill, and the difficulty of the incoming shot that you're reacting to (just like in other racket sports). On the court and after the clinic, I was always amazed at the difficulty of the shots I was reacting to. They had to be harder than the ones the other players in the clinic were getting; there was no other way to explain why my own shots weren't as good as theirs. After all, I'd been play-ing the game about as long as they had, was a generally athletic guy, and was clearly better at the sport than the evidence from the clinic would indicate. The weekly memo from my press secretary was always the same: *Due to a sta-tistical fluke, you got harder shots hit at you today than the other players did.*

Did I know that I wasn't as good as I thought I was? To paraphrase Kurzban, the question is pretty bad and the answer is largely meaningless.

---

* Even as I typed that sentence, my press secretary was resisting the idea that the incident was my fault.

† Despite the obvious similarities between the two sports, most squash players look down on racquetball and will have nothing to do with it. The squash courts at my gym were often crowded while the racquetball ones were almost always empty. In all the times that I couldn't get a squash court or had to wait for one, it never once occurred to me to play racquetball.

The part of my brain that understands basic statistics could have worked out the (extremely low) probability that by chance I always received more difficult shots than everybody else. But the press secretary is also part of my brain, and one with a close connection to my self-image. And it kept telling me how good I was. The parts of my mind responsible for my self-image and presentation to others were eager to read the self-deceptive memos drafted by the press secretary, because "Andy is good at squash" is better for my confidence than "Andy is lousy at squash." Same thing with "Andy is principled," "Andy is a good friend and a trustworthy ally," "Andy is benevolent and kind," "Andy is smart and productive," and so on. It even makes great ultimate sense for me to be self-deceptive about "Andy is self-aware."

My reaction to the squash clinics demonstrates that the press secretary module thrives on plausible deniability. As long as there's some way to make the case that I'm good at squash (or good in whatever way), and to plausibly deny evidence pointing in the opposite direction, the press secretary will keep doggedly making the case. It doesn't even have to be all that plausible—just plausible enough to keep alive the idea of my excellence. I finally stopped playing squash because I kept losing to people who I didn't think were as good as I was. The score kept showing, however, that they were better. After a while there was no plausible way for even my press secretary to deny that. So I hung up my racquet, having thoroughly absorbed tennis player Andre Agassi's insight that "a win doesn't feel as good as a loss feels bad, and the good feeling doesn't last as long as the bad. Not even close."

It used to be that whenever I heard politicians say outrageous things that had no basis in reality, I would ask myself: "They can't actually believe that, can they?" But the more I learn about the press secretary module, the more I think that's actually not a useful question. The press secretary excels at giving us reason to believe; that's its job, and it's very good at it.

Almost all of us (politicians included) have said things that we know to be bald-faced lies.* But for most of us, those kinds of falsehoods are rare.

---

* There appear to be some people who lie very infrequently. They probably don't go into politics.

Flat-out lies are at one end of what we can call the range of self-awareness — the end where we're absolutely aware of the veracity of what we're saying. Most of us don't say a lot of falsehoods at that end of the range, in large part because the press secretary can't operate there. I never told my friends in San Francisco, "I beat the pro at my squash club yesterday." It's not just that I was worried my falsehood would get back to Cambridge, where I live; it's that my press secretary couldn't help me say that sentence with any confidence.

The split-brain patient who participated in the experiment described above was all the way at the other end of the range of self-awareness. He had absolutely no idea that he was giving a false explanation for his responses. Most of the time, most of us operate in the murky middle of the range of self-awareness, where plausible deniability exists and where the press secretary really shines. For years, I easily told my friends in San Francisco, Cambridge, and everywhere else, "I'm one of the better squash players at my club," because my press secretary could plausibly draft that false memo.*

We see press secretaries operating in the murky middle throughout Kahneman's story about how badly he and his colleagues underestimated their textbook project. Seymour Fox had a great deal of knowledge about how long such projects actually took. Yet in response to Kahneman's initial request for an estimate, Fox's press secretary drafted a memo that *this* project would only take a couple years. And after Kahneman elicited Fox's knowledge about how long comparable projects actually took, and how their inexperienced team would probably take longer, everyone involved found it plausible to deny that inconvenient truth. As Kahneman recalls, "All we could see was a reasonable plan that should produce a book in about two years, conflicting with statistics indicating that other teams had failed or had taken an absurdly long time to complete their mission."

As these examples show, the press secretary excels at ignoring inconvenient information. What's even more striking, though, is how good it is at incorporating anything and everything that *is* convenient — that can be used to confirm to ourselves that we're more competent than we actually are.

---

* I haven't played squash in a decade, but it still hurt to type the word *false* there.

Or more virtuous or moral or anything else that will improve our standing in the eyes of others. As we saw at the start of this chapter, confirmation bias is right up there with overconfidence on the list of pervasive and sticky cognitive biases.

Because of confirmation bias, we have to be very careful when designing efforts to help people make better decisions. There's a real danger that these efforts could backfire. For example, we often think that giving people more information will help. But replace the word *people* there with *press secretaries,* and the risk becomes clear: the press secretary module will pick out the most self-serving bits and use them to draft even more convincing memos.

This is not just a hypothetical risk. In one study, people who were well-informed about contentious issues like gun control and affirmative action couldn't come up with even a single argument against their own position. People with less knowledge, meanwhile, could articulate multiple opposing points. As philosopher Michael Hannon summarizes, "The most politically knowledgeable individuals tend to be the most partisan, and... the most knowledgeable and passionate voters are also the most likely to think in corrupted, biased ways... Attempts to remedy voter ignorance are problematic because partisans tend to become more polarized when they acquire more information."

If you think of us humans as wise *Homo sapiens,* the remedy for this kind of biased thinking is clear. It's self-improvement. It's becoming aware of our biases and training ourselves to overcome them. Two of my favorite recent books about how to do this are Adam Grant's *Think Again* and Steven Pinker's *Rationality,* both published in 2021. I learned a lot from both of them, and hope that they've made me a more clear, less biased thinker.

But when I switch from the *Homo sapiens* to the *Homo ultrasocialis* perspective, I see a risk with this approach to making better decisions. Training ourselves to think again and be more rational has many benefits, but it also gives our press secretaries powerful new material to work with. They can add to their memos sentences like, "Since you've worked so hard on your reasoning, you can be more sure that you're correct in this case."

In chapter 3, I suggested that mainstream individual-level ethics training wouldn't make people behave more ethically at work. We see now that such training might even make them behave *worse,* because it'll give graduates' press secretaries a new sentence to include in their memos: "You have been through ethics training; therefore you are now a highly ethical individual." In other words, the training could provide moral licensing—permission to behave badly under cover of the self-deceptive belief that you're a good person. Psychologist Sonya Sachdeva and her colleagues observed this licensing in a study where they had participants write a story about themselves, emphasizing either positive or negative traits. They were paid for this work, then offered the chance to donate some of the money they'd just received. On average, those who wrote a positive self-story donated only a fifth as much as those who wrote a negative one. The researchers "suggest that affirming a moral identity leads people to feel licensed to act immorally."

Science as Cognitive Jiu-Jitsu

All of these insights about overconfidence, confirmation bias, and our tireless press secretary modules seem to leave us in a hopeless place. They show that our press secretaries keep us from being rational evaluators of the information we receive. Instead, these mental modules pick out all the remotely plausible bits of information that make us look good, draft memos based on these bits, then send these memos to the parts of our minds that interface with our fellow ultrasocial human beings. It's extraordinarily difficult to get our press secretaries to stand down—to train ourselves not to be overconfident, and not to succumb to confirmation bias. Our press secretaries simply make use of this training and, like jiu-jitsu experts making use of their opponents' moves, draft memos telling us that we don't need to worry about overconfidence anymore—because, after all, we've had training!—when we absolutely still do. Being presented with more information doesn't do the trick against overconfidence and confirmation bias. Even being Danny Kahneman doesn't do the trick.

Yet things are clearly not hopeless. We irrational, overconfident, confirmation-obsessed people still manage to get smarter and better over time. Biologists and medical practitioners around the world no longer believe in the miasma theory of disease. Geologists *do* believe in plate tectonics, whereas a hundred years ago most of them didn't. And as we saw in chapter 3, it took us less than two centuries to go from briefly leaving the Earth's surface in a balloon to landing a spaceship on Mars.

How do we accomplish these remarkable, improbable feats of progress? How do we chronically self-deceiving humans keep getting closer to a rational and accurate understanding of the universe, and also keep improving our ability to shape it? Adopting a *Homo ultrasocialis* perspective helps solve this riddle.

To see how, let's go back to the ultimate geek ground rule: *Shape the ultrasociality of group members so that the group's cultural evolution is as rapid as possible in the desired direction.* Since we know what kind of cultural evolution we're seeking here, we can be more specific: *Shape the ultrasociality of group members so that the group makes better decisions and predictions.* We also know that overconfidence and confirmation bias are two of the main things that keep us from getting better at these tasks. Finally, we know that while the *Homo sapiens* approach of training ourselves to be better, more rational thinkers is helpful, it's unlikely to make our press secretaries stand down, and might even give them new material to work with as they draft their biased memos.

Now let's adopt the *Homo ultrasocialis* perspective and ask two related questions. First, instead of trying to fire or silence our press secretaries, can we instead employ them to help the group make better decisions? In other words, can we put them to work to help the group become more accurate, instead of more biased? And second, have we *Homo ultrasocialis* evolved any defenses against other people's press secretaries? After all, deception is a common evolutionary strategy across Earth's species, and it rarely goes unchallenged. When a predator develops better camouflage, for example, its prey develops better eyesight (or goes extinct). So have we developed defenses against all the deceptive press secretaries out there? We've seen that we're typically unaware of our own press secretaries. Are we better at detecting others'?

We get answers to both of these questions by exploring how science works. But as I'm sure you've noticed, there's a huge amount of disagreement on that topic. If you ever want to start a long and loud debate in a room full of overeducated people, just say something like, "Hey, what *is* the scientific method, anyway?"

I'm not even going to try to summarize that debate. Instead, I want to highlight one viewpoint that makes a great deal of sense to me, that addresses both of our questions, and that yields practical advice for companies and their leaders. It's a viewpoint laid out by philosopher Michael Strevens in *The Knowledge Machine*. Geek companies run as if their founders got their hands on this book well before it was published and have been using it as a blueprint.

Strevens studied the enormous literature about science and the scientific method, and came to a brilliantly simple conclusion—science is an eternal argument governed by an "iron rule of explanation":

1. Strive to settle all arguments by empirical testing.
2. To conduct an empirical test to decide between a pair of hypotheses, perform an experiment or measurement, one of whose possible outcomes can be explained by one hypothesis...but not the other.

One important thing to realize right away about the iron rule is that it's a norm: an expected standard of social behavior, or habit of groupmind. It takes for granted that there are always going to be disagreements among people about the nature of reality and specifies how to resolve them: *with evidence*. Not seniority or charisma or past performance or rhetoric or philosophizing or appeals to morality or aesthetics, but evidence. In particular, evidence that distinguishes between the rival hypotheses, and therefore helps to settle the disagreement.

This norm sounds commonsensical, but it's actually deeply unnatural. We humans really don't want to do the evidence-gathering part of the iron rule. Listening to our press secretaries tell us that we're right is effortless, natural, immediate, and pleasant. Gathering actual evidence is none of these things. It takes time, effort, and meticulous attention to detail; it's often no fun at all. Strevens tells the story of Roger Guillemin and Andrew Schally, two endocrinologists who raced each other throughout the sixties to be the first to specify the structure of an important brain hormone known as TRH. This race involved gathering about 1 million sheep and pig brains and processing them in order to obtain enough TRH for analysis.

Looking back, Schally reflected that the key factor in his success was "not the money, it's the will...the brutal force of putting in sixty hours a week for a year to get 1 million fragments." Many of his rivals dropped out because of "the immense amount of hard, dull, costly, and repetitive work" required. The race was a grueling ultramarathon. Schally and Guillemin completed it at about the same time, and shared the 1977 Nobel Prize in Physiology or Medicine.

The brilliance of the iron rule is how it focuses people who want to win the race of science. As Strevens writes of such people, "All of their need to win, their determination to come out on top—all of that raw human ambition...is diverted into the performance of empirical tests. The rule thereby harnesses the oldest emotions to drive the extraordinary attention to process and detail that makes science the supreme discriminator and destroyer of false ideas."

Once we decide that we want to win at science, and once we realize that that means following the iron rule, our press secretaries get to work. But they don't draft memos intended for other scientists describing how brilliant we are. Those memos would fall on deaf ears, since in communities that have decided to follow the iron rule all that matters is evidence that stands up to the harshest scrutiny.

Instead, our press secretaries start writing memos to ourselves about how good we are at producing this kind of evidence: our hypotheses are surely correct, we're amazing evidence gatherers, and we're clearly going to win the race. These memos inspire us to do the hard work of coming up with evidence to support what we believe. The underappreciated part of the scientific method is that it's a bias-reducing activity that doesn't even try to reduce the individual biases of its participants. Instead, it harnesses these biases, making participants overconfident in their own ability to survive empirical testing of their ideas. This is virtuoso cognitive jiu-jitsu.

The iron rule harnesses our deceit-detection capabilities, which are excellent as long as they're aimed at someone else. As we've seen, we're really bad at assessing the products of our own minds: we're chronically overconfident and self-deceptive. But it turns out that we're excellent at assessing and critiquing the products of other people's minds. Just like we're oddly bad at evaluating ourselves, we're oddly *good* at evaluating others.

Our press secretaries make us con artists, offering overconfident versions of ourselves to the social world. But habitually believing con artists is a really bad idea. So we don't. Instead, most of us evaluate others' arguments naturally and automatically, and are good at rejecting the bad ones. This is by design, and evolution, of course, is the designer.

We saw in chapter 3 that evolution crowdsourced the knowledge about making fire from the individual to the group. Something very similar has happened with ideas: evolution has crowdsourced evaluating them to the group, not to the individual who originated them. Our minds are deeply justificatory with their own ideas, and just as deeply *argumentative* with others'. This is the viewpoint laid out by cognitive scientists Hugo Mercier and Dan Sperber, who offer an ultimate perspective on how reasoning works in us *Homo ultrasocialis.*

In this perspective, individuals' ideas get evaluated by group-level discussion and debate. Bad ideas get rejected, and sound ones accepted. A lot of us walk around with the stereotype that (other) people will believe almost anything, but the evidence says otherwise. Most of the time we're actually quite good at the back-and-forth of probing somebody else's argument and evaluating its quality.* In fact, Mercier and a team of colleagues found that

---

* The big exceptions here are arguments that activate our morality or our tribal identity. As we'll see in the next chapter, we humans are deeply and innately tribal, and our morals are largely determined by our tribe. Evolution has programmed us to want to be members in good standing of our tribe, which sometimes means shutting our ears to opposing tribes' arguments, even if they're sound. American society has become so polarized and tribal that solid, evidence-backed scientific arguments for getting vaccinated against the virus responsible for a deadly global pandemic are not being accepted by large numbers of people. This polarization is a worrying trend.

we become better at ignoring our press secretaries and evaluating our own ideas *if they're repackaged and fed back to us as coming from someone else*. In an experiment the team asked participants to solve short logic problems on their own and provide reasons for their answers. Just a few minutes later, the team gave each participant a set of answers and reasons that came from other subjects in the experiment and asked the participant to evaluate each reason.

You see where this is going, right? One of the reasons in the set came not from someone else in the experiment, but instead from the participant themselves. In other words, each participant was asked to evaluate a reason that they had come up with only minutes before. About half the time, participants did not realize that this was the case; they thought that they were evaluating someone else's argument. And in more than half of those cases, they rejected their own arguments. Mercier and Sperber write that "reassuringly, there was a tendency for participants to be more likely to reject their own bad reasons than their own good reasons."

In their book, *The Enigma of Reason,* Mercier and Sperber conclude that

> solitary reasoning is biased and lazy, whereas argumentation is efficient not only in our overly argumentative Western societies but in all types of cultures, not only in educated adults but also in young children.

The word "argumentation" has a negative connotation in many cultures, and it's true that it's usually less fun to have someone disagree with you than applaud your flawless brilliance. But you've already got a press secretary to do that applauding. What you and I and everybody else need is to have our ideas stress-tested. And that's what other people are really good at, just like *we're* really good at stress-testing *their* ideas. Argumentation is how we distinguish good ideas from bad ones.

The power of the iron rule is how it narrows our arguments. It specifies that arguments are to be settled with evidence. According to Strevens, the iron rule began to be widely followed by scientists in the second half of the eighteenth century. This was due in part to the enormous influence of Isaac

Newton, whose genius was almost matched by his meticulous attention to conducting empirical tests and presenting evidence in support of his theories. However it happened, the norm of evidence-based arguing spread throughout scientific communities and they became knowledge machines. We started to make much faster progress at understanding the universe.

Earlier in this chapter we took the ultimate geek ground rule—*shape the ultrasociality of group members so that the group's cultural evolution is as rapid as possible in the desired direction*—and started customizing it for the norm of science. We got as far as: *Shape the ultrasociality of group members so that the group makes better decisions and predictions.* Now we can use the iron rule to finish the customization job: *Conduct evidence-based arguments so that the group makes better decisions and predictions.*

The Coca-Cola Company got into deep trouble with New Coke because it only followed the evidence-gathering part of this norm. The Pepsi challenge was a kind of A/B test, and evidence from the tests indicated that people preferred the taste of Pepsi over (old) Coke. Coca-Cola even replicated this test internally, and got the same empirical results. The mistake they made was not arguing enough about them.

More argumentation would have revealed that there was a small problem with using the results of the Pepsi challenge to justify New Coke, and also a gargantuan problem. The small one was mistaking a sip of cola for a glass or bottle full of it. Many cola drinkers preferred the sweeter taste of Pepsi when they were only having a sip (as was the case in the Pepsi challenge), but when drinking more their preference changed.

The gargantuan problem was thinking that people drank Coke because of how it tasted. Instead, they mainly drank it because of what it meant. For nearly a century before New Coke came along Coca-Cola had been an unvarying part of the American experience. Its place in the country's psyche was already established by 1938 when William Allen White, a Kansas newspaper editor, described it as "a sublimated essence of all that America stands for, a decent thing honestly made." White might have written those words after adding a bit of moonshine to his Coke, but he captured something about how people felt about this particular carbonated sweet beverage.

Goizueta involved very few people in the decision to switch over to New Coke. If he had consulted more widely with colleagues, some of them would surely have argued about the evidence he'd collected. Not its validity, but its relevance. Instead of asking which of two sips of cola tasted better, did the New Coke team ask people how they'd feel about a big change to a beverage they'd known all their lives, and a piece of Americana? Did they A/B test "alter the 'sublimated essence of all that America stands for'" versus "don't alter it"? The huge blunder with New Coke didn't come from the taste tests. It came from not also doing many other kinds of evidence gathering and arguing about what changing Coca-Cola would mean to the people who drank it. Constance Hays, the author of a book about Coke, summarized the debacle: "It wasn't only about the taste. It was about heartbreak. It was about the loss of a product that people considered almost a part of them, the gratuitous bashing of something that held meaning for them. Goizueta hadn't weighed that factor in all his calculations and assessments." But if he had followed the iron rule and engaged in the essential argumentative part of science, someone would certainly have pointed these things out to him.

Data, Demos, Debates

As the New Coke fiasco shows, the business world is very much like the world of science in one fundamental way: incorrect hypotheses don't last. If you're wrong about what customers want or how the market will evolve you will learn that you're wrong, and you will learn it more quickly in more competitive environments. Such environments are inhospitable to companies that are incorrect a lot. Be wrong enough times, and you won't be in business anymore.

It's great news, then, that companies can import the iron rule from science and use it to guide them. The rule helps a company be less wrong in exactly the same way that it helps the entire scientific community become less wrong over time: by specifying that disputes are to be resolved with evidence that's able to distinguish between rival hypotheses.

As we saw in chapter 1, the use of the iron rule in the business world entered a new golden era early in 2000, when Google ran the first known A/B test on a web page. Every such test is a tight little application of the iron rule. There are two or more versions of a page. Each is a rival hypothesis about what users want. Which one is best? Rather than relying on HiPPOs or press secretary memos, let's instead agree in advance about what evidence related to user behavior we're going to rely on to determine which is best, generate that evidence with an experiment (that is, an A/B test), and then use that evidence to decide which vision to roll out widely.

That evidence-producing infrastructure should be used to "test literally everything," according to Ranker.com founder and CEO Clark Benson. In other words, don't just run experiments on things that you think will make a big difference; run them also on things that you have no reason to think will make any difference at all. Even an online veteran like Benson is "constantly amazed with minor, minor factors having outsized value in testing." Our press secretaries draft memos all the time telling us that we know what customers and other important constituencies want. But a lot of these memos are wrong.

Just like every pig or sheep brain yields only a tiny amount of TRH, however, each A/B test is likely to improve overall corporate performance by only a small amount. So it's important to do a *lot* of them. As Google's chief economist, Hal Varian, told me in 2017,

> One of the things that we did at Google very early on, which is really important, is we built an experimental infrastructure. So we could do A/B testing of different ideas: different ideas on user interface, different ideas on ad ranking, different ideas on search ranking, and so on. And we could run actual experiments on little slices of the population, 1 percent or 2 percent, and see if they really improved our metrics. And if they did, then we can implement them more broadly. So having that experimental infrastructure available was really critical to Google's success.

So far the great geek norm of science sounds pretty impersonal and mechanized: stop relying on HiPPOs and judgments of "experts," set up an infrastructure for experimentation, and let it do its thing. But any such infrastructure is really only a tiny part of how science is practiced at geek companies. Most of the rest of it is deeply social, involving a great deal of back-and-forth among people.

An example of following the iron rule in a way that's relatively light on evidence comes from Apple, a company that's fond of demos. By the middle of the 2010s the company's iPhones had become famous for their ability to take great pictures of all kinds of things, including people. High-end portraits often have blurred backgrounds (an effect called *bokeh*), and Apple wanted to incorporate this capability in some of its upcoming iPhone models. However, there was debate about how to do so. The camera team's initial implementation allowed users to see the blurred background only *after* they'd taken the photo. The human interface (HI) design team thought that this was the wrong approach, and that users should be shown the blurriness and given some control over it while they were setting up the photo. The matter was settled once HI team member Jonny Manzari gave a demo of the "preview the blur" approach, which showed how powerful it was. The demo ended the argument. Previewing the blur became part of the iPhone's Portrait mode, which was introduced with the iPhone 7 Plus model in 2016 and became known as "one of the coolest camera features on the iPhone."

As this example shows, following the iron rule doesn't have to involve fancy statistical tests or massive experimentation infrastructures. Those things are often useful and sometimes essential, but they're not what the geek norm of science is all about. That norm is simply about coming up with a hypothesis (users will like this version of a web page better, Coke drinkers will prefer New Coke, iPhone owners want to be able to see exactly what a portrait will look like before taking the picture, and so on), figuring out how to test the hypothesis with evidence, and producing and interpreting that evidence—and talking, collaborating, and arguing all the while.

In the mid-1990s, a mathematical physicist gave a description of the iron rule that emphasized talking and collaborating. As the physicist put it, science is "a very gregarious business, it's essentially the difference between having [my office] door open and having it shut. If I'm doing science, I have the door open. That's kind of symbolic, but it's true. You want to be all the time talking with people . . . It's only by interaction with other people in the building that you get anything interesting done; it's essentially a communal enterprise."

At about the same time, a couple of business geeks provided a great illustration of the argumentative aspect of the iron rule. In 1996 a war was brewing between upstart Netscape and incumbent Microsoft for dominance in software to power the World Wide Web. Netscape had recently gone public after launching the first commercially successful web browser, but Microsoft was preparing its own major moves. Ben Horowitz was in charge of some of Netscape's important strategic countermoves, which were going to be announced at a splashy launch event in New York on March 5, 1996.

However, these countermoves were revealed a couple weeks early by Marc Andreessen, the inventor of one of the first web browsers and, at the age of twenty-two, cofounder of Netscape. Andreessen revealed Netscape's strategy in an interview for *Computer Reseller News*. Horowitz was not pleased about the interview, and wrote Andreessen a short email:

To: Marc Andreessen
Cc: [Horowitz's boss]
From: Ben Horowitz
Subject: Launch

I guess we're not going to wait until the 5th to launch the strategy.
— Ben

In less than fifteen minutes, Andreessen wrote back:

To: Ben Horowitz

Cc: [Horowitz's boss], [Netscape CEO], [Netscape Chairman]

From: Marc Andreessen

Subject: Re: Launch

Apparently you do not understand how serious the situation is. We are getting killed killed killed out there. Our current product is radically worse than the competition. We've had nothing to say for months. As a result, we've lost over $3B in market capitalization. We are now in danger of losing the entire company and it's all server product management's fault.

Next time do the fucking interview yourself.

Fuck you,

Marc

Ignore Andreessen's swearing for now (we'll come back to it soon). Instead, observe how he follows the geek norm of science. In his email, Horowitz advanced the hypothesis that the interview was a mistake. In his reply, Andreessen offered a very different hypothesis—that Netscape had lost significant value and was getting "killed killed killed" in part because "we've had nothing to say"—and backed it up with evidence. This is the iron rule being practiced.

Upon receiving the email, Horowitz was worried he'd be fired. He wasn't. As he wrote in his 2014 book, *The Hard Thing About Hard Things,* "More shocking, Marc and I eventually became friends; we've been friends and business partners ever since...With Marc and me, even after eighteen years, he upsets me almost every day by finding something wrong in my thinking, and I do the same for him. It works." It works well enough that the pair cofounded the venture capital firm Andreessen Horowitz, or a16z, in 2009.

In a 2016 interview with podcast host Tim Ferriss, Andreessen agreed that productive debate was at the core of his relationship with Horowitz and advised listeners not to stick around organizations that weren't argumentative:

So one [thing that demonstrated Horowitz's value as a colleague] is he would talk back to me...He wouldn't just roll over. He would argue right back. And if you just observe a lot of companies over time or investment firms or whatever, there's the temptation of everything wants to become a hierarchy. And people have trepidations about speaking truth to power. And a lot of what I've always found the really wise and smart leaders are trying to do is they're trying to actually find the people in the organization who will actually talk back...There are certain organizations where the way to get ahead is to talk back to the leadership. That's how you get noticed.

By the way, there are other organizations where that doesn't work at all, and I would recommend getting out of those as fast as possible. We try to be, at least Ben and I want this organization to be one where people will actually speak truth to power and argue back at us just like anybody else, which is why he and I argue so much...because we want to set the precedent.

All the alpha geeks I talked to when researching this book stressed the importance of argumentation at the highest levels of the company. This back-and-forth helps the executive team get important decisions right, and also sets a model for the rest of the organization. There's a mythos in tech (as well as in science) that lone geniuses are responsible for many of the biggest breakthroughs, but this belief doesn't hold up to scrutiny. I kept getting told by people who are in a position to know that in geek companies even the biggest talents and the biggest egos listened to others. They have to, in order to keep their companies on top.

I asked former Google CEO Eric Schmidt how geek companies avoided the problem of people who don't listen or stop listening to others because of their success. He acknowledged that it was a challenge, but said that many people who really want to win the race of business are forced into argumentation because they see that it works so well. As he told me, "The successful ones are forced to listen to you, even if they're screaming. If you look at Steve

Jobs, who I knew well,* Steve was very, very tough, but he also bended to reality."

Where Geeks Are Weak

Jobs was famous for hurling blistering insults at colleagues, business partners, and anyone else who disappointed him. Andreessen finished an email to a junior colleague with "Fuck you, Marc." These examples indicate that geeks might sometimes struggle to create cultures that feature high levels of psychological safety.

This concept, which dates to the mid-1960s, is defined by management scholar Amy Edmondson as

> a climate in which people are comfortable expressing and being themselves. More specifically, when people have psychological safety at work, they feel comfortable sharing concerns and mistakes without fear of embarrassment or retribution. They are confident that they can speak up and won't be humiliated, ignored, or blamed. They know they can ask questions when they are unsure about something. They tend to trust and respect their colleagues... Psychological safety is a crucial source of value creation in organizations operating in a complex, changing environment.

Edmondson highlights that psychological safety is not a personality trait like agreeableness or extraversion that an individual possesses to some degree. Instead, it's a characteristic that a group possesses to some degree.

Psychological safety is a norm—a habit of groupmind—and a critically important one. It's a requirement for following the iron rule and actually practicing science. People with good hypotheses, good ideas for tests, and good evidence at their disposal have to feel comfortable bringing them forward and challenging even their bosses and their seniors with them. It's

---

* Schmidt was on the board of Apple from 2006 to 2009.

obvious from his previous quote that Marc Andreessen believes psychological safety separates excellent organizations from miserable ones. So then maybe he should have signed off in his email differently?

I'm pretty sure that he does by this point; his salty closing to Horowitz is more than twenty-five years old. But I can tell you from experience that he remains a highly argumentative person. When he disagrees with your ideas he will rebut them forcefully, at length, and with energy. When he and I clash his arguments are filled with evidence, not insults, but they're still more than a little intimidating. I've spent my whole career in academia, where debate is as natural as talking about the weather, but Andreessen and many other geeks take argumentation to a whole new level.

Why is this? It's probably due in part to the fact that tech is still a male-dominated industry, and men are generally more assertive than women. Tech also attracts a lot of neuroatypical people who excel at thinking about abstract ideas but struggle to empathize with others and read their emotional cues. Such people might not be able to tell when their arguments have gone too far and are perceived as hurtful or belligerent. For whatever reasons, many business geeks find themselves in a position that's simultaneously enviable (they argue well) and precarious (they go about it in an alienating way).

Sage Sharp started working on the open-source Linux operating system while an undergraduate at Portland State University, and by 2013 was being employed by Intel to contribute to the Linux kernel—the heart of the operating system. However, they (Sharp uses they/them pronouns) kept seeing that the online conversations about the kernel were full of insults and abusive language, some of which came right from the top—from Linux founder Linus Torvalds himself.

Torvalds had begun work on Linux in 1991. He soon invited others to join him in the effort, and many did. Linux became the largest open-source software project in the world, with more than eighty thousand improvements and bug fixes made in 2017 by a global community of programmers. Torvalds remained a towering figure in this community. He was directly responsible for maintaining and developing the kernel, but his true role was conveyed by his informal job title: "benevolent dictator for life."

In many online interactions, however, he appeared downright malevolent. He swore frequently and leveled personal attacks, saying things like, "Just kill yourself now. The world will be a better place." When others criticized him for such language, a typical response was, "Jokes are often offensive. If you get offended, the problem is solidly at your end. Think about it for a while."

On the public Linux kernel mailing group Sharp appealed to Torvalds to change his approach: "Linus, you're one of the worst offenders when it comes to verbally abusing people and publicly tearing their emotions apart... *No one* deserves to be yelled at IN ALL CAPS in email, or publicly ridiculed. You are in a position of power. Stop verbally abusing your developers." Torvalds didn't budge, and kept justifying his behavior: "I curse when there isn't any argument. The cursing happens for the 'you're so f*cking wrong that it's not even worth trying to make logical arguments about it, because you have no possible excuse' case."

Sharp continued to try to improve how the Linux community argued. In 2015, they advocated for a code of conduct. What they got instead was an online mechanism for filing complaints, the name of which was one more needless affront. It was called the Linux Code of Conflict.

Eventually, Sharp had enough. In October of 2015, they announced that they would no longer be a Linux kernel developer, because of a lack of psychological safety. As they wrote,

> I finally realized that I could no longer contribute to a community where I was technically respected, but I could not ask for personal respect. I could not work with people who... argued that maintainers should be allowed to spew whatever vile words they needed to in order to maintain radical emotional honesty... I feel powerless in a community that had a "Code of Conflict" without a specific list of behaviors to avoid and a community with no teeth to enforce it.

There's an ending to this story, but I have trouble seeing it as a happy one. In 2018, Torvalds stepped down from his duties at Linux after he was confronted by *The New Yorker* magazine about his online behavior. He wrote:

> I really had been ignoring some fairly deep-seated feelings in the community...
>
> This is my reality. I am not an emotionally empathetic kind of person and that probably doesn't come as a big surprise to anybody. Least of all me. The fact that I then misread people and don't realize (for years) how badly I've judged a situation and contributed to an unprofessional environment is not good.
>
> This week people in our community confronted me about my lifetime of not understanding emotions. My flippant attacks in emails have been both unprofessional and uncalled for. Especially at times when I made it personal. In my quest for a better patch, this made sense to me.
>
> I know now this was not OK and I am truly sorry.
>
> I am going to take time off and get some assistance on how to understand people's emotions and respond appropriately.

As we all know, a leader's behavior sets the tone for an organization and deeply influences its norms. In a later chapter, we'll explore the ultimate reasons why this is the case. For now let's take note of this sad example of argumentation becoming abuse. Psychological safety was in short supply throughout the Linux community, due in large part to Torvalds himself. The absence of safety drove out Sharp and countless other people who wanted to contribute their energy and talent to the effort. It eventually even forced out Torvalds, who very much wanted to continue to be involved in what he'd started.

This is a shame, all the more so because it was so avoidable. The first rule of healthy debate is to focus on the issue and not make personal attacks. In the pages ahead, we'll see many positive examples of healthy practices that support the great geek norms of science, ownership, speed, and openness.

Can There Be *Too Much* Science?

Is it possible to go too far with the geek norm of science? I often hear the concern that a company can become overly obsessed with measuring everything, and with trying to get key metrics to move in the right direction. This obsession can lead to undesirable behavior if it leads people to ignore other activities — or, even worse, deliberately engage in counterproductive ones — in order to get the numbers trending the right way. In 1995, the shareholders of Computer Associates approved a compensation plan for three top executives, including then-COO Sanjay Kumar, that included large bonuses if the company's stock price remained over $53.33 for sixty days in a row. This feat was accomplished in May of 1998, and the three officers shared $1.08 billion, one of the largest bonuses in corporate history at the time.

Stories began to circulate, however, that the company was only able to hit its share price targets thanks to accounting practices that were legally questionable. It booked a lot of the revenue from some long-term software contracts immediately, and at the end of the quarter kept its books open for a few extra days in order to recognize additional revenue (a practice that came to be known as the "thirty-five-day month"). The SEC filed securities fraud charges in 2004, and in April of 2006 Kumar, who had been Computer Associates' CEO from 2000 to 2004, pled guilty; he was sentenced to twelve years in prison.

There are endless variations on the theme of reacting inappropriately to numeric targets. By the early 2010s the Wells Fargo bank was well known for a hard-charging sales culture that featured cross-selling, or getting customers to use more of the bank's products (not only a checking account, for example, but also a credit card, a mortgage, and so on). Bank branch employees were given aggressive targets, some of which were practically impossible to hit. The St. Helena, California, branch had the goal of selling 12,000 new products one year, even though there were eleven other financial institutions in the area and only 11,500 potential customers. Many employees reacted to this pressure by simply setting up new accounts and other products for customers without their knowledge or permission. Investigations revealed that as many as 3.5 million fake accounts were created, many of which imposed fees on owners who were unaware of their existence. Wells Fargo paid more than $2.5 billion in fines over its false account scandal.

The endless supply of examples like these has led some people to believe in Goodhart's law, which states that "when a measure becomes a target, it ceases to be a good measure." In other words, getting people to pay close attention to a metric—by, for example, tying their compensation to it—is almost sure to backfire somehow.

Yet most of the business geeks I've talked to don't let Goodhart's law get in the way of their mania for measurement and all the things that accompany it—observation, experimentation, analysis, argumentation, and so on. There are a couple reasons for this. One of them is that the geeks believe Goodhart's aphorism is not so much a law as a caution against overly simplistic measurement and reward schemes. If you tie a huge executive reward to a single metric like the share price, don't be surprised when the execs in question come up with an elaborate scheme to boost that metric just high enough for just long enough, whether or not the scheme actually benefits the company. Or is even legal. If you strongly encourage bank employees to sell more new products than there are potential customers in an area, you should expect to see a lot of fake checking and savings accounts created.

Like a lot of geek business leaders, Stripe CEO Patrick Collison is a self-acknowledged "instrumentation freak."* As he put it to me, "I'm always pushing people, how will we measure that? How do we know whether it's working? If you have the measurement, why is it increasing or why is it not increasing?" When I asked if he was worried about Goodhart's law, he replied, "Univariate metrics are almost always inadequate, so for any area across Stripe we have our primary metrics. And we also try to choose counterbalancing metrics to control for or assess the most obvious kind of pathologies that could arise if you only optimized one of them. And we also have all sorts of secondary metrics that we

---

* Strong evidence that Collison is in fact an instrumentation freak came on a Sunday in June of 2019 when he tweeted a photo of himself with his brand-new fiancée and announced, "Hit our engagement metrics this weekend! 🎉"

just have to keep an eye on. And with like fifteen metrics on this product or area of our business or whatever, I don't worry too much about Goodhart."

As Collison highlights, a key part of the geek response to Goodhart's law is to pay attention to an entire dashboard of metrics, instead of any single number. Another key is to understand that measuring something does not automatically mean tying important rewards like compensation and promotion to it. A lot of my MBA students find this approach odd; after all, why measure something if you're not going to do anything about it? The geek response here is that talking about a measurement—referring to it often, arguing about how to get it to improve, and being clear about who's responsible for it—is in fact doing a lot about it.

Venture capitalist John Doerr is another instrumentation freak, so much so that he wrote an entire book called *Measure What Matters*. But like many other geeks, Doerr does *not* advocate tightly linking what he calls objectives and key results (OKRs) with compensation. Examples like Computer Associates and Wells Fargo show that this is a clumsy and outdated approach to motivating behavior. As Doerr puts it, "In today's workplace, OKRs and compensation can still be friends. They'll never totally lose touch. But they no longer live together, and it's healthier that way."

Liane Hornsey, the chief people officer of cybersecurity company Palo Alto Networks, agrees with Doerr. She draws a sharp distinction between using data to help a person's professional development versus using it to assess their performance (and hence their compensation and other rewards). As she explained to me, "Development is using the data to help people improve. So for example, if I get my performance review and there's something in there, I would share it with [Palo Alto CEO Nikesh Arora] and he would mentor me and help me improve. Performance, on the other hand, is saying 'Liane, your review was crap. And I'm gonna give you a really, really poor performance grade.' That is a very, very important difference." Arora added, "I think the difference is that a development organization is an empathetic organization, while a performance organization is more mercenary. And the empathetic ones usually get a better outcome in the long run because in a mercenary organization when crap hits the fan, people bail."

Hard Fun

The geeks know that it's possible to overemphasize a single measure. But they don't worry much about overemphasizing science. Instead, they keep trying to do more of it, because science is a process for learning more about the universe. While it's not the only thing worth doing—I want to live in a society that has a lot of painters and novelists and songwriters and actors and essayists and teachers and muckrakers in it, as well as a lot of scientists—it's an extremely important thing to do well.

We humans got much, much better at science once we started rigorously following the iron rule. We began to conduct science by formulating hypotheses, testing them, and arguing at every step along the way while agreeing to use evidence to settle the arguments. Michael Strevens correctly points out that all of this is hard work, infinitely harder than just continuing to confidently repeat whatever our press secretaries are telling us. But an eight-year-old robot builder reminded us a while back of something else that's fundamental about science.

This kid was working with Lego/Logo construction kits, which were developed at the MIT Media Lab in the 1980s. The kits featured the familiar Lego bricks as well as motors, sensors, wheels, and other things helpful for navigating the physical world. These elements could be programmed via the Logo language, which was developed for children. In 1989, the Lego/Logo group showed off some of its young creators' work at a press event. In his book *Being Digital*, Media Lab founder Nicholas Negroponte described the day's highlight:

A zealous anchorwoman from one of the national TV networks, camera lights blazing, cornered one child and asked him if this was not just all fun and games. She pressed this eight-year-old for a typical, "cute," sound-bite reply.

The child was obviously shaken. Finally, after her third repetition of the question and after considerable heat from the lights, this sweaty-faced, exasperated child plaintively looked into the camera and said, "Yes, this is fun, but it's hard fun."

"Hard fun" became a mantra at the Media Lab. I think it's also a good one for science as a whole, whether practiced in research labs or in geek companies. Following the iron rule is a grind, but it's also a delight. Not all the time, of course, but often. Learning something new, seeing a hypothesis hold up, watching an idea of yours survive tough scrutiny: these are all wonderful things. And arguing can be wonderful, too. The evidence is strong that we ultrasocial human beings are wired for it, and are good at it. We are excellent evaluators of others' ideas; it's the flip side of being lousy at evaluating our own.

The more psychologically safe I feel with colleagues and friends, the more I argue with them. Once I feel like they trust and respect me, and once I'm confident that they know I trust and respect them, I let my inherently argumentative nature loose. As we've seen, the geeks can take this argumentation too far and be insensitive and alienating about it. These tendencies have to be corrected if real science, which depends on open and egalitarian back-and-forth, is going to take place. If and when a group can get this to happen, a lot of progress and a lot of hard fun ensue.

Let me end this chapter with two quotes about science that capture its most important aspects: its ability to overcome the deep-seated human capacity for self-deception, and its inherently social — not solitary — nature. The first is from biologist Robert Trivers, who says, "If you are trying to... transmit knowledge more quickly, you will be drawn to science itself, which is based on a series of increasingly sophisticated and remorseless anti-deceit and anti-self-deception mechanisms."

The second is from the sixteenth-century French philosopher Michel de Montaigne, who wrote that he learned more from arguing than even from reading:* "The study of books is a languishing and feeble motion that heats not, whereas conversation teaches and exercises at once. If I converse with a strong mind and a rough disputant, he presses upon my flanks, and pricks

---

* Even though Montaigne said that he learned more from conversation than from books, he still isolated himself from almost all human interaction for nearly ten years while he was working on his famous book *Essais* (*Essays*), which was first published in 1580.

me right and left; his imaginations stir up mine; jealousy, glory, and contention stimulate and raise me up to something above myself."

Now that we see how the great geek norm of science works, we also see how it contributes to geek companies' remarkable ability to be simultaneously excellent at agility, execution, and innovation.

A company that settles debates about which features to include with demos, as opposed to anything like "Trust me; I'm the expert here," or "I'm the boss, and I like this one," is going to do a better job creating products that delight customers and are perceived as innovative.

An organization where people are comfortable speaking truth to power and arguing with those higher up on the org chart is going to do a better job spotting new trends early, and not getting held up by the worldviews of its most senior members. In other words, it's going to be a more agile organization.

A team that believes in A/B testing just about *everything,* and that sets up an experimentation platform to do lots of tests and continually incorporate the results into its offerings, is going to be good at execution. In fact, many geek companies even run tests in which they knock out part of their own infrastructure to see how smoothly and quickly they can recover. This high-wire technique is called chaos engineering, and it's only used by companies that are already pretty confident in their execution ability.

As we examine the other great geek norms, we'll see the same pattern: they help build cultures and companies that excel at execution, agility, innovation, and other activities that contribute to strong and sustained performance. The success of geek companies isn't a mystery: a lot of it comes from focusing on a few habits of groupmind—science, ownership, speed, and openness—and making sure that these habits permeate the organization and remain robust over time. As we'll see in the next chapter, these norms can even help combat one of the scariest words in the corporate lexicon: *bureaucracy.*

Chapter Summary

We humans are chronically overconfident and subject to confirmation bias. As a result, we make poor decisions and poor forecasts.

The ultimate explanation for overconfidence is that it's beneficial for us ultrasocial human beings to appear confident to others. So evolution has equipped us with a mental press secretary module that constantly generates a favorable self-image.

Our press secretaries deceive us not just about the quality of our ideas and judgment, but also about many other things: our generosity, our morals and ethics, our social status, our looks—any arena where it would be advantageous for us *Homo ultrasocialis* to be perceived favorably by others.

Because of the press secretary, we're bad at evaluating our own ideas. But we're excellent at evaluating the ideas of others. Our minds are inherently *justificatory* about their own ideas, and *argumentative* about the ideas of others.

The geek norm of science is all about arguing. It also specifies how to win arguments: with evidence. Not seniority or charisma or past performance or rhetoric or philosophizing or appeals to morality or aesthetics, but evidence.

For the norm of science, the ultimate geek ground rule is: *Conduct evidence-based arguments so that the group makes better decisions and predictions, and estimates.*

Business geeks have to watch out as they argue, because they can fail to create cultures with high levels of psychological safety.

Survey for Your Organization

These ten statements can be used to assess how well an organization follows the great geek norm of science. Respondents reply to each with a number between one and seven, where one means "strongly disagree" and seven means "strongly agree."

1. We rely on evidence to make important decisions.
2. We don't conduct a lot of tests or experiments.*
3. Senior people here frequently override data-driven recommendations based on their judgment or gut instinct.*
4. At this organization, debate is seen as a normal and healthy part of making decisions.
5. The more important a decision is, the more likely we are to spend time debating and gathering evidence about it.
6. We do not have a data-driven culture.*
7. In debates, people here support their positions by saying things like "Trust me; I'm the expert," or "I've been in this area for the longest, so I know best," or "I'm the boss, so we're doing it my way," instead of presenting data and analysis.*
8. People here are reluctant to bring up evidence that doesn't support their boss's views.*
9. People here frequently change their mind and change course after being shown new evidence.
10. When we can't agree on how to proceed, our usual approach is to run a test or experiment to help us decide which way to go.

---

* Scores for these statements need to be reversed. To do this, subtract the respondent's score from eight. For example, if the respondent answered with six, the reversed score would be two.

CHAPTER 5

Ownership

Tearing Down the Giant Machinery Operated by Dwarves

> Bureaucracy [is]...a heavy curtain drawn between
> the right thing to do and the right person to do it.
> — *Honoré de Balzac*

If you want to help win the war, inflict standard corporate operating procedure on the other side.

That's a conclusion you're likely to reach after reading the *Simple Sabotage Field Manual,* which was produced in 1944 by the US Office of Strategic Services (the predecessor of the CIA). When I first heard about this document I thought it was an urban legend, but it's real. It was declassified in 2008 and is now discussed on the CIA's website.

The manual was aimed at people living in Norway, France, and other countries occupied by the Nazis during World War II. It offers advice to "citizen saboteurs" on how to vex their occupiers by doing everything from starting fires to clogging up toilets. But not all the recommended damage is physical; some of it is organizational. As the manual states, "[One] type of simple sabotage requires no destructive tools whatsoever...It is based on universal opportunities to make faulty decisions, to adopt a noncooperative attitude, and to induce others to follow suit."

Here are some of its "universal opportunities" for making things worse:

Insist on doing everything through "channels." Never permit short-cuts to be taken in order to expedite decisions...

Be worried about the propriety of any decision — raise the question of whether such action as is contemplated lies within the jurisdiction of the group or whether it might conflict with the policy of some higher echelon...

Multiply the procedures and clearances involved in issuing instructions, paychecks, and so on. See that three people have to approve everything where one would do.

Sound familiar? Many companies' current practices seem like they were copied straight from the *Simple Sabotage Field Manual.* If that sounds like an exaggeration, let's watch Jennifer Nieva try to get her job done. In 2005, Nieva was working as a manager at Hewlett-Packard. She was put in charge of a project for which she needed to spend $200,000 on outside consultants. As she describes it:

The consultants were available now, but if I waited too long, they'd be reassigned to another client.

I followed the process and entered a request for spending approval into the HP procurement system. Then I looked over everything. There were TWENTY names that needed to sign off before I could get started. My boss, my boss's boss, my boss's boss's boss, but also over a dozen names I'd never heard of, people I soon learned were sitting in our procurement department in Guadalajara, Mexico.

Was I going to lose these consultants I'd taken so long to find? My boss signed, her boss signed, his boss signed. Then I started calling the procurement department, first daily and later hourly. Most of the time no one answered. Finally, I called a woman named Anna who picked up. I used every ounce of charm I could to get her to help me. The approval took six weeks and I called Anna so many times that, when she made the next step in her career, she asked me to write a LinkedIn recommendation for her.

The creators of the *Simple Sabotage Field Manual* would have been thrilled if a partisan behind enemy lines had been able to put this process in place at a Nazi organization.

The Tale of the Red Tape

A lot of us would describe the approval process Nieva encountered at HP as bureaucractic. But "bureaucracy" itself is not the problem. That's just the label for, as *Britannica* puts it, a "specific form of organization defined by complexity, division of labour, permanence, professional management, hierarchical coordination and control, strict chain of command, and legal authority." Most companies I'm familiar with meet that definition.*

Some hierarchy, management, and division of labor—some bureaucracy, in other words—is necessary to accomplish the goals of any corporation. As Max Weber, one of the founders of sociology, put it a hundred years ago: "However many people complain about the 'red tape,' it would be sheer illusion to think for a moment that continuous administrative work can be carried out in any field except by means of officials working in offices... The needs of mass administration make [bureaucracy] completely indispensable." The problem comes when companies turn into the kinds of bureaucracies that Nieva ran into: organizations so full of red tape that it becomes hard to get actual work done.

Nieva's experience sounds extreme, but it might not be all that rare. In 2017, management scholars Gary Hamel and Michele Zanini conducted a survey on bureaucracy with *Harvard Business Review* readers. They found a lot of it.

Based on responses to twenty questions, Hamel and Zanini constructed

---

* In late 2013 the online shoe retailer Zappos began experimenting with holacracy, a management system that did away with hierarchy and well-defined management roles in favor of "distributed authority." It was not universally popular. When CEO Tony Hsieh announced in March 2015 that all employees would have to fully commit to the new system, 18 percent of the workforce instead took a buyout. In January 2000, the *Quartz* website announced that "Zappos has quietly backed away from holacracy."

a "bureaucracy mass index" (BMI), which ranged from 20 to 100. Any score above 60 was considered at least moderate bureaucratic drag, while any score below 40 showed "a relative absence of bureaucracy." Fewer than 1 percent of respondents scored less than 40, and fully three-quarters of these low-bureaucracy responses came from people who worked in companies with fewer than a hundred employees.

It will surprise no one to learn that the situation was very different at large companies. Those with at least five thousand employees averaged a BMI of 75. Eighty percent of respondents from large companies reported that bureaucracy was significantly slowing them down, as evidenced by the fact that at those companies it took twenty days, on average, to get approval for an unbudgeted expense.

Overall, companies don't seem to give their people much autonomy. Only 11 percent of all respondents said that they had "substantial" or "complete" freedom to do things like set priorities and decide on work methods. And just 10 percent reported that they were empowered to spend $1,000 without first getting approval from higher up in the organization.

Economist Larry Summers warns about the dangers of the "promiscuous distribution of the power to hold things up," which is a concise description of excessive bureaucracy. Governments seem to specialize in distributing this power more and more widely over time, to the point that they can become what the political scientist Francis Fukuyama calls vetocracies. The Code of Federal Regulations, which records all of the permanent rules of the US federal government, grew 40 percent faster than the American economy did between 1950 and 2019. State and local regulations also increased, and have slowed down many projects. The Anderson Memorial Bridge, which spans the Charles River in Massachusetts and connects the cities of Boston and Cambridge, was built in less than a year in 1915. A century later, however, completing relatively minor repairs to the structure took more than five years thanks to what Summers called "a gaggle of regulators and veto players, each with the power to block or to delay."

Red tape has become a cultural cliché. We now expect large organizations both public and private to be harmfully bureaucratic in the same way that we expect, say, a supervillain to listen to classical music or a kid from the wrong side of the tracks to get a frosty reception from the parents of the rich girl he loves. The expectation of suffocating bureaucracy in big companies is so ingrained that in the 2019 movie *Ford v Ferrari* it's taken for granted by both the filmmakers and the audience that Ford is the *underdog* in the clash.

Think about that for a minute. In the mid-1960s, when the events depicted in the film took place, Ford was the second-largest company in the world.* Ford came close to buying Ferrari outright in 1963 for $16 million, or 3 percent of Ford's profits that year. So the American company was not cash constrained. Nor did it lack drivers and car builders who knew how to win. It's true that Ferrari was dominant at Le Mans in the early '60s. But Ford's racing team hired Carroll Shelby, a legendary American car designer and driver who had won the race in 1959, and the equally talented English driver and engineer Ken Miles.

The setup for the movie, then, is that Ford enters the Le Mans competition with immense spending power and top talent. And yet the movie's basic premise, which is so obvious that it never needed to be spelled out, is that the American giant is unlikely to win because of bureaucracy—because it can't get out of its own way enough to let its world-class innovators do their jobs. Most of the movie's conflicts are not Ford versus Ferrari; they're Ford versus Ford.

An executive who knows nothing about racing meddles and second-guesses the team's decisions. In order for Shelby to get the autonomy he needs (because "you can't win a race by committee"), he has to literally bet his company; he promises that if he and Miles don't finish first at a Le Mans warm-up race he'll give Shelby Racing to Ford outright. He also has to stage a high-stakes intervention. He puts Henry Ford II in a race car and takes

---

* Ford was the second-largest company in America, which was by far the largest economy in the world, having grown by more than 50 percent during World War II while most other large countries' productive capacities were ravaged by the conflict. So I'm pretty comfortable asserting that among all the world's companies in the mid-1960s, only General Motors was bigger than Ford.

him on an exhilarating and terrifying drive that leaves the CEO in tears of joy, finally willing to eliminate the red tape that's getting in the way of excellent performance on the track. The film's happy ending is that the good guys at Ford eventually triumph over the bad guys, who are also at Ford. The team's victory at Le Mans itself is almost an afterthought.

I can't resist including one more telling anecdote about Ford, Ferrari, and bureaucracy that's not part of the movie: according to Enzo Ferrari's personal secretary, the reason the 1963 purchase by Ford fell apart was a clause in the contract that would have required Ferrari to obtain prior approval from his new bosses for any increase in the racing team's budget, which was then around a quarter of a million dollars. This was something like 0.05 percent of Ford's 1963 profits, and less than 0.003 percent of its revenue. When Ferrari learned that he would be subjected to that kind of pettifogging oversight he exploded in curses and left the negotiating table, never to return.

Our Most Bottomless Appetite

Why is there so much excess bureaucracy? It's dispiriting. It's a drag on morale and productivity. It wastes huge amounts of time and energy. It's universally disliked. And it runs counter to the principles of trust, empowerment, and autonomy that so many companies espouse. So then why is it still so common? Is it the result of large-scale industrial espionage — are tons of companies getting infiltrated by agents from rival firms and hostile governments who put in place the measures described in the *Simple Sabotage Field Manual*? No, but the fact that modern companies still sometimes operate as if they'd been sabotaged should give us pause. Here we are in the third decade of the twenty-first century, still dealing with one of the oldest ailments of the industrial era — one that the French novelist Honoré de Balzac was already complaining about in the 1830s when he called bureaucracy a "giant machinery operated by dwarves." Why are we still building so much of this machinery?

No one at HP would get out a blank sheet of paper and design a spending approval process that distributed the power to hold up an important project among twenty different people spread across multiple countries. No organization wants that. But the organization is the wrong unit of analysis here. The right one is the individual within the organization. And instead of thinking about those individuals as wise *Homo sapiens* who realize that high productivity and healthy profits will be beneficial to them, we should instead think of them as *Homo ultrasocialis* who know way deep down that high status will be beneficial to them.

Status is central to the lives of many social animals. Chickens, for example, really do have a pecking order. If you collected a bunch of them into a flock, the biggest and healthiest birds, both roosters and hens, would immediately start displaying their formidability and sizing each other up. They'd puff themselves up, strut around, face off, and squawk at each other until one backed down. If neither did, the pecking would start, and it could get nasty, bloody, and even deadly.

When this competition died down the flock would have a clear status hierarchy based on dominance. The birds at the top of the pecking order would get the best nesting and roosting spots, and first access to food and dust baths. The roosters at the top would also get the most mating opportunities; roosters lower down the pecking order typically don't try to mate, or even crow, when the number 1 is around.

High status, in short, leads to high fitness, which is why many social animals like birds and mammals have clear and hard-fought status hierarchies. Are we humans an exception to this pattern? Let's turn that question around a little bit: *Why would you think that the planet's only ultrasocial species wouldn't care about social status?* Evolution has wired us to care about status for exactly the same reason that it's wired chickens, elephant seals, gorillas, and chimpanzees to care about it.

The importance of status for us *Homo ultrasocialis* is hard to overstate. As journalist Will Storr writes in his book *The Status Game,* "We are... driven by a multitude of desires. We want power. We want sex. We want wealth. We want to change society for the better. But it's also true that the status game is deeply implicated in these great human hungers." The psychologist and pioneering ultimate researcher David Buss finds that higher status is clearly associated with a person having higher-quality mates, healthier children, and longer, healthier lives. We humans like power, but for most of us our desire for more of it tapers off after a while. The same thing is true for money: we like it a lot, but in one survey of office workers fully 70 percent chose a higher-status job over a higher-paying one. Our desire for higher status, meanwhile, appears to be bottomless. In a series of experiments, sociologist Cecilia Ridgeway found that "there was no point at which preference for higher status leveled off."

Ridgeway thinks we chase after status so relentlessly because we know it's hard to hold on to: "Since [status] is esteem given by others, it can always, at least theoretically, be taken away." We are desperate to avoid that. For social animals like us, losing status is extremely bad news. It's not just that it reduces access to important resources and mating opportunities. There's another major problem: low status stresses individuals out and makes them sick.

This association between status and health in humans came through clearly in the famous Whitehall studies of British civil servants, the first of which was published in 1978. Even after controlling for age, weight, height, blood pressure, smoking habits, leisure time, and other factors, people in lower employment grades had significantly higher rates of chronic heart disease than their higher-ranking colleagues did. This was true for both men and women, and the health differences were massive; middle-aged workers lowest on the hierarchy had death rates fully four times higher than their most elite counterparts. When researchers manipulated the social status of baboons, they found that health changed in lockstep with status change. As epidemiologist Michael Marmot summarized, "It was the new position, not the one [a baboon] started with, that determined the degree of [cardiac disease] they developed. And the differences were dramatic."

It appears that social mammals like humans and baboons perceive a threat when their status drops, and that their bodies respond just as they would to a physical threat. They increase inflammation in order to accelerate healing from wounds and decrease viral response to save energy. These responses might be appropriate for a short physical attack, but are harmful over the long haul. And they're deeply rooted. According to professor of medicine Steve Cole, "Several studies have related objective indicators of low social status to increased expression of pro-inflammatory genes and/or decreased expression of antiviral genes. Being beaten down in the rat race naturally changes what you expect from tomorrow, and that does seem to filter down into the way your cells prepare for tomorrow."

Losses of status, especially steep and sudden ones, are also associated with higher rates of suicide. And because status is always relative, we can feel the pain of losing it even when nothing has changed in our own circumstances, as long as others have moved ahead. As sociologist Jason Manning puts it, "Suicide is encouraged not just by falling, but by falling behind." Will Storr summarizes that "to our brains, status is a resource as real as oxygen or water. When we lose it, we break."

Because status is so real and vitally important to us, we humans are adept at figuring out who has it and who doesn't. We make social comparisons all the time. Some of these comparisons are conscious and deliberate but most of them happen far at the other end of the range of awareness, where judgments are subconscious and almost instantaneous. After just glancing at candid photos of colleagues interacting in a workplace, for example, subjects in one study made "exceedingly accurate" assessments of who had higher status.

After we figure out where we ourselves are on the local status ladder we act accordingly, and here again we often act without conscious thought. When two people talk, the lower-status one generally changes the low-frequency tones of their voice to match those of their higher-status counterpart. Sure enough, when talk show host Larry King interviewed Hollywood legend Elizabeth Taylor, he shifted his low tones closer to hers. However, when he interviewed Vice President Dan Quayle, who was generally not considered to be among America's great statesmen, it was Quayle who did the shifting.

Two Routes to the Top

We *Homo ultrasocialis* are like many other social animals in that we are aware of status, willing to fight for it, and desperate to keep it. But we play especially rich status games. In our nearest evolutionary relatives, physical dominance plays a starring role in determining status hierarchies. Violence is always an option, and dissent—even with body language, and even from bystanders *of another species*—is not tolerated. When anthropologist Christopher Boehm turned his research attention from humans to chimps, some tough lessons were in store:

> Even with excellent advice, I had to learn the hard way that a frail human body is ill suited for the bruising that attends daily life with this physically powerful and frequently agonistic species. One day, in a mood of experimentation, I inadvertently gave the alpha male of the study group the impression that I was competing with him politically. I painfully discovered that high-ranking male chimpanzees are preoccupied with dominance, jealous of their prerogatives, and quick to put down potential rivals.

Like chimps, we humans are highly attuned to rank and dominance and highly averse to getting beaten to a pulp. As a result, we have good radar for formidability, or a person's ability to inflict physical harm and other costs on a target. At a conference a few years ago I was wandering around during a break when I felt my brain trying to tell me something. It wasn't exactly fear. Instead, it was a deep-seated kind of "hey, you might want to watch your step" alert. As I was trying to figure out what was going on I looked up and saw the boxer Mike Tyson. Now, Tyson was not being aggressive or threatening in any way. He was just standing there holding a cup of coffee. But he's the most formidable human being I've ever come across.* I'm pretty sure that before I looked directly at him I saw him out of the corner of my eye; that quick, fleeting glimpse was enough to trigger an alert. Just as

---

* Tyson was described as "perhaps the most ferocious fighter to step into a professional ring." He won his first nineteen fights as a professional by knockout; twelve of those fights did not go past the first round. He took his first heavyweight title at the age of twenty. In 1992, he was convicted of rape and spent nearly three years in prison. In 1997, he bit off part of boxer Evander Holyfield's ear while in the ring with him during a heavyweight championship bout.

chimps do, we ascribe dominance status to those who can coerce us into giving them what they want. Because of his formidability, I experienced Tyson as dominant when I encountered him. Companies have clear dominance hierarchies (even if they're not filled with ex-boxers) because our bosses can coerce us via some version of "Do it or you're fired."

I've also met Yo-Yo Ma a few times. He's clearly another high-status person. But he's no Mike Tyson. Yo-Yo (as he likes to be called) is a great illustration that among humans there are two routes to high status. In addition to dominance, there's also prestige.

Prestige is more subtle than dominance, and it appeared more recently in our evolutionary history. What's its ultimate purpose? What's the function of prestige? One compelling theory is that it arose because it helps accelerate cultural evolution.

As we saw in chapter 3, we humans are uniquely good at learning from others. An important part of this is figuring out who to learn *from*. If I learn from the absolute best salesperson, I'll be better at closing deals. But who is the best? When I'm still a novice I can't tell on my own whose sales tactics and strategies are the best. But as a member of an ultrasocial species, I am wired to be aware of who holds the floor when they talk about selling, or whose opinions people defer to, or who people crowd around in the bar at the hotel where the sales conference is being held. *That's* the best seller, and so that's the person I want to learn from. In short, I let the group tell me who's prestigious, then mimic that person to acquire their skills.

In experiments, three- and four-year-olds show exactly this tendency. They're much more likely to mimic people who get watched by others. We humans accord prestige by observing who gets observed; we then seek to learn from these folk, and cultural evolution speeds up (we'll look more closely at learning and cultural evolution in the next chapter). Yo-Yo's extraordinary talent meant that a lot of people paid attention to him, starting when he was a child. Those of us who are not part of the music world at some point started to hear or read about this stellar new talent that the music world was paying attention to, and we started to pay attention as well. So Yo-Yo's prestige grew.

Even for someone who attains their status via prestige, though, the expectation is that they'll be willing to use dominance to keep it or get it back. As psychologist Dan McAdams puts it, "The human expectation that social status can be seized through brute force and intimidation, that the strongest and biggest and boldest will lord it over the rank and file, is very old, awesomely intuitive, and deeply ingrained. Its younger rival—prestige—was never able to dislodge dominance from the human mind."

The Ultimate Danger of Bureaucracy

Once we take into account the universal, "old, awesomely intuitive, and deeply ingrained" human drive for status—and the fear of losing it—bureaucratization becomes much easier to understand. In fact, it becomes hard to understand how an organization can wind up with anything *other* than an elaborate bureaucracy. It's what we should expect to see as we ultrasocial, status-obsessed human beings try to improve our lot as we interact with each other day after day in the workplace. Excess bureaucracy is a bug for anyone who wants a company to run efficiently, but it's a feature for the *Homo ultrasocialis* who seek to gain status in the organization. They'll invent work so that they can be part of it. They'll want to participate in more and more activities over time. They'll strive to be consulted on lots of decisions, and if possible have veto power over them.

The more explicit the status hierarchies become, the more we'll fight for high status, and the more bureaucratic things will get. We'll create twenty-signature approval processes like the one Jennifer Nieva encountered at Hewlett-Packard, and power struggles like those dramatized in *Ford v Ferrari*. We'll continually try to acquire symbols of organizational status: bigger budgets and more people working for us. All the while, we'll tell ourselves and others that we're doing all these things because they're good for the company and the bottom line. And we'll believe it; our press secretaries are really good at their jobs.

There's a story, perhaps apocryphal, that circulates in the military about how quickly the human quest for higher status and its symbols can get out of hand. The story goes that after World War II ended more quickly than expected, tens of thousands of American soldiers were sent home to army bases to wait for their discharge papers to be processed. The colonel in charge of Lincoln Air Field in Nebraska felt it was important to keep the new arrivals there busy, so he summoned a major and said, as retired four-star general Bill Creech tells it,

> "I want you to take these fifty people and keep them busy. Idle hands are the devil's workshop, and they're sitting around with nothing to do. I don't care what you do with them, just keep them busy. Report back to me in two weeks and by that time we should have discharge instructions." The major saluted smartly and and went off to corral the fifty people. In a week, he was back. The colonel said, "I thought I told you two weeks." And the major replied, "I need more people."

The common organizational result of all these status games is a highly bureaucratic workplace — one in which getting things done is anything but straightforward. A 2010 study by management scholar Ruthanne Huising investigated how bureaucratization affected one company's ability to get its work done. Huising recorded the reactions of people to a wall-sized flow-chart of the processes actually in use at their company for common customer service activities. It was a mess. The flowchart showed that "tasks that could be done with one or two handoffs were taking three or four...Data painstakingly collected for decision-making processes were not used...Work-arounds, duplication of effort, and poor communication and coordination were all evident on the map." One employee used vivid language after seeing this big picture: "People are only seeing the surface...They really can't see down to the bottom and see where the rocks are piled up and see where the tree branches have gotten snagged and where the dead bodies are rotting that is causing all of the churn on the top of the water...They really don't get a picture that if you cleared out all of those rocks and stumps and tree branches and dead bodies how fast the stream could really flow and how clear it could be." The company's CEO also used vivid language: "This is even more fucked up than I imagined."

Veteran investor Charlie Munger says, "Show me the incentive and I'll show you the outcome." This guidance becomes even more helpful when we realize that for us *Homo ultrasocialis* some of the strongest incentives are social. When the corporate drive to create profits clashes with the human drive to create status via bureaucracy, it's clear which is likely to win. This remains true even after bureaucracies become so elaborate that they prevent any actual work from getting done, and exist only to perpetuate themselves. The German army officer Claus von Stauffenberg is best known for spearheading an almost successful attempt to assassinate Adolf Hitler in 1944. But his name also lives on in some circles because of an insight about human behavior attributed to him. The von Stauffenberg principle holds that "any bureaucratic entity of forty or more people can stay busy ten hours a day, six days a week, with no inputs and no outputs."

If that sounds to you like too harsh and cynical a judgment, let's take a look at what happened at Microsoft in the early 2000s.

Windows, Office, Quagmire

Microsoft took the standard history of an industrial-era corporation and compressed it. It went from birth through impressive growth to sclerosis and stasis not over the course of a century, but instead within just a few decades.

The company was founded in 1975 and soon found a lucrative niche writing operating systems for personal computers. Its first big hit was MS-DOS, which was followed by Windows. Microsoft went public in 1986, and in 1990 released Microsoft Office, a bundle of its spreadsheet (Excel), presentation application (PowerPoint), and word processor (Word).

Windows and Office became a popular and lucrative combination as the PC revolution spread throughout businesses, schools, and homes. Microsoft came to have such a dominant position in the PC industry (while, some observers felt, abusing this position with anticompetitive practices) that the U.S. Department of Justice brought an antitrust case against the company in 1994. The next year, CEO Bill Gates wrote a memo about another important development: the birth of the World Wide Web. He wrote that "the Internet is a tidal wave. It changes the rules. It is an incredible opportunity as well as [an] incredible challenge." The "Tidal Wave" memo spurred quick action at Microsoft; in 1996, the company started bundling its Internet Explorer web browser into its Windows 95 operating system.*

Microsoft battled the government charges and embraced the web throughout the rest of the decade, and continued to grow rapidly. As the year 2000 dawned it was the most valuable publicly traded company in the world, with a market capitalization of almost $620 billion. Twelve years later it was worth less than half that.

Much of that decline happened quickly. Like other large technology companies Microsoft saw its share price plummet when the dot-com bubble burst in March of 2000. But in the years that followed, the company didn't bounce back. Instead, it seemed to lose its ability to innovate, join the trends that were reshaping the high-tech industry, or impress investors. Microsoft fell far behind on Internet, mobile, and cloud computing technologies. Windows and Office continued to generate revenue and profits, but little the company did generated much excitement. As it stumbled along year after year, Microsoft became a farce to many observers and a tragedy to its investors. Its share price was about as flat as a corpse's EKG from the start of 2001 through the end of 2012. At the end of that dozen-year period of enormous innovation in digital industries and some of the fastest growth the global economy has ever seen, the verdict of the market was that Microsoft was *less* valuable than it had been at the turn of the millennium (after taking inflation into account), despite having spent well over $80 billion on research and development.

Thanks to some excellent reporting we have a rich account of what happened inside the company during those years. In a 2012 *Vanity Fair* article

---

* The Justice Department took a dim view of this practice.

journalist Kurt Eichenwald captured the deep trouble Microsoft was in. He found that "what began as a lean competition machine led by young visionaries of unparalleled talent has mutated into something bloated and bureaucracy-laden, with an internal culture that unintentionally rewards managers who strangle innovative ideas that might threaten the established order of things." He documented that the seeds of Microsoft's decline were planted years in advance of any external threat, and were planted by the company's own people.

Microsoft had no shortage of the kind of dysfunction we explored in the previous chapter: bad decisions made by overconfident executives who listened to their internal press secretaries instead of testing their beliefs with evidence. In 2003, for example, a junior programmer working on the MSN Messenger instant messaging product noticed that friends of his who were still in college used a competing product called AIM. What's more, they kept it prominently displayed on their computer screens even when they weren't using it. Why? Because AIM allowed users to post short messages to update their network about where they were or what they were doing or thinking.

These messages, of course, would in a few years blossom into a new, planetwide mode of self-expression enabled by Facebook, Twitter, Instagram, and other social media companies. As early as 2003 it was clear to the young Microsoft programmer that apps centered around updates and messages would be popular. As Eichenwald tells it,

> The developer concluded that no young person would switch from AIM to MSN Messenger, which did not have the short-message feature. He spoke about the problem to his boss, a middle-aged man. The supervisor dismissed the developer's concerns as silly. Why would young people care about putting up a few words? . . .
>
> "He didn't get it," the developer said. "And because he didn't know or didn't believe how young people were using messenger programs, we didn't do anything."

There were plenty of examples of press secretaries triumphing over evidence at Microsoft in the early years of this century, but what hamstrung the company wasn't a set of bad decisions. It was instead a long descent into stifling bureaucracy.

As Eichenwald tells it, once the smooth escalator ride to an ever-higher stock price stopped operating in 2000, it was replaced by a situation that von Stauffenberg would have recognized immediately:

"People realized they weren't going to get wealthy," one former senior executive said. "They turned into people trying to move up the ladder, rather than people trying to make a big contribution to the firm."

And so, the bureaucratization of Microsoft began...

More employees seeking management slots led to more managers, more managers led to more meetings, more meetings led to more memos, and more red tape led to less innovation.

Bureaucracy accumulated over the years. One of its most obvious and pernicious effects was an increase in the time and effort required to get anything done. The never-ending quest for more status resulted in the promiscuous distribution of the power to hold things up. As Eichenwald puts it,

Marc Turkel, a product manager, told me about an initiative he oversaw around 2010 that involved multiple groups. At the same time the new project began, workers were breaking ground for construction of a 12-story building that would occupy a square block; Turkel's office window looked out on the construction site.

Turkel began negotiating with the different managers, then their supervisors, and then *their* supervisors as he tried to get the project finished. "It was amazing the amount of buyoff that was required," he said. "It was something, without all that time we wasted, that should have taken six weeks at most."

Finally, one day, Turkel was running another interminable meeting when he looked out the window. The building was finished. The project was not.

"I pointed to the building and said, 'When we started this, that building didn't exist,'" Turkel told me. "It was unbelievable."

In 2011 Microsoft made its bad situation worse by introducing a performance review system called stack ranking. It required managers to rank the members of their teams, and to designate the lowest-ranking ones as "below average" or worse. This had the immediate effect of making status rivalries both more common and more intense. No matter how successful or prestigious they were, people were forced into competition with their colleagues. Stack ranking created a clear human pecking order. Those that wound up highest on it got raises and promotions; those at the bottom often got fired. The resulting fights weren't literally bloody, but they were otherwise as vicious as anything seen in chicken pens. And they were essentially never-ending, since new rankings were required twice a year.

Eichenwald found that "every current and former Microsoft employee I interviewed—every one—cited stack ranking as the most destructive process inside of Microsoft." It led to infighting, Machiavellianism, and warring factions. One thing it didn't lead to was better results for the business. According to former Microsoft engineer Brian Cody, "I was told in almost every [performance] review that the political game was always important for my career development. It was always much more on 'Let's work on the political game' than on improving my actual performance." The political game was not characterized by fair play. As another engineer complained, "People responsible for features will openly sabotage other people's efforts. One of the most valuable things I learned was to give the appearance of being courteous while withholding just enough information from colleagues to ensure they didn't get ahead of me on the rankings."

The dysfunctions generated by the stack ranking system kept growing. The twice-yearly review sessions to assign rankings dragged on for days as managers rearranged Post-it notes with employee names on them and traded favors and threats with each other. A software designer remembered that "people planned their days and their years around the review, rather than around products. You really had to focus on the six-month performance, rather than on doing what was right for the company." Employees also had to focus on making sure that managers throughout the company knew what they were working on, so that they'd be widely seen as top performers. As Brian Cody put it, "Whenever I had a question for some other team, instead of going to the developer who had the answer, I would first touch base with that developer's manager, so that he knew what I was working on. That was the only way to be visible to other managers, which you needed for the review."

A Steady State of Dissatisfaction

One manager who had left Microsoft told Eichenwald, "I wanted to build a team of people who would work together and whose only focus would be on making great software. But you can't do that at Microsoft." This rueful conclusion highlights one of the worst things about excessive bureaucracies: their inescapability. They're disheartening because you can't rise above or go around them. Instead, you have to slog through them. You have to get all of the approvals if you want to spend the money. You have to attend all the product review meetings if you want to launch a product. You have to negotiate with the other managers if you want them to give high rankings to your people. And so on.

Sclerotic bureaucracies are stable and durable even though they make most of their constituencies miserable. This is a deeply counterintuitive situation. Most of us have the notion that a stable situation — an equilibrium — must be one that most participants, or at least the most powerful ones, are satisfied with. Another commonsense view is that an equilibrium must benefit the group as a whole, even if it leaves some participants worse off.

But both of those intuitions are wrong, as the great toilet paper shortage of 2020 showed us. Early that year, as the COVID-19 pandemic spread and economies around the world shut down, people stayed home and stocked up.

A lot of us were particularly keen to make sure that we had enough toilet paper. It's an important household item, after all, and substitutes that don't clog up plumbing or irritate sensitive skin are rare. So we did the rational thing in an uncertain time and made a larger-than-usual toilet paper purchase at the start of the shutdown.

The problem came when we went back to the store and noticed that all the toilet paper shelves were bare due to everyone's bigger-than-normal purchases. So a lot of us (myself included) made a mental note: "I really don't want to run out of toilet paper at home, so I'd better buy a lot of it the next time I see any for sale." And we did.

For a while we became a nation of toilet paper binge-buyers and hoarders. Even people who weren't worried about the SARS-CoV-2 virus itself had to binge and hoard. Why? Simply because so many other people were binge-buying that the shelves were empty most of the time. This meant that on the rare occasions when the shelves *weren't* empty you too had to binge-buy enough to last you through all the upcoming empty-shelf visits you had learned to expect. People quickly realized that the pre-pandemic way of buying toilet paper—when you run low, just buy a few rolls from a well-stocked shelf—didn't work anymore. By March of 2020 stores were seeing full-blown stampedes toward the toilet paper aisle as soon as they opened.

Most of us didn't like to shop like this. Most stores didn't like it either; constant stockouts make customers unhappy. The only people who really did like it were the toilet paper speculators who cropped up early on, driving vans and SUVs from supermarket to supermarket, buying up all their toilet paper, then selling it online at a large markup. This kind of opportunism didn't last long, though, as Amazon and other sites clamped down on it.

Still, the shortages continued. Walmart's CEO went on the *Today* show in April to ask Americans to change their new binge-and-hoard habit. (They didn't.) In November, Walmart reported it was once again seeing "pockets of lower than normal availability" during the second wave of lockdowns. It's not that we didn't learn. We *did* learn. We learned that if we wanted to be sure of having toilet paper in the house during a COVID wave, we had to binge and hoard.

Bingeing and hoarding was no fun for anyone involved, but it was still the right move—right in the sense that it beat all the alternatives. It was therefore a stable situation, one that an economist would label a Nash equilibrium. The reasoning that economist and pioneering game theorist John Nash came up with to explain such situations doesn't include any notion of good or bad, desired or loathed. His reasoning was clean, simple, and heartless: if no player in a game can benefit by unilaterally defecting, then you have a Nash equilibrium. In the "game" of buying toilet paper during the COVID pandemic, a lot of us settled on the strategy of binge-buying and hoarding. Defecting from that strategy—trying to buy toilet paper another way, in other words—didn't benefit shoppers. It instead left them worse off. So they stopped trying to defect, and the binge-buying and hoarding continued.

As with pandemic toilet paper shopping, so too with excess bureaucracy; individuals don't help themselves out by defecting. An engineer at Microsoft who cared about her career during the era of stack ranking would have to run her work by lots of managers so that she'd have a solid reputation when the next round of evaluations happened. She might even have to withhold help from her colleagues in order to look better than them, especially if they were doing the same to her. There was no effective way for her to be successful by "going rogue" in these situations—no way to thrive by taking shortcuts around the thicket of processes and practices and layers of bureaucracy. She and all of her colleagues were in a Nash equilibrium, even if they didn't want to be there.

Microsoft's descent into bureaucracy and sclerosis was unusually well documented. It might also have been unusually fast for such a large company. But I don't think its story is exceptional. Instead, I think the company followed the standard industrial-era trajectory of a rise followed by a particular kind of takeover from within. This kind of takeover is unplanned and uncoordinated, and it's not explicitly hostile. It's not carried out by people who want the organization to fail. Instead it's executed by people who want to succeed at the ultimate human goal of achieving higher status. In other words, it's a strategy executed by *Homo ultrasocialis.*

The Unleashed Organization

The problem for Microsoft, as for so many other organizations, was that the main routes to high status within the organization became increasingly disconnected from the goals of the company. No external force caused this to happen; the ultrasocial, status-obsessed people within the company did.

Like many other business geeks, Stripe CEO Patrick Collison is aware how easy it is for individuals' goals to diverge from those of their organizations. When I asked him what kinds of behaviors, if he observed them on a walk around his company, would leave him feeling pessimistic about its future, he replied, "I think anything that one would categorize as antisocial rather than prosocial. I think that the ratio between those is actually very important. There are a million definitions of 'startup' that one could use. I think there are fifty-person organizations that don't feel like a startup. I think there are five-thousand-person organizations that do. And I think the difference is the degree to which people are acting prosocially and actually trying to achieve the organization's stated goals."

With his last sentence, Collison comes close to articulating our second geek ground rule. Recall that the general form of the ultimate ground rule is, *Shape the ultrasociality of group members so that the group's cultural evolution is as rapid as possible in the desired direction.* For the great geek norm of science, the specific ground rule is, as we saw in the previous chapter, *Conduct evidence-based arguments so that the group makes better decisions, predictions, and estimates.* For the great geek norm of ownership—the subject of this chapter—the specific ground rule is, *To reduce bureaucracy, take away opportunities to gain status that aren't aligned with the goals and values of the company.*

This is a very different ground rule from encouraging communication and cooperation. The geeks realize that because these behaviors come so naturally to us ultrasocial human beings, they don't need to be encouraged. We band together to create groups that advocate for a change ("This incident shows that we need tighter control over our spending") and then benefit from it ("Our office must approve all spending requests over $1,000"). When we see another group making a play for higher status ("They just got invited to the product review meeting"), we join in ("We need to participate in product reviews"). We do this in formal and obvious ways ("Here's the new org chart with my allies at the top") and informal and subtle ones ("Next time, could you give us a heads-up before you launch?"). And we do all of it much more if a system like stack ranking sets up an explicit pecking order. There was no shortage of cooperation during Microsoft's decline; people were helping each other beat the system all over the place. They just weren't helping the company as they did so.

The net effect of all this activity is a bureaucracy that just keeps growing, creating ever-larger gaps between the goals of the company and its actual activities. To use Balzac's language, it's a curtain drawn between the right thing to do and the right person to do it. That curtain eventually gets so heavy that it brings down the entire organization.

To prevent such a collapse, the business geeks take a radical step: they stop a lot of coordination, collaboration, and communication. It's hard to overstate how big a change this is from the dominant approach of the late industrial era. When I was starting my academic career in the mid-1990s, business process reengineering was all the rage. This approach to improving performance was based on defining key business processes that cut across several functions (taking an order for a hundred widgets from a customer, for example, involved looking up inventory at the warehouse, having finance do a credit check, telling accounts receivable to generate an invoice, and so on), then specifying in great detail all the coordination required to make the process run smoothly. Reengineering and other approaches that emphasized cross-functional processes and well-defined coordination and collaboration were extremely popular. Executives loved the idea of having a tightly syn- chronized company that operated like an orchestra in which everyone was playing from the same sheet of music. In 1995, a group of CEOs in conversa- tion on the Harvard Business School campus described the virtues of sychro- nized business processes:

PAUL ALLAIRE [CEO, XEROX]. After all, if you have processes that are in control, you know how the organization is working. There's no guesswork, because variances are small and operating limits are well defined. You get quality output without a lot of checking…

CRAIG WEATHERUP [CEO AND PRESIDENT, PEPSI-COLA NORTH AMERICA]. I agree with you one thousand percent. A process approach is liberating. It helps us build reliability and winning consistency, and our people love to win. So over time, they've bought in completely.

JAN LESCHLY [CEO, SMITHKLINE BEECHAM]. People have a tough time understanding what it means for processes to be reliable, repeatable, and in control,…and it will take us years before we can honestly say that all 50,000 people at SmithKline Beecham understand what it means to standardize and improve a process.

Amazon and its leader took a very different view, and were happy to tell the world about it. Since 2010 Jeff Bezos has closed all of his shareholder letters with the words "It's still Day 1." The 2016 letter opens with an explanation of what this means:

"Jeff, what does Day 2 look like?"

That's a question I just got at our most recent all-hands meeting.

I've been reminding people that it's Day 1 for a couple of decades. I work in an Amazon building named Day 1, and when I moved buildings, I took the name with me. I spend time thinking about this topic.

"Day 2 is stasis. Followed by irrelevance. Followed by excruciating, painful decline. Followed by death. And *that* is why it is *always* Day 1."

To be sure, this kind of decline would happen in extreme slow motion. An established company might harvest Day 2 for decades, but the final result would still come…

As companies get larger and more complex, there's a tendency to manage to proxies. This comes in many shapes and sizes, and it's dangerous, subtle, and very Day 2.

A common example is process as proxy. Good process serves you so you can serve customers. But if you're not watchful, the process can become the thing. This can happen very easily in large organizations. The process becomes the proxy for the result you want. You stop looking at outcomes and just make sure you're doing the process right. Gulp... The process is not the thing. It's always worth asking, do we own the process or does the process own us? In a Day 2 company, you might find it's the second.

So if the process is not the thing at Amazon, what is? The great geek norm of ownership, or clear and sole responsibility for an agreed-upon goal.

One example of this norm is Amazon's emphasis on "single-threaded leaders." As former Amazonians Colin Bryar and Bill Carr explain in *Working Backwards,* their book about the company's culture and practices, single-threaded leadership is "an Amazon innovation... in which a single person, unencumbered by competing responsibilities, owns a single major initiative and heads up a separable, largely autonomous team to deliver its goals."

Single-threaded leadership grew out of two-pizza teams, an earlier attempt to foster a culture of ownership at Amazon (and one with a catchier name). These teams were small—ideally containing no more people than could be fed by two large pizzas—responsible for a clearly defined objective like selling more shoes in Germany, and conceived to be as autonomous as possible. The whole point of setting up two-pizza teams was to *minimize* the amount of coordination and communication needed with other Amazonians, and the number of dependencies the team had with the rest of the business. Instead of starting from the assumption that important business efforts require a lot of coordination, involvement, and buy-in from many groups, two-pizza teams were born out of the opposite assumption: the more important an effort is, the more its dependencies should be reduced and the more the team responsible for it should be given sole ownership and complete autonomy.

Technology analyst Benedict Evans describes how Amazon's small, autonomous teams give bureaucracy fewer places to take root:

Amazon is hundreds of small, decentralized, atomized teams sitting on top of standardised common internal systems. If Amazon decides that it's going to do (say) shoes in Germany, it hires half a dozen people from very different backgrounds, maybe with none of them having anything to do with shoes or e-commerce, and it gives them those platforms, with internal transparency of the metrics of every other team, and of course, other people (and Jeff) have internal transparency to their metrics...

The obvious advantage of a small team is that you can do things quickly within the team, but the structural advantage of them, in Amazon at least (and in theory, at least), is that you can multiply them. You can add new product lines without adding new internal structure or direct reports, and you can add them without meetings and projects and process in the logistics and e-commerce platforms. You don't (in theory) need to fly to Seattle and schedule a bunch of meetings to get people to implement support for launching makeup in Italy, or persuade anyone to add things to their roadmap.

You don't, in other words, create opportunities for status seeking that aren't strictly aligned with the goals of the company.

As two-pizza teams were getting rolled out across Amazon, the company found that the ones that worked hardest early on to reduce their dependency on the rest of the organization were the most successful over time. When it became clear that some teams needed to be bigger than the two-pizza limit would allow, the phrase "single-threaded leader" became common, but the core idea remained the same: a strong sense of ownership within teams, and very little communication, coordination, or interdependence among them. At Amazon, the dependencies that industrial-era companies were so fond of came to be associated with one of the most hated words in business. As Bryar and Carr write in *Working Backwards,*

"We found it helpful to think of such cross-functional projects as a kind of tax."

The geeks' distaste for coordination can seem extreme. They often don't even want teams to talk with each other, or with the higher-ups in the company. They believe that cross-team communication can be harmful because it often turns into a soft form of bureaucracy. In our never-ending quest for status, we ultrasocial humans insert ourselves into more discussions at work, expect to be consulted and informed, want to be included when new ideas and projects are "socialized," and want to leave our mark on them.

The business geeks really don't like this kind of socializing. So while teams aren't encouraged to be unhelpful, they're also not encouraged to coordinate their efforts or seek approval. Sebastian Thrun, an alpha geek computer scientist, executive, and entrepreneur, gave me a status-based explanation why this is. As he put it,

> You take a good idea and you communicate up the management chain, every manager will of course want to change it because they want to take credit for the invention. And before you realize it, something very simple at the base becomes really complicated at the top, and as it comes back down to the individual that invented it, they often face so-and-so complexity that wasn't even there, just because the managers wanted to justify their existence.

Jeff Bezos agrees. Colin Bryar recalls, "In my tenure at Amazon, I heard [Bezos] say many times that if we wanted Amazon to be a place where builders can build, we needed to eliminate communication, not encourage it."

How to Lead a Swarm

The great geek norm of ownership provides high autonomy but has two obvious weaknesses. The first is that it can be abused. People can take advantage of the lack of required prior approvals and other checks to commit fraud, embezzle, or otherwise enrich themselves. The second potential weakness is chaos. There's no guarantee that a bunch of atomized teams will, in aggregate, act in ways that advance the goals of a company. In fact, it seems almost guaranteed that they won't. As Max Weber reminded us, some level of bureaucracy is required to accomplish the goals of almost any organization. So how can bureaucracy-phobic geeks get their swarms of teams to move in the right direction? These are both serious challenges. Let's look at fraud first.

If enough people are given freedom to act without prior approval, it's a near certainty that there will be some bad actors. At Netflix, for example, employees were more fond of business class travel than the company might like. One employee even treated himself to $100,000 worth of luxury vacations before he was found out and fired. The geeks fight back against these kinds of behaviors with two main weapons. The first is ongoing reminders of expected behavior. These reminders, especially when they come from prestigious leaders, are an important part of establishing and maintaining norms. An employee at Netflix was fired after a spot check by their boss revealed that they were expensing meals that had no relation to work. As Erin Meyer writes, "At the next Quarterly Business Review (QBR) leadership meeting, Netflix's chief talent officer at the time got up onstage and told [the] story to the 350 attendees, detailing the abuse but not identifying [the employee] by name or department. She asked participants to share the situation with their teams so everyone understood the gravity of cheating the system... Without this degree of transparency, freedom from expense approvals doesn't work." In chapter 7, we'll look in more detail at how norms are set and maintained. Norms require a lot of upkeep, and the words and actions of senior and prestigious people matter a great deal.

The second big geek weapon against divergent behavior is one we've already seen: evidence. The geeks' mania for collecting evidence comes in handy for the very simple reason that people are less likely to misbehave if they know that their bad acts will be observable. Cash registers, for example, don't make it impossible for cashiers to steal money; the bills and coins are right there every time the register is opened. Registers reduce theft not by making it impossible to commit, but instead by making it easier to observe after the fact. They keep a record of sales over the course of a cashier's shift. If (cash in register at start of shift) plus (total sales) doesn't equal (cash in register at end of shift), there's going to be an investigation.* As cashiers became aware of this, they became less likely to steal, to the point that cash registers soon became known as incorruptible cashiers. The automated travel and expense audits routinely conducted now by Netflix and many other companies are modern technologies that do the same thing cash registers do; they increase observability and monitoring, and decrease unwanted behavior.

What about the other big weakness, chaos? Autonomous, self-directed teams sound great in many ways, but how can anyone ensure that their work will be aligned with the strategy and goals of the company? The vision of a company reengineered and tightly orchestrated to do just what its leaders want is an extremely clear and enticing one. It's a lot less clear how a bunch of uncoordinated teams can be counted on to do the same.

To ensure that autonomous teams remain aligned with the company's overall goals, geek companies rely on a bureaucracy that's powerful yet tightly constrained. Its job is to oversee the work of translating the company's high-level vision and strategy into team-level goals and associated metrics — the objectives and key results (OKRs) we saw in the previous chapter. This alignment process specifies what each team's goals are and how it's going to be measured, but does *not* tell teams how to best hit their metrics and meet their objectives, or who they should work with. That's for the teams themselves to decide.

At the cloud-based software company Salesforce, for example, the alignment bureaucracy revolves around a management process called V2MOM, or vision, values, methods, obstacles, and measures. It came about because of cofounder Marc Benioff's frustration at a previous job. As he writes in his book *Behind the Cloud,*

---

* After the first cash registers were introduced, some inventive cashiers got around their recording capabilities by simply not using them at all, and pocketing the cash received from customers. Register manufacturers dealt with this by including the now-familiar bell that rings with each sale. If the bell doesn't ring before customers walk away from the sales counter with their purchases, the store owner knows something is amiss.

When I was at Oracle, I struggled with the fact that there was no written business plan or formal communication process during our growth phase... What I yearned for... was clarity on our vision and the goals we wanted to achieve. As I started to manage my own divisions, I found that I personally lacked the tools to spell out what we needed to do and a simple process to communicate it. The problem only increased as the teams that I was managing increased.

As Salesforce was getting off the ground in 1999, Benioff created a quick first version of a written plan to provide clarity throughout the company. He grabbed an envelope, wrote the five words "Vision, Values, Methods, Obstacles, and Measures" on the back of it, and filled in a few entries under each of them. His cofounder, Parker Harris, kept the envelope, had it framed, and presented it to Benioff the night before Salesforce went public in June of 2004.

Since then, as Benioff writes,

we've expanded the scope of the V2MOM to both individuals and teams across the company: Each year, every single department and every single employee drafts their own. As a result, this practical exercise... courses through the entire organization from top to bottom.

And to foster transparency, we publish every V2MOM on our corporate social network...

Anyone can look up any employee's V2MOM to see how each plans to contribute to our company's future. We even built an app that allows every employee to track their progress on each item in their V2MOM.

Salesforce's annual V2MOM process starts with Benioff's document, which gives goals and metrics for the entire company, then cascades downward and throughout the organization. V2MOMs aren't static; they can be updated at any time in response to changing circumstances. My friends who work at Salesforce tell me that they really are important and widely used documents. Before meeting with someone, for instance, it's common practice to look up their V2MOM so that their agenda is clear.

There are lots of varieties of OKR and V2MOM processes across geek companies. They all support a fundamentally similar approach to getting work done while avoiding sclerosis: give teams a great deal of autonomy, use an alignment process to establish their goals and monitor progress toward them, and then get out of the way and let teams work with high autonomy. Working through the alignment process isn't fast or easy, but many business geeks feel that it's worth the effort. Benioff says, for example, that "the biggest secret of Salesforce.com is how we've achieved a high level of organizational alignment and communication while growing at breakneck speeds,... with the help of" the V2MOM process.

Many industrial-era companies, on the other hand, seem unable to keep their people aligned with the organization's goals and strategies. In 2001 management scholars Robert Kaplan and David Norton found that "a mere 7 percent of employees today fully understand their company's business strategies and what's expected of them in order to help achieve company goals." Things didn't improve much as the twenty-first century progressed. Gallup's 2015 "State of the American Manager" report found that "only 12 percent of employees strongly agree that their manager helps them set work priorities, and just 13 percent strongly agree that their manager helps them set performance goals." Overall, Gallup consistently found that only about half of all employees surveyed knew what was expected of them at work.

Companies that put in place a norm of ownership—that give their people and teams high autonomy while maintaining alignment throughout the organization—can achieve something impressive. They can reverse the promiscuous distribution of the power to hold things up, and instead promiscuously distribute the power to get things done. They can replace bureaucracy and vetocracy with simultaneous agility, innovation, and execution.

One important point here is that while the business geeks believe strongly in sole ownership of a project, they don't believe in sole ownership of a market opportunity. James Manyika, a longtime McKinsey consultant and researcher who became Google's first senior vice president for technology and society in

2022, emphasized this point to me. Manyika was chairman of the McKinsey Global Institute, the firm's internal think tank. In 2018, MGI published research on global superstar firms, many of which were headquartered in our Northern California circle. The research found that one of the things that stood out about the superstars was that, as Manyika put it,

> they're not trying to optimize everything. They tolerate some flex and redundancy. For example, they tolerate trying several different things in parallel. They might say, "We're going to run ten parallel experiments. Sure, only one of them will pan out; that's fine. We're chasing a big opportunity, and the ten teams are going about it in very different ways." You often find an executive from what I'll call the old world say, "That's wasteful. How can you have ten different teams working on the same thing with different methods? That's a waste of money." The superstar's response is, "It's worth having all ten teams because the market size is so large, and who knows where the most innovative way to crack that market is going to come from?"

The great geek norm of ownership often conflicts with traditional notions of business efficiency. Instead of centralizing responsibility for important efforts, the geeks tend to distribute it, because distribution increases the chance of finding a breakthrough. This approach works as long as there's not a huge career penalty for people who aren't on the "winning" team. In other words, for distributed ownership to work it has to be okay to fail periodically. In chapter 7 we'll look at how the business geeks have let go of the fixation on winning all the time and embraced some kinds of failure.

In the previous chapter we saw that the great geek norm of science works not by trying to get rid of overconfidence among us *Homo ultrasocialis,* but instead by channeling it. Science makes us overconfident evidence producers, and then subjects our evidence to group-level scrutiny and argumentation that is highly effective at getting rid of bias and getting to the truth. Something similar happens with the great geek norm of ownership. It doesn't try to get rid of the status seeking that's innate to being an ultrasocial human.

It instead channels our status seeking into activities that would make a customer or investor happy, and does this simply by eliminating other activities. If there's no giant machinery of bureaucracy, there's no way to get ahead by getting good at operating it. Working hard to be in the loop more often—having veto or approval power over more requests or decisions, controlling a resource that others have to ask for (like engineering talent or a database), being part of meetings to socialize new initiatives—is a bad strategy in a company that wants to have as few loops as possible.

A much better strategy is accomplishing your objectives and hitting your key metrics. In a culture with a strong norm of ownership, doing those things will give you prestige and high rank in your work environment. Because that environment is so important to us *Homo ultrasocialis*—remember, a lot of us spend as much time there as we do asleep—our drive for status at work is very strong. Geek companies align that drive with the goals of the organization by pruning away the kinds of status that get in the way of achieving those goals.

This is a very clever trick. It's also a difficult one. There are both technical and organizational barriers—high ones—to putting in place a norm of ownership at most companies. Let's look at how business geeks have dealt with both kinds, starting with the technical hurdles.

The Soul of a New Machinery

Amazon hasn't always had a culture of ownership and autonomy. In its early years, in fact, it found itself on its way to becoming the kind of process-heavy Day 2 company that Bezos later warned against. Amazon grew quickly after it was founded in 1994, and it developed an elaborate and pervasive bureaucracy. All Amazonians knew about it and no one liked it, but it seemed essential since it coordinated the company's innovation efforts.

The bureaucracy existed to administer the "new proposed initiative" (NPI) process, which was all about cross-functional dependencies. Four times a year, any team with an idea for a new project would write it up in a short proposal that specified what the team needed from other parts of the company. If the proposal passed two initial reviews, it went before the NPI final decision makers. The proposing team then waited to see which of three emails they would receive:

Congratulations, your project has been approved! The other teams you need to help complete your project are ready to get started too.

The bad news is that your project was not chosen, but the good news is that none of the approved NPI projects require work from you.

We're sorry that none of your projects were approved and you were probably counting on them to hit your team goals. There are, however, approved NPI projects for other teams that require resources from you. You must fully staff those NPI projects before staffing any of your other internal projects. Best of luck.

The second note reveals a deep truth about bureaucracies: it's good news when they leave you alone. The third note highlights the fact that they often don't, and that they can give nothing while asking much in return. Because of NPI, Amazonians could periodically get the unwelcome news that they had just become less likely to reach their own goals because they had to contribute to someone else's projects. As Bryar notes with some understatement, "The NPI process was not beloved. If you mention NPI to any Amazonian who went through it, you're likely to get a grimace and maybe a horror story or two... [It] was deflating for morale."

The NPI process and accompanying bureaucracy were considered critical for the company, but were miserable for most people involved with it. This is a potent combination for encouraging bad behavior. I can only imagine how intense the status games and organizational infighting were around NPI.

The dysfunctions and disappointments of the NPI process were instrumental in sparking a 180-degree shift at Amazon away from trying to define and manage dependencies and toward trying to flat out eliminate them.

This was a shift away from a culture in which management exercised a great deal of control, toward a culture in which management encouraged high levels of ownership. It led to two-pizza teams, single-threaded leaders, and many other organizational innovations. But before that shift could begin in earnest, Amazon needed to rewrite just about all of its software in a way that had never been done before.

By the early years of this century the code that powered Amazon's website and operations was being held together by "duct tape and WD-40 engineering," as technology executive Werner Vogels put it. The company had grown more than twentyfold in just the five years leading up to 2001, and its databases and applications were having trouble keeping up, as were the developers and engineers who looked after them.

Amazon's information technology desperately needed an upgrade, which would be a huge and difficult project (after all, the company needed to continue to operate while something like its brain and nerves were being replaced). But Bezos wanted to do more than just modernize his company's information systems; he also wanted to make them as separable and modular as the two-pizza teams that were then being envisioned.

Without this modularity, business innovation teams would have to ask for support from the IT function in order to make any code or database changes they needed. This would mean submitting and prioritizing requests. It would mean, in other words, re-creating some version of the NPI bureaucracy. And whatever the initial version was like, it would probably become more elaborate and sclerotic over time if human nature and previous organizational history were any guide.

So Bezos set out to do something very different. A CEO who, according to former Amazon engineer Steve Yegge, "makes ordinary control freaks look like stoned hippies," mandated that his company would build a software architecture that devolved control to teams throughout the company, allowing them to access data and software without having to ask anyone for permission or support (and without crashing the entire company). Yegge wrote that this mandate "was so out there, so huge and eye-bulgingly ponderous, that it made all of his other mandates look like unsolicited peer bonuses."

179

It took several years, but Amazon pulled it off. It rebuilt its systems for super-high modularity (in technical terms, it adopted a service-oriented architecture). Teams could use and combine these modules without needing to ask anyone for access or permission. The company learned so much from this effort and developed so many innovations that it launched a new business, Amazon Web Services, to sell modular technology infrastructure to other companies (thereby helping to create the cloud computing industry). It also permanently shut down the NPI bureaucracy and replaced it with a process that aligned teams' activities with corporate goals. Amazon eventually settled on two annual alignment processes, called OP1 and OP2. They are detailed, but also narrow: their aim is only to specify OKRs for teams, and *not* to tell them how to do their work or who they need to interact with. Instead, as Werner Vogels (who eventually became Amazon's CTO) puts it, "The [new, modular] Amazon development environment requires engineers and architects to be very independent creative thinkers... You need to have a strong sense of ownership."

How Microsoft Hit Refresh

Earlier we saw how Microsoft descended into excessive bureaucracy. Let's end this chapter on an encouraging note, by showing how the company climbed out of its sclerosis under the leadership of Satya Nadella.

When Nadella became the third CEO of Microsoft in February of 2014, the company was moribund. Its main product lines of PC operating systems and productivity applications were fading in importance, and it was far behind in the red-hot areas of online apps and mobile and cloud computing. The people who worked at Microsoft knew this and were dispirited. As Nadella wrote in his 2017 book, *Hit Refresh,*

> Our annual employee poll revealed that most employees didn't think we were headed in the right direction and questioned our ability to innovate. [Focus groups revealed that people] were tired. They were frustrated. They were fed up with losing and falling

behind despite their grand plans and great ideas. They came to Microsoft with big dreams, but it felt like all they really did was deal with upper management, execute taxing processes, and bicker in meetings. They believed that only an outsider could get the company back on track. None of the names on the rumored list of internal CEO candidates resonated with them — including mine.

In his first speech, Nadella told his colleagues that Microsoft needed to rediscover its soul. In an all-hands email sent the same morning, he wrote that "every one of us needs to . . . lead and help drive cultural change . . . [and] find meaning in our work." These aren't exceptional words; they're pretty standard for a new leader in charge of a company that needs a turnaround. But Microsoft's performance under Nadella has been anything but standard. During his first eight and a half years on the job, the company's market capitalization increased over six and a half times and grew at an annual rate of more than 25 percent. By comparison, in the eight and a half years before Nadella took the top job, the company's valuation grew at less than 2 percent per year.

Microsoft under Nadella has made several smart strategic moves, including investing heavily in mobile and cloud computing, embracing open-source software, shuttering its disastrous acquisition of Nokia, and developing software for platforms other than Windows. But remember, culture eats strategy for breakfast. If Nadella didn't succeed at getting his company out of the bureaucracy, sclerosis, and infighting described earlier in this chapter, the new strategies would have had no chance of succeeding. They'd have been smothered, just like so many other good ideas had been during the long years of Microsoft's stagnation.

So what did Nadella actually *do* to revive his company? He helped Microsoft get back to its roots by embracing all four of the great geek norms: science, ownership, speed, and openness. Before turning our attention to ownership, let's look briefly at the other three.

We saw in the previous chapter that evidence and measurement are core to science, and that geek companies often embrace OKRs to track their progress. Nadella told me, "We're also converting pretty much all of Microsoft to an OKR system. I buy that because having the objectives on which people can converge is a very helpful thing. I think having a management system overall that allows you to have a top-down, bottom-up, and continuously calibrating system is a very important one."

The norm of science involves not just collecting evidence but also arguing about it. In *Hit Refresh,* Nadella writes of Microsoft's senior leadership team (SLT), a small group of the most senior executives in the company, that "debate and argument are essential. Improving upon each other's ideas is crucial. I wanted people to speak up. 'Oh, here's a customer segmentation study I've done.' 'Here's a pricing approach that contradicts this idea.'"

As we'll see when we discuss the great geek norm of speed in the next chapter, "agile" approaches to developing software and running large projects of all kinds can be surprisingly effective at both improving quality and reducing delays and unpleasant surprises. Nadella saw this firsthand earlier in his career when he was in charge of Bing, Microsoft's search engine. As he writes, "I found that the key was agility, agility, agility. We needed to develop speed, nimbleness, and athleticism to get the consumer experience right, not just once but daily. We needed to set and repeatedly meet short-term goals, shipping code at a more modern, fast-paced cadence." He stressed to me that "speed of iteration matters. So one of the fundamental things we do is in any project review, we look at not just what was the input and the output but also the speed of the input-to-output iteration."

The great geek norm of openness is, as we'll see in chapter 7, essentially the antithesis of defensiveness. Defensive thinking and behavior are often rooted in a zero-sum mindset where gains in one area must be accompanied by losses in another—where I perceive your victory as my defeat. Nadella told me that an outlook of "in order for me to win, I gotta be able to point very clearly to somebody who's losing" was common at Microsoft when he took over. As he writes in *Hit Refresh,* "Our culture had been rigid. Each employee had to prove to everyone that he or she knew it all and was the smartest person in the room. Accountability—delivering on time and hitting numbers—trumped everything." Being accountable for hitting targets is important, but when it "trumps everything" people get defensive and think of their work environment in zero-sum terms.

Defensiveness is corrosive. It eats away at a team's ability to innovate, take risks, and work well together. Nadella learned just how defensive even the most senior people at Microsoft had become when he invited psychologist Michael Gervais to attend the regular SLT meeting. Gervais opened by asking if the people in the room wanted to have an "extraordinary individual experience." Everyone of course said yes. Gervais then asked for a volunteer to stand up. No one did for a long time, until CFO Amy Hood bravely got to her feet. As Nadella recalls, "Dr. Gervais was curious: Why wouldn't everyone jump up? Wasn't this a high-performing group? Didn't everyone just say they wanted to do something extraordinary?... The answers were hard to pull out, even though they were just beneath the surface. Fear: of being ridiculed; of failing; of not looking like the smartest person in the room... 'What a stupid question,' we had grown used to hearing."

Gervais had a simple but savvy technique for starting to break down this deep defensiveness: he simply got people to talk about themselves—to, as we say, *open up*. Nadella writes that at the meeting

> we shared our personal passions and philosophies. We were asked to reflect on who we are, both in our home lives and at work. How do we connect our work persona with our life persona? People talked about spirituality, their Catholic roots, their study of Confucian teachings, they shared their struggles as parents and their unending dedication to making products that people love to use for work and entertainment. As I listened, I realized that in all of my years at Microsoft this was the first time I'd heard my colleagues talk about themselves, not exclusively about business matters. Looking around the room, I even saw a few teary eyes.

To be clear, the goal of openness isn't to turn every meeting into a therapy session. Instead, it's to get people comfortable with not always being in control or victorious, and less concerned about projecting an image of infallibility and invincibility. The SLT meeting Nadella describes was important for Microsoft's transformation because it got the top leaders of the company to at least start thinking about behaving less defensively. Such behavior stood a good chance of spreading, because it originated with the most senior and respected people in the company. As we saw earlier in this chapter, we ultrasocial human beings consciously and subconsciously pay attention to prestige. If the most prestigious people around us start acting differently, we're likely to mimic this new behavior, even if we're not always aware that we're doing so. Some kinds of change, like greater openness or defensiveness, really do come from the top—from the most prestigious people in an organization.

This chapter is about the great geek norm of ownership and the accompanying work of alignment. The SLT meeting described by Nadella not only started to chip away at the defensiveness that prevailed at the company; it also started to increase alignment. It did this by reminding the team of "their unending dedication to making products that people love to use for work and entertainment." In other words, it got Microsoft's senior leaders to think of themselves as members of the same tribe.

This matters because we *Homo ultrasocialis* are such an intensely tribal species. We *have* to be part of a tribe, given how helpless we are as individuals. As we saw in chapter 3, throughout most of our evolutionary history we needed to be part of a group in order to simply stay alive and learn the most basic tasks necessary for survival. So we're deeply wired to associate ourselves with a group; adopt its worldview, values, norms, and so on; and strive to be members in good standing.

But an immediate implication of our tribalism is that there's not just an "us"; there's also always a "them."* Our innate tendency to separate the social

---

* Psychologist Leda Cosmides and anthropologist John Tooby stress that an undeniable consequence of human tribalism is our tendency to wage war. As they explain in a lyrical and emphatic paragraph: "War is older than the human species. It is found in every region of the world, among all the branches of humankind. It is found throughout human history, deeply and densely woven into its causal tapestry. It is found in all eras, and in earlier periods no less than later. There is no evidence of it having originated in one place, and spread by contact to

world into in-groups and out-groups is deeply rooted and remarkably easy to activate. As Robert Trivers puts it:

> Such groups, in and out, are pathetically easy to form. You need not stoke Sunni or Catholic fundamentalism to get people to feel the right way; just make some wear blue shirts and others red and within a half-hour you will induce in-group and out-group feelings based on shirt color.

When Nadella became CEO, Microsoft was a demonstration of just how right Trivers was. The company was deeply factionalized, and groups fought with each other, both openly and covertly, over resources, people, promotions, "ownership" of a product or customer segment, and anything else that was worth fighting over. The constant intergroup conflict at Microsoft throughout the 2010s was an enormous handicap. Nadella knew he had to bring it way down and get the company to become a single tribe—"one Microsoft," as he put it.

One important move toward one Microsoft was to eliminate existing profit centers (for the Windows operating system, Office application suite, and so on) and replace them with a single corporate profit and loss (P&L) statement. This eliminated product group A's tendency to see group B's fast-growing product as a looming threat that needed to be reined in or even sabotaged. As Nadella explained to me, "We became a functional organization, so there were no P&Ls except one P&L for all of Microsoft. Instead we gave everybody cost targets. This unconstrained the organization and oriented it on the future. We basically moved the P&L risk up to the corporate level."

Nadella's second major move to restore alignment was to take away from individual groups ownership of important assets like code, data, and data

---

others. War is reflected in the most fundamental features of human social life. When indigenous histories are composed, their authors invariably view wars—unlike almost all other kinds of events—as preeminently worth recording. The foundational works of human literature—the *Iliad*, the Bhagavad Gita, the Tanakh, the Quran, the *Tale of the Heike*—whether oral or written, sacred or secular—reflect societies in which war was a pervasive feature."

centers. As we've discussed, owners of such assets have a strong tendency to gain status by acting as gatekeepers. In exchange for access, they demand to be consulted, to be "brought into the loop," and so on. Nadella worked to do away with this gatekeeping:

> Nobody can own code or data inside Microsoft. So in some sense we have one corporate resource that anyone can use, obviously subject to all the rules and regulations on it. But that said, any team can stand up and say, "Hey, I have an idea. I want to train a large-scale AI model to go do, for example, GitHub Copilot [an AI tool that generates computer code based on natural language instructions from a human]. I want all the code, I want all the data." Yes, you absolutely can have it because no team can hoard it.

In *Hit Refresh*, Nadella describes a pivotal moment right before the start of his tenure as CEO:

> In an intense prep session two days before the announcement [my chief of staff] Jill [Tracie Nichols] and I sparred on how to inspire this disheartened group of [employees]. In some ways, I was annoyed by what felt like lack of accountability and finger pointing. She stopped me mid-riff with "You're missing it, they are actually hungry to do more, but things keep getting in their way."

Seeing that the barriers to real organizational change are the obstacles people face, rather than the people themselves, became core to Nadella's worldview. In 2022 I asked him about an often-heard frustration related to organizational change: that the CEO and frontline employees want it, but middle managers don't. Instead, they cling tightly to the status quo and thwart attempts to move away from it. I found his answer fascinating. It illustrates what kind of leader he is, and why he's been so successful. He began by highlighting that like virtually all CEOs, he used to *be* a middle manager:

People talk about the "frozen middle." I resist that characterization, because for most of my professional career I was in the middle. And I think the jobs I had in the middle were the hardest because you got the squeeze from the top and the bottom. All the constraints were being managed by the middle. So one thing that I like to say is no one in top leadership should ever throw middle managers under the bus because without them you have no company... Most of the time, middle managers are not sitting there not wanting to do the right thing; it's just that they're overconstrained. As a top leader, if you're giving your teams five things that all need to be top priority you're not doing your job. You're just squeezing them. And so no wonder they look at this and say, I might as well hide. To me, instead of thinking about the frozen middle, really empowering the middle so that they can help the organization move forward is one of the most important managerial tricks.

Nadella realized that the fight against bureaucracy and sclerosis isn't a fight against some group of bad actors. It's instead a fight against a badly configured environment—one that lets us *Homo ultrasocialis* gain status in ways that aren't tightly aligned with the goals of the organization. Geek leaders like Nadella work hard to create very different environments. Doing so entails rejecting a lot of the received wisdom of the industrial era about how important communication, cooperation, and cross-functional coordination are and instead striving to build autonomous and aligned organizations that unconstrain people and give them ownership.

Chapter Summary

Companies have a puzzling tendency to become excessively bureaucratic even though bureaucracy frustrates people and hurts performance. It's an undesirable Nash equilibrium.

The ultimate explanation is that dense bureaucracy is the result of status seeking by us status-obsessed *Homo ultrasocialis*. We invent work so that we can be part of it. We strive to be consulted on lots of decisions, and if possible have veto power over them. Excess bureaucracy is a bug for anyone who wants a company to run efficiently, but it's a feature for the *Homo ultrasocialis* who seek opportunities to gain status in the organization.

To fight against bureaucracy and sclerosis, business geeks take a radical step: they stop a lot of coordination, collaboration, and communication and instead establish a norm of *ownership,* or clear and sole responsibility for an agreed-upon goal.

The geeks' distaste for coordination can seem extreme. They often don't even want teams to talk with each other, or with the higher-ups in the company. They believe that cross-team communication can be harmful because it often turns into a soft form of bureaucracy.

To ensure that their autonomous teams remain aligned with the company's overall goals, geek companies rely on a bureaucracy that's powerful yet tightly constrained. Its job is to oversee the work of translating the company's high-level vision and strategy into team-level objectives and key results.

For the norm of ownership, the ultimate geek ground rule is: *To reduce bureaucracy, take away opportunities to gain status that aren't aligned with the goals and values of the company.*

Survey for Your Organization

These ten statements can be used to assess how well an organization follows the great geek norm of ownership. Respondents reply to each with a number between one and seven, where one means "strongly disagree" and seven means "strongly agree."

1. There is a lot of red tape in this company.*
2. We have a bias for action over planning and coordinating.
3. The best way to succeed at this company is to help it accomplish its stated goals.
4. I am free to act autonomously in the areas that are most important for my work.
5. I have to coordinate my work with many other teams across the company.*
6. Bureaucracy prevents us from moving quickly to seize opportunities.*
7. I spend a lot of time in cross-functional meetings and other coordination activities.*
8. I am rewarded for taking the initiative.
9. I have to spend a lot of time asking for the resources I need to do my work.*
10. It's clear to me how my work fits in with the overall strategy and goals of the company.

---

* Scores for these statements need to be reversed. To do this, subtract the respondent's score from eight. For example, if the respondent answered with six, the reversed score would be two.

CHAPTER 6

Speed

From Lying to Learning

Yeah, you go back, Jack, do it again
Wheel turnin' 'round and 'round
— *Steely Dan*

Volkswagen learned recently that when it comes to developing a modern car, the hardest part isn't any of the moving parts.

In 2015 VW decided to create an entirely new platform for electric vehicles (EVs) instead of modifying any of the ones it was using for internal-combustion vehicles. Of course, software would be a huge part of this "modular electric power train" platform. The company showed a nonfunctioning EV in October of 2016 at the Paris auto show and announced a new all-electric brand, ID., which stood for "intelligent design, identity, and visionary technologies."

In September of 2019, VW unveiled its final version, the ID.3, at the Frankfurt auto show. The vehicle was a hit. By the end of the show, more than thirty-three thousand people had put down a deposit for one. Factory production was to start in November, and the first deliveries were due in mid-2020.

On the Road, but Not over the Air

At about the 90 percent mark of the car's original development timeline, however, word of a serious problem leaked out. In December 2019 Germany's

Manager Magazin reported that at least the first twenty thousand ID.3s produced would not have the ability to update their software over the air (OTA, or remotely and wirelessly), a capability the startup EV manufacturer Tesla had pioneered with its all-electric cars in 2012. These initial all-electric VWs off the assembly line were to be parked in rented lots until a software update could be installed—via wire—that would allow future updates to be done over the air.

In late February of 2020, the same magazine reported on a frantic, all-hands-on-deck effort involving around ten thousand people to fix the ID.3's software problems. Hundreds of engineers and technicians were flown in from sister companies Porsche and Audi each Monday, then back again on Friday. Test drivers reported scores of new bugs every day. Rumors flew that delays of up to a year were possible, but sources close to VW head Herbert Diess dismissed them as "complete nonsense." In June, however, VW announced that the first deliveries of the ID.3 to customers would not happen until September, and that these cars would still not allow full OTA updates. Also that month, VW's board stripped Diess of his title as CEO of the Volkswagen division, although he remained CEO of the entire VW automotive group.

In February of 2021, more than a year after the initial reports of VW's troubles with OTA updates, photos circulated of long rows of ID.3s parked in what appeared to be a temporary structure. Each car was connected to a laptop via a cable, presumably to receive software updates. The timing was unfortunate for VW, since that same month a video posted to TikTok showed a huge parking lot full of Teslas receiving OTA updates at night. "It looks like aliens are landing," wrote journalist Fred Lambert of the empty cars' lights flashing in large-scale patterns as their software updated automatically and wirelessly.

In September of 2021, VW finally announced, "Effective immediately, all ID. models will receive regular software updates via mobile data transfer... The company plans to provide its customers with free software around every twelve weeks." For at least some ID.3 owners, however, that announcement proved premature. On July 22, 2022, more than two years after ID.3s capable of OTA software updates were supposed to be available, the *Handelsblatt* website reported, "After months of delays, the ID models delivered over the past two years are now getting a new software update. To do this, more than 150,000 e-cars in Europe have to spend a whole day in the workshop." The article included a promise that may have rung hollow to some customers: "Future updates can then be installed wirelessly and without having to visit the workshop." The same day the *Handelsblatt* article appeared, Herbert Diess announced that he was stepping down as CEO of the VW Group. As Bloomberg journalist Stefan Nicola put it, "It says a lot about the state of the auto industry and where it's going that software problems have cost the CEO of a carmaker his job."

Tesla, meanwhile, sent seventeen OTA updates to its Model 3 fleet in 2019, twenty-two in 2020, and nineteen in 2021. Some of these were minor bug fixes, but approximately half were more substantial changes, such as improved navigation and driver-assistance technologies, a new tire-pressure monitoring system, 5 percent greater power for the vehicle as a whole, and more video games.

Why Are Things Late?

VW's experience with the ID.3 is not an isolated example. Many organizations have real trouble getting important projects done anywhere near on time (and therefore on budget), whether they involve software, hardware, or a combination of both, and regardless of whether they're public or private efforts. Sometimes, in fact, major efforts yield nothing at all. The Standish Group has been collecting data on the results of large software projects for almost thirty years. Failure rates have held steady at about 20 percent, and the fraction of "challenged" projects now hovers near half. It has become "all but impossible," as the *New York Times* put it in November 2021, "to complete a major, multibillion-dollar infrastructure project in the United States on budget and on schedule over the past decade."*

---

* Japan's Monju nuclear reactor shows that the problems are not confined to the US. Construction on Monju began in 1986; it achieved its first sustained chain reaction on schedule in 1994, and was commissioned in 1995. But then a series of accidents and problems kept it offline for fifteen years. It was recommissioned in 2010, but soon afterward a three-ton machine fell into the reactor vessel. In 2013, all work to prepare Monju for commercial use

As with bureaucracy, the question around lateness is, *Why is there so much of it?* Why is it so chronic, and hard to eliminate? Customers resent delays and people get fired over them, so why are they still so common?

There's no single answer. Late projects are like Tolstoy's unhappy families: each has its own problems. But there are some consistent themes. One of them is something we've already seen: overconfidence. Our press secretaries tell us that we're above average in all things, including our ability to get things done on time. And we listen to our press secretaries. As we saw in chapter 4, Danny Kahneman is both professionally and personally familiar with overconfidence. He writes, "Overly optimistic forecasts of the outcome of projects are found everywhere." He and his frequent collaborator, Amos Tversky, thought the phenomenon was so widespread that it deserved its own label; they called it "the planning fallacy."*

There's also an obvious relationship between bureaucracy and delays. Endless meetings, approval loops, and reviews don't lend themselves to getting things done on time.

In 2010, when mobile phone maker Nokia was down but not yet out, journalist Mikko-Pekka Heikkinen talked to more than a dozen former employees for the Finnish newspaper *Helsingin Sanomat.* They kept talking about how slowly things moved as the power to hold things up got more and more widely distributed. As Heikkinen tells it:

[A] former manager offers a graphic example...

A designer responsible for the mobile phone's integrated digital camera works out how the picture quality could be improved by a change in algorithm that would demand a couple of weeks'

---

was halted, and the plant was permanently closed in late 2016. Over its thirty-year life it generated electricity for one hour, at a total expense of $30 billion. It will cost $12 billion more to fully decommission the facility and will take thirty years, assuming everything goes according to schedule.

* Did I complete the manuscript for this book on time? I did not.

work to sort out. He reports on this to his immediate superior, who then feeds the matter into the requirements analysis [RA] matrix.

A week later the matter is noticed at an RA follow-up session and further information is sought...

Another week goes by.

The next RA follow-up session looks at the answer and decides to send the request on for prioritisation.

After a week, the requirements are examined in a prioritisation meeting, and a decision is made to go back to the team...to understand...the scale of risk.

The team comes up with a risk analysis in a day or two.

Another week goes by.

A prioritisation meeting resolves to approve the initial request, if a suitable "lead product" can be found for it—

A month later, one product reports back that, yes, we could take the improvement on, if it does not add to the risk of a timebox overrun.

Back to the team.

Another week goes by, and the prioritisation meeting gives the second-highest priority to the camera request.

It determines that the algorithm change can be embarked on, just as soon as any more important work has been completed.

The more important matters take two months.

By the point when the algorithm team should then be getting down to work, it turns out that the scheduling of the lead product has progressed too far and the timebox window has closed.

Another lead product must be found instead.

And so it goes on, until a competitor gets rave press reviews for the improved image quality of its integrated camera.

And someone expresses shock, and wonders why it is that Nokia has not come up with a similar improvement.

The former product development manager sips his coffee and recalls his feelings:

"It made you feel like shouting out: 'For Christ's sake, can't you just bloody DO it and stop all this passing the buck!' And there were many chains of events just like this one, and worse besides."

In other words, Nokia's product development process was bureaucratic, stiff, and painfully slow.

As we saw in the previous chapter, bureaucracy also strangled Microsoft's ability to get things done in the first decade of this century. The extent of its sclerosis became clear with Windows Vista, an upgrade to the company's cornerstone PC operating system that turned into an embarrassing debacle. When work began in May 2001 under the code name Longhorn, it was envisioned as an eighteen-month project with a release in late 2003. But Microsoft was still working on Longhorn in April 2005 when Apple released its Mac OS X Tiger operating system, scooping many of the innovations Microsoft was planning. After throwing out a huge amount of the code it had written and reengineering its overall process for developing software, Microsoft announced that Vista would ship in late 2006, in time for the holidays. It didn't; it was released in January of 2007. Most users didn't think it was worth the wait. *PCWorld,* then the magazine of record for the computer industry, named Vista its biggest tech disappointment of 2007, asking, "Five years in the making and this is the best Microsoft could do?"

In thinking about why large projects are late, we shouldn't be naive about the fact that some of them are designed that way from the start. The people and organizations proposing them know that they won't be finished on time or on budget. In 2013, after Willie Brown retired from nearly a half-century career in elected office—first as a California state representative, eventually rising to Speaker of the House, and then as the mayor of San Francisco—he wrote a few frank paragraphs in a newspaper column about a downtown bus station:

News that the Transbay Terminal is something like $300 million over budget should not come as a shock to anyone.

We always knew the initial estimate was way under the real cost. Just like we never had a real cost for the Central Subway or the Bay Bridge or any other massive construction project. So get off it.

In the world of civic projects, the first budget is really just a down payment. If people knew the real cost from the start, nothing would ever be approved.

The idea is to get going. Start digging a hole and make it so big, there's no alternative to coming up with the money to fill it in.

The approach Brown described might not have been ethical, but it was effective. If people won't approve a $1.5 billion project, tell them that it will only cost $1.2 billion (the initial budget for the Transbay Terminal). In other words, do what it takes to "start digging a hole." It can take extra time, as well as extra money, to fill such holes. The first phase of the Transbay Terminal was finished in August of 2018, a year late. Brown's estimate of a $300 million cost overrun for this phase was optimistic; the final cost was $2.4 billion, or twice the initial budget. (Six weeks after the terminal was opened, workers found structural flaws that shut it down to most bus traffic for another year.)

Even after taking all these factors into account, though, it's still puzzling why delays are so common and so severe. When it actually matters whether an effort is done on time—when the competition is breathing down your neck, for example, or when you might actually get fired if you're too late— why is it *still* so hard to finish on schedule, or even to see signs of trouble early?

When 90 Percent Isn't Even Close

We get an intriguing answer to this question—one that helps us understand more about how we ultrasocial human beings can act in counterproductive ways when we get together—from management researchers David Ford and John Sterman. They wondered why so many big projects are completed late, and decided to study the phenomenon. As they gathered evidence they uncovered an odd pattern.

Ford and Sterman worked with an unnamed manufacturer of application-specific integrated circuits (ASICs), or customized computer chips. The researchers selected two projects, code-named Python and Rattlesnake, and tracked their progress against their original schedules. Both were expected to take around forty weeks, and at twenty weeks both efforts were close to being on time. They started to slow down, but not too badly. Python was about 75 percent done by its original completion date, and Rattlesnake almost 80 percent.

Then the trouble began. At Python, progress crept along, with none of the big jumps forward that had occurred earlier in the effort. Things got slower as the project was pushed further back. Python finally slithered over the finish line on week 69, 77 percent overdue.

The people on the Rattlesnake project, meanwhile, probably wished that they were working on Python. Rattlesnake didn't just slow down; it actually went *backward*. Serious problems uncovered shortly before week 50 meant that the project had to be restarted almost from scratch. It made up time quickly, and got back close to the finish line in ten more weeks. But then another unforeseen bad problem cropped up, and took Rattlesnake back to being only about 10 percent finished. It was finally done after eighty-one weeks, more than twice as long as scheduled.

As Ford and Sterman looked at projects across a wide range of companies and industries, they kept seeing the same phenomena: late surprises, high uncertainty, and badly missed due dates. A manager they interviewed summarized the grim situation: "The average time to develop a product is 225 percent of the projected time, with a standard deviation of 85 percent. We can tell you how long it will take, plus or minus a project."

Python, Rattlesnake, and the VW ID.3 all suffered from the 90 percent syndrome. In the early 1980s, software researcher Robert Laurence Baber defined the syndrome: "Estimates of the fraction of work completed [increase] as originally planned until a level of 80–90% is reached. The... estimates then increase only very slowly until the task is actually completed." It's a pattern that shows up over and over again, in everything from chip design to software, consumer electronics to construction. Python and Rattlesnake might not have gotten to 90 percent complete before their slowdowns occurred, but they're still emblematic of this failure mode for large efforts.

As Ford and Sterman were conducting their field research on the 90 percent syndrome, they got a deep insight about its causes from a project team's weekly meeting at a large defense contractor. The insight came not from anything that was said or done at the meeting, but from the team's informal name: the liar's club. Ford and Sterman describe the meeting's ground rules:

> Everyone withheld knowledge that their subsystem was behind schedule. Members of the liar's club hoped someone else would be forced to admit problems first, forcing the schedule to slip and letting them escape responsibility for their own tardiness. Everyone in the liar's club knew that everyone was concealing rework requirements and everyone knew that those best able to hide their problems could escape responsibility for the project failing to meet its targets.

Did the researchers just stumble across a particularly dysfunctional or unethical company? The prevalence of the 90 percent syndrome suggests otherwise. It indicates instead that liar's clubs are pretty widespread, meeting regularly at organizations all around the world. In other words, the prevalence of the liar's club indicates that, like bureaucracy, it's a Nash equilibrium—a steady state—under the right conditions. As we saw in the previous chapter, the Nash equilibrium is one of game theory's most important concepts. We can use game theory, then, to understand both why liar's clubs are so common and how to break them up.

Game of Unknowns

Let's reframe the liar's club as a game played by project teams all over the world in their weekly meetings. We'll call it the "Are you on time?" (AYOT?) game. A critical feature of this game is that *observability* is low for most of a project's timeline; it's hard to know from the outside whether a given team member is falling behind. At some point far down the line, observability will get a lot better—the microchip will overheat during a test, the car won't accept an OTA software update, or something—but until that fateful moment, observability is generally low.

At each meeting, players in the AYOT? game can answer either yes or no to the all-important question. If they're on track and on schedule, they of course answer yes. But as time goes by, more and more of the players are no longer going to be on time, because they were overconfident and succumbed to the planning fallacy, or because an unpleasant surprise occurred, or for any of a thousand other reasons. Project teams rarely sprint ahead of their initial schedule; they're much more likely to fall behind.

Let's focus exclusively on these late players in the AYOT? game. Each week they have a choice between two strategies: be deceptive (and say "Yes, we're on time") or be honest (and say "No, we're behind"). What are the pay-offs associated with each of these strategies? Well, if they're honest, the pay-off is that their reputation suffers and they get chewed out by the boss, blamed for throwing the whole effort off schedule, subjected to increased scrutiny and work as well as decreased career prospects. If that sounds too harsh or cynical to you, my guess is that you haven't worked on a lot of big projects at industrial-era companies.

What's the payoff to being deceptive in the AYOT? game? It depends on whether your overall project manager knows your team's running behind. If so, the payoff is all the bad things listed above *plus* gaining the reputation of being a liar. That's bad. But remember, observability is low in this game. It's unlikely that the manager knows who's late (if they knew, why would they bother to ask?). So the most common payoff for players who are late and deceptive is the same as the payoff for players who are on time and honest: escaping further scrutiny and going back to work with an intact reputation.

The players in the AYOT? game who are late thus face a choice between a highly negative payoff if they're honest, and a chance at that same negative payoff if they're deceptive. To say the same thing a bit differently, they face a choice between a highly negative payoff and a chance at avoiding a highly negative payoff. That is a really easy strategic choice. They engage in deception, and hope to get back to work unscathed.

Note that the choices made by players in the AYOT? game don't depend on their knowledge about other players' lateness. "Say you're on time" is the right move regardless of how much you know about how the rest of the project is doing. Players don't need high observability in order to make their moves. Once they realize that everyone else faces the same payoffs as they do, a liar's club spontaneously forms, with no explicit coordination required.

The AYOT? game is a version of the prisoner's dilemma, one of game theory's most important concepts. It's a dilemma because the deception benefits the individual but harms the organization as a whole. It's also not advantageous to honest players who make the strategic mistake of admitting that they're behind schedule. And yet, deception among those who are late is a stable Nash equilibrium in the AYOT? game. The fact that the 90 percent syndrome and late projects of all kinds are so common shows us that the simple game described here is a decent model of what happens in the real world of trying to get big, complex projects done.

But in the real world, aren't there several ways to fight the liar's club that aren't part of our simple AYOT? game? For example, there are whistleblowers—people who know how late a particular team is and expose its deceptions. And there are project managers, who are probably veterans of many liar's clubs themselves and so know how the game is played. Haven't they learned from their ample experience how to deal with all the deception? Finally, what about good old-fashioned morals? Lying is wrong, after all. Most of us have that simple point drilled into us over and over at home and school, in houses of worship and ethics classes. So why do liar's club members keep lying? Are they just lousy people?

No, they're just people. And every person, as we saw in chapter 4, has a press secretary—a mental module that paints our behavior in the most favorable light possible and comes up with justifications for our actions. To see the press secretary in action, think of the things we say to ourselves when we're falling behind:

Yes, we're a bit late, but I know we can make up the time.
We've been distracted by other assignments. Once we can focus more on
    this project we'll make fast progress.
We'll have to work a bit harder, but I have faith in the team.
This latest solution we just found will definitely get us back on track.
There's no way we're as far behind as those jerks down the hallway. I'm
    not taking the fall so that they can escape repercussions.
There's no way we're as far behind as those jerks *up* the hallway. I'm not
    taking the fall so that they can escape repercussions.

When project team members say these things they *believe* them, even if they shouldn't based on the cold, hard facts. The press secretary module provides plausible deniability of those facts, and makes it easy and natural for liar's club members to say "We're on time" when it's their turn in the AYOT? game. In other words, self-deception—the press secretary's main job—makes deception easier. Remember, our intelligence is highly *justificatory;* we effortlessly come up with reasons why our ideas and actions are righteous, whether or not those reasons will pass muster with our Sunday school teacher, rabbi, priest, or ethics professor.

In fact, I'm confident that many liar's club members *are* Sunday school teachers; regular attendees at mosques, synagogues, and churches; parents who take seriously their responsibilities as role models; and so on. They're moral people, and yet they're not inwardly full of shame and self-loathing at their behavior during the project team's weekly meeting. The payoffs of the prisoner's dilemma and the tireless, plausible-deniability-providing press secretary module combine to make individual morality not much of a factor in the AYOT? game.

If we can't rely on morality to disband the liar's club, what about whistleblowers? Most participants are aware that there's a lot of deception going on in the AYOT? game. And it probably wouldn't be too hard to find smoking-gun evidence that those jerks up or down the hallway are way behind, even though they keep saying they're not. So why don't we see more cases where people are blowing the whistle on their deceptive colleagues and blowing up the liar's club?

Because the rewards to whistleblowers are rarely worth the risks and costs. In the AYOT? game, the clearest reward for whistleblowing is seeing another group take the heat for being late. Is there anything beyond that, like the gratitude of a project manager or a faster promotion? Maybe. Or maybe the manager mentally labels you as a snitch, and someone who can't be trusted with sensitive information. What's more, there's the risk that gossip about your disclosure will spread and you'll get a reputation as a tattletale and "not a team player." This is a huge risk, since your reputation matters greatly at work (and everywhere else).

Such considerations deter many kinds of whistleblowing behavior. Several years ago, I got a late-night phone call from an extremely tough-minded friend. I'd never heard her so distraught. She told me that she was at a corporate retreat and had just been assaulted in her room by a senior colleague. I encouraged her to call the police immediately, but she resisted. The scene she imagined—of giving a statement to uniformed police officers, her coworkers looking on, the patrol car's red and blue lights flashing constantly in the background—was too distressing. She anticipated being whispered about in the hallways at work from that point forward, and she didn't want that (this was well before the #MeToo movement changed how workplace assault allegations are perceived and handled). Later on, she did decide to come forward in order to stop her assaulter from doing to other women what he'd done to her. It was a brave move. (Her company opened an investigation and disciplined her assaulter, who left the firm soon afterward. My friend did not press criminal charges against him.)

Our interactions with work colleagues are best thought of as *repeated games*. They're not one-off encounters. Instead, they happen over and over again. A new round of the AYOT? game is played in every meeting of every liar's club. Behavior is different in repeated games because of "the shadow of the future." Players have to think about their payoffs not just in the current round, but in all the rounds to come. As we'll see in the next chapter, getting a reputation as someone who's not a team player is harmful in a lot of ways. So we shouldn't expect a lot of whistleblowers in the AYOT? game.

A last potential line of defense against deception in liar's clubs is the project managers who preside over weekly status meetings. These managers are experienced veterans; they definitely know how liar's clubs work and how common they are. They've certainly *been* members of those clubs at different points in their careers. But without good observability into exactly which parts of a project are behind schedule, general knowledge that things are late does managers little good.

When managers are presiding over liar's clubs but don't know who exactly the liars are, the managers are often reduced to bluster and meaningless threats, as a veteran of the auto industry pointed out to Ford and Sterman:

> [One] executive engineer used to have what I would call "fighting meetings." ... His attitude was we should tell everybody that they're all [behind schedule], they're all failing, they have to make changes faster, [and that] if we don't make changes right now, we're going to shut the whole division down.

Ford and Sterman dryly note that "the consequence, of course, is to create even stronger incentives for concealment."

I find this strategy of undirected yelling and unenforceable threats kind of pathetic. But I have to admit, I've engaged in it myself. Once when I was teaching an MBA class at Harvard I heard the door in the back of the classroom open and shut while I was writing on the board at the start of class. I turned around as soon as I was done to identify the tardy student who had just come in, but whoever they were had already found their seat and blended in. Without giving myself a chance to think, I opened my mouth and created a very dumb version of the AYOT? game by saying "Okay, fess up: who just came in late?"

I apparently thought that some combination of my dominance, prestige, and moral authority would cause the latecomer to self-identify. Or that the school's flagship semester-long ethics course would have provided them with the grounding they needed to do the right thing. Or that a whistleblower would speak up. Nope. All I got were blank looks and innocent smiles. The latecomer knew that I didn't know who they were, knew I didn't have any good way to find out, and was confident that no one in the room would snitch.

Once I caught up to this reasoning, I realized I was beat. I forget what I said before I turned back to the blackboard and kept writing; it was probably a sad attempt at face-saving, like "This is *not* over!" The altruistic part of me hopes that student has gone on to a brilliant career in which they frequently use game theory. The vindictive part of me hopes otherwise.

The Manifesto That Broke Up the Liar's Club

Chronic delays and liar's clubs are very hard problems to fix. But hard problems are catnip for geeks. So on a February weekend in 2001, seventeen veteran coders got together at a ski resort in Utah to pursue an ambitious goal. They wanted to do more than just address the 90 percent syndrome: they wanted to completely change how software gets written.

They succeeded. As journalist Caroline Mimbs Nyce put it, "This small, three-day retreat would help shape the way that much of software is imagined, created, and delivered—and, just maybe, how the world works." The movement that was sparked that weekend, called Agile programming, has transformed how many if not most companies in the high-tech industry develop code.

It also helped establish our third great geek norm: speed. But speed here doesn't really mean velocity: it's not how fast people and projects are moving toward a finish line. Rather, it's the speed of *iteration:* how quickly a team can create something that works in a meaningful and measurable sense, present it to a customer, and get feedback on it.

Prior to the Utah meeting there was very little iteration or feedback in most software development projects. Instead, there were a lot of meetings, a lot of planning, and a lot of document-writing before the actual programming started; a lot of unpleasant surprises and delays during the actual coding; and lots of dissatisfaction and finger-pointing afterward. The way we were writing software in the industrial era would have made the authors of the *Simple Sabotage Field Manual* proud.

For decades, large software development efforts had usually followed the waterfall approach, so called because its sequential steps reminded some of a waterfall splashing down a sequence of pools. The waterfall approach sounded sensible enough. The first steps defined what the software needed to do—exactly what its requirements were. These were written down in a comprehensive document that was given to the programmers (software lore is full of stories about how many thick binders were required to contain some requirements). The programming team designed and wrote the software according to the requirements, then submitted it for testing. Once testing and bug fixing were done, the software was delivered to the customer; it entered production and "went live."

That was the theory, anyway. The reality was almost always much messier. Requirements changed, which meant negotiations about how much more time and money would be needed to accommodate them. The 90 percent syndrome appeared, which meant that programming took a lot longer than expected. When at last the finished system was delivered to its customers, they often found that it didn't give them what they thought they had asked for. The U.S. Department of Defense mandated waterfall approaches for its software projects throughout the 1980s and '90s. It then had the excellent idea to see how well this approach was working. In one sample of projects, it found that fully 75 percent failed or were never used.*

The programmers who came together in Utah all had ample experience

---

* It's unfair to blame the waterfall method's originator for its shortcomings. In the 1970 paper that first described waterfall, computer scientist Winston Royce stressed that proceeding from step to step without seeking and incorporating feedback was a bad idea, one that "is risky and invites failure." He even predicted that doing so would lead to something like the 90 percent syndrome.

with these kinds of projects, and wanted no more of them. They were also true geeks—mavericks with little respect for the niceties of corporate life. As Jim Hightower, one of the participants, put it, "A bigger gathering of organizational anarchists would be hard to find." Because the problem they were tackling was so big, and because the group had its share of prickly personalities and big egos, some of the attendees weren't expecting to accomplish too much. Bob Martin, who sent out the invitations, recalled, "It was one of those things where you think, 'You know, you're gonna get a bunch of people in a room and they're going to chitchat and nothing's going to happen.'"

But, Martin continued, "that's just not what happened. This group of people arranged themselves, organized themselves, and produced this manifesto. It was actually kind of amazing to watch." The manifesto, which took shape on a whiteboard, was a repudiation of waterfall's linearity and rigidity and a clear vision of how geeks preferred to work:

> We are uncovering better ways of developing
> software by doing it and helping others do it.
> Through this work we have come to value:
> ## Individuals and interactions over processes and tools
> ## Working software over comprehensive documentation
> ## Customer collaboration over contract negotiation
> ## Responding to change over following a plan
> That is, while there is value in the items on
> the right, we value the items on the left more.

After a lot of discussion, the group settled on a name for this declaration: it would be the Manifesto for Agile Software Development. It was posted online by attendee Ward Cunningham in 2001.* It then did for

---

* Cunningham is the developer of the wiki software that underlies Wikipedia. As he was looking for a name for the software he'd created, which allowed anyone to quickly make edits to a web page, he remembered the Wiki Wiki Shuttle at the Honolulu airport. "Wiki" is the Hawaiian word for "quick."

software geeks much the same thing that the Netflix culture deck did for business geeks eight years later: it quickly spread among them and galvanized them into action.

In addition to the manifesto, the group also posted a set of twelve principles. A few of them reflect the two great geek norms we've already seen: science and ownership. The seventh principle, "Working software is the primary measure of progress," for example, plays the same role that the iron rule of explanation does in science: it specifies how to move forward. In science, progress is made by arguing about evidence. In agile software development, progress is made by showing working code.

Two of the other principles are squarely about ownership: "Build projects around motivated individuals. Give them the environment and support they need, and trust them to get the job done," and "The best architectures, requirements, and designs emerge from self-organizing teams." It's probably not a coincidence that right around the time that Amazon was completely rebuilding its software to support Bezos's vision of highly autonomous teams, the Agile Alliance's geeks were advocating that such teams were also the right units for building great software.

Across the manifesto's principles, though, the theme of speed—of rapid iteration and fast feedback—is the one that appears most often. Here are five of the twelve principles (emphasis added):

Our highest priority is to satisfy the customer through *early and continuous delivery* of valuable software.

Welcome changing requirements, even late in development. Agile processes *harness change* for the customer's competitive advantage.

Deliver working software frequently, from a couple of weeks to a couple of months, with a *preference to the shorter timescale.*

Business people and developers must *work together daily* throughout the project.

At regular intervals, the team reflects on how to become more effective, then tunes and adjusts its behavior accordingly.

Over the two decades since the manifesto was published a consensus has formed that Agile programming is just flat-out better than waterfall and other older, more planning-heavy approaches to developing software. A 2015 survey of over a thousand large projects in several industries found that, as authors Pedro Serrador and Jeffrey Pinto put it, "Agile use improves time, budget, and scope goals and is most effective at improving stakeholder satisfaction." Agile Manifesto coauthor Alistair Cockburn maintains that "even badly done, Agile outperforms all of the alternatives, or at least, the main older alternative [waterfall], which is out there." Statistics collected by the Standish Group support this assertion. The group's 2020 report found that across fifty thousand software projects, those that took an agile development approach succeeded 42 percent of the time. Waterfall projects, in contrast, had a success rate of only 13 percent. Failure rates were similarly uneven: 28 percent for waterfall; 11 percent for agile.*

One of the main reasons agile approaches work better is that they change the game of managing large projects. As we've seen, these projects often feature liar's clubs whose members play a weekly AYOT? game in which deception is common because observability is low and plausible deniability is high.

Agile reverses the situation. To see how, let's look at observability first. To allow everyone to see if they're living up to the principle of delivering working software frequently, agile projects often feature visible displays of progress like kanban boards. These are typically whiteboards with cards posted on them. Each card represents a unit of work on the project, often called a "story." The board is divided into columns showing stages of progress such as To Do, In Progress, Testing, and Done. As each story progresses, its card moves from column to column.

Agile coach Max Rehkopf says, "Kanban only has two rules: Limit work in progress and visualize your work." Visualization is critical because it provides constant observability: the progress of everyone's work becomes

---

* The third category of project outcome, between success and failure, was "challenged"; agile projects were challenged 47 percent of the time, waterfall projects 59 percent.

obvious to everyone when all story cards are visible on a kanban board. Rehkopf's other rule, to limit work in progress, also relies on the observability provided by the board. If work in progress is piling up—if, for example, there are lots of cards being added to the Testing column but not very many leaving that column—the problem soon becomes clear to everyone. The nasty surprises that characterize the 90 percent syndrome become much less likely, and the kanban board indicates when and where the teams need to take action to get the project back on track.

When it matters most, though, teams don't get to move their own story cards. Each story has a customer outside the team, and only the customer gets to decide when the story moves to the all-important Done column. The principle of "deliver working software frequently" drives down plausible deniability for two reasons. The first is the "working" part. That determination isn't made by the team that writes the code; it's instead made by a downstream team that will make use of it and gets to sign off on it. As a result, teams can't plausibly deny—to themselves, their peers, the project manager, or anyone else—that they're writing good software when their customer hasn't accepted it.

The second reason that agile methods decrease plausible deniability is indicated by the word "frequently." The original manifesto advocated delivering working software to customers on a cadence ranging from a couple weeks to a couple months, but modern business geeks move even faster. Today, agile "sprints"—think of them as the time available to get all the story cards all the way across the kanban board—typically last from one to four weeks. This fast pace of iteration limits how long a group can live in a state of denial. It's very hard for a team to get months behind schedule when it has to deliver every couple weeks (or be the center of a lot of attention if it doesn't).

The unpleasant surprises VW experienced with the software for the ID.3 strongly indicate that observability wasn't high enough throughout the development effort, and that plausible deniability was too high. The project became a classic example of the 90 percent syndrome, the root cause of which is the inability to see what progress is actually being made.

Software problems at the VW Group didn't stop with the ID.3. They also delayed the planned introduction of new Porsche and Audi models by at least two years each, and jeopardized the promise made by Bentley to be all-electric by the end of the decade. A May 2022 story in *Der Spiegel* on these woes reported that the VW Group's supervisory board was contemplating a reorganization of its Cariad software subsidiary because "processes should be simplified and decisions accelerated." According to *Der Spiegel,* a study commissioned by Audi and performed by the consultancy McKinsey determined that "the various parties involved in the process find it difficult to communicate with one another. That jeopardizes the schedules."

It sure does. Poor communication and jeopardized schedules are signs that an organization isn't following the principles of the Agile Manifesto, and is likely to keep experiencing unpleasant surprises and the 90 percent syndrome. The founders of agile development were adamant not only about delivering working software, but also about communication, interaction, and constantly receiving and responding to feedback. Look at the manifesto's language: "customer collaboration," "responding to change," "Welcome changing requirements, even late in development," "Business people and developers must work together daily throughout the project," "harness change," "At regular intervals, the team reflects on how to become more effective, then tunes and adjusts its behavior accordingly." It's striking how much of the short manifesto is devoted to seeking and incorporating new information during agile development efforts. To see why, let's look at a team exercise where kindergartners routinely outperform MBA students.

Soft Treats That Provide Hard Lessons

When Peter Skillman was working at the design consultancy IDEO in the early 2000s, he came up with a simple exercise for small teams: in eighteen minutes, using twenty pieces of spaghetti, one meter of masking tape, one meter of string, and a marshmallow, build the tallest tower possible on a tabletop. The only constraints were that the tower had to remain motionless for three seconds after it was finished, and the marshmallow had to be on top.

Consultant Tom Wujec picked up Skillman's marshmallow challenge and gave it to a wide variety of groups. In a 2010 TED talk, he summarized his findings: The average tower height was about twenty inches. CEOs were a little better than average, lawyers significantly worse. The group with the shortest overall towers were business-school students. Kindergartners did at least two and a half times better than the B-schoolers, and a bit better than the CEOs. In fact, the only unfacilitated groups that did better than the young children were professional architects and engineers. And the children made by far the most interesting-looking structures.

Why are kindergartners so much better than B-school tycoons-in-training? Because they "don't waste time in status transactions," Skillman explains. "There's no discussion about who's going to be CEO of Spaghetti Corporation. They just jump in and do it. They don't sit around talking about the problem." Maria Montessori probably wouldn't have been surprised by these results. She knew that children are innately curious, are eager to get their hands on things, and learn fast when they're given the chance.

Wujec stresses how beneficial it is to be childlike and just jump in and do it. His description of the standard adult approach to the marshmallow challenge sounds very much like the waterfall methodology. And the results of this approach are about as disappointing as we'd expect, right down to the 90 percent syndrome—the appearance of unforeseen problems late in the schedule:

> Most people begin by orienting themselves to the task. They talk about it, they figure out what it's going to look like,...then they spend some time planning, organizing, they sketch and they lay out spaghetti. They spend the majority of their time assembling the sticks into ever-growing structures. And then finally, just as they're running out of time, someone takes out the marshmallow, and then they gingerly put it on top, and then they stand back, and— ta-da!—they admire their work. But what really happens, most of the time, is that the "ta-da" turns into an "uh-oh," because the

weight of the marshmallow causes the entire structure to buckle and to collapse.

In sharp contrast, the young kids naturally adopt an agile development approach. As Wujec describes, "What kindergartners do differently is that they start with the marshmallow, and they build prototypes, successive prototypes, always keeping the marshmallow on top, so they have multiple times to fix when they build prototypes along the way... With each version, kids get instant feedback about what works and what doesn't work."

In his breakout 2011 book, *The Lean Startup*, Eric Ries advocates that entrepreneurs should act like kindergartners making marshmallow towers: they should make something quickly, get it to customers, get feedback from them about what works and what doesn't, and incorporate this feedback as they quickly make the next version. The obvious objections to this approach are that many customers don't like getting a buggy prototype instead of a polished and finished product, nor do they like using something that changes over time instead of remaining constant.

Ries acknowledges these objections. As he writes about the first company where he tried the lean startup approach:

> We do everything wrong: instead of spending years perfecting our technology, we build a minimum viable product, an early product that is terrible, full of bugs and crash-your-computer-yes-really stability problems. Then we ship it to customers way before it's ready. And we charge money for it. After securing initial customers, we change the product constantly — much too fast by traditional standards — shipping new versions of our product dozens of times every single day.

This seems like a guaranteed way *not* to have satisfied customers. Why, then, has the lean startup approach been so successful? The idea of a "minimum viable product" has become widespread enough among startups that it's become an acronym; entrepreneurs everywhere talk about what their

MVP should be. The success of the lean startup approach depends in part on finding early customers who are tolerant of faults and rapid changes. But most of the success stems from the value of feedback and rapid iteration. Ries and countless others in the lean startup movement have learned that customers will stick with you and work with you if you do two things: give them a product that—even if it's flawed—satisfies a real need, and keep improving that product over time. The agile approach to building software, and the kindergartners' approach to building marshmallow towers, achieve these goals better than planning-heavy methods do.

The "launch early and improve quickly" path to building products and companies has become so entrenched among the business geeks that investor and LinkedIn cofounder Reid Hoffman has turned it into something of a personal mantra: "If you're not embarrassed by the first version of your product, you've launched too late." Entrepreneur and programmer Sam Corcos advises startup founders on the critical next step: how to rapidly become less embarrassed by later versions. The key, he says, is to think like a scientist instead of a HiPPO. Don't keep planning and building product features that you think customers will like (that's what a HiPPO does). Instead, as he explained to me, "start with what you want to learn, not what feature you want to build, and don't work on the next iteration until you get the learning back." In other words, think of your product road map as a series of experiments, and make sure you know what the goal—the learning—of each experiment is.

The speedy, iteration-heavy approach to development has another benefit—one that's hard to see unless we adopt an ultimate perspective and investigate how we *Homo ultrasocialis* got so good at so many complicated things well before we adopted the evidence-and-argue approach of modern science. To see what this benefit is, let's go back once more to the high-performing kindergartners in the marshmallow challenge. The ultimate reason kindergartners do a better job than most adults is that the kids naturally tap into our *Homo ultrasocialis* superpower, which is trying something, observing what works, and copying the most successful models. In other words, the kids are faster at practicing cultural evolution.

Carbon Copiers

Thanks to a lot of research, we now know a great deal about how cultural evolution takes place and how to make it as fast as possible. One of the central insights from this work is that most of the learning that's at the heart of cultural evolution doesn't come from classroom instruction. Instead, it comes from less formal teaching, learning, and copying. We learn how to safely prepare food, run a tight meeting, heal the sick, close a sale, find food, deal with difficult colleagues, make a tall marshmallow tower, quickly write code that works, and so on by watching others, listening to them, and imitating them.

And who should we imitate? Research shows that we use three main cues to answer this critical question. The first is age. We're more likely to copy from older people, because they've had more time to amass useful knowledge. Also, the fact that someone has lived a long time indicates that they must have learned to do important things well, and not make too many costly mistakes. In virtually all preindustrial societies we know about, the elderly are listened to and emulated until their cognitive capabilities are clearly in decline.

The second big cue we use for finding learning models is one we encountered in the previous chapter: prestige. We figure out who to copy by observing who everyone else is looking at. Every young cello player today knows that Yo-Yo Ma is a great model to learn from, simply because of his towering reputation. Prestige is a magnet for learners; it draws them closer.

A third and final cue, related to prestige, is skill, or clear and obvious excellence at a task that the learner wants to master. When I was a kid with dreams of playing big-league baseball the Cincinnati Reds were a dominant team. They'd frequently come to Chicago and beat up on my hometown Cubs. The Reds' second baseman was the perennial all-star and future Hall of Famer Joe Morgan, who had the unusual habit of pumping one of his arms up and down while waiting for the pitch. He said he did it in order to start his swing correctly, but I really didn't care. He was Joe Morgan and it was working for him, so it was good enough for me. I imitated it. It did me no good whatsoever, but that didn't deter me.*

A huge amount of evidence shows that our imitative learning is essentially constant and that it happens all across the range, from fully conscious, planned, and deliberate to totally unconscious and spontaneous. In *The Right Stuff*, his history of the US space program's pilots and astronauts, journalist Tom Wolfe explained how it came to be that all US commercial airline pilots sounded the same. Without being aware of what they were doing, they started imitating the accent of the most skillful and prestigious of all the pilots of the postwar era.

> Anyone who travels very much on airlines in the United States soon gets to know the voice of the airline pilot... that tells you, as the airliner is caught in thunderheads and goes bolting up and down a thousand feet at a single gulp, to check your seat belts because 'uh, folks, it might get a little choppy'... Who doesn't know that voice!... That particular voice may sound vaguely Southern or Southwestern, but it is specifically Appalachian in origin. It originated in the mountains of West Virginia... In the late 1940s and early 1950s this up-hollow voice drifted down from on high... It was amazing... Military pilots and then, soon, airline pilots, pilots from Maine and Massachusetts and the Dakotas and Oregon and everywhere else, began to talk in that poker-hollow West Virginia drawl, or as close to it as they could bend their native accents. It was the drawl of the most righteous of all the possessors of the right stuff: Chuck Yeager.

A startling demonstration of how powerful and far-reaching our subconscious learning can be comes from studies conducted by psychologist Ken Craig. Craig administered painful electric shocks to volunteers, some of whom were in the presence of an apparently tough person who, you guessed it, was actually part of the team of experimenters. The tough person always

---

* The mockery of my teammates eventually deterred me.

rated the shocks as being only three-quarters as painful as the study participants found them to be.

The participants quickly imitated this model, and learned to hurt less.
Compared to people who hadn't been in the presence of toughness, these
participants rated subsequent shocks as being only half as painful. And their
bodies backed up their words. They maintained more consistent and lower
heart rates while being shocked, and exhibited fewer physical signs that they
were under threat. When our innate capacity for imitation can quickly and
effortlessly reduce our experience of pain, we know it's a powerful part of our
mental hardware.

As we copy our models and evolve our cultures, two things usually happen. The first is that, no surprise, we don't copy perfectly. (Can you make the
dish as well as the chef on the Food Network, or follow your ski instructor
turn for turn down the mountain?) The second feature of our copying is
much odder: we overimitate. We copy exactly, including even steps that are
clearly nonessential or irrelevant. Pilots hoping to fly as well as Chuck Yeager
didn't just try to copy his aerial maneuvers; they also copied his accent.
Chimps and other primates don't overimitate, so why do we?

The ultimate explanation for this odd human behavior is that because
our cultural tools and techniques—even the apparently simple ones—are
complex, it's not at all clear if any of the steps involved in making them are
superfluous. So the safe thing to do is just to copy everything as closely as
possible. Evolution has given us *Homo ultrasocialis* a mental "copy exactly"
module that helps us maintain our cultures across generations.

How to Improve (Almost) Anything

But if we humans are all trying to copy our models exactly, generation after
generation, how do innovation and improvement ever happen? "Copy
exactly" seems like it would ensure cultural stasis, not cultural evolution. If
anything, it seems like we're designed for cultural *degradation* across generations, since most of us can't copy our models exactly; we're not as good as
they are. So why do human cultures generally evolve instead of backsliding?

Because of the standouts. Some imitators are better than their models; some students are better than their teachers. They're a Simone Biles or a Mozart. What's more, in large enough groups at least a few people tend *not* to copy exactly. They take the examples they're presented with and tinker with them. They're like Joni Mitchell or Pablo Picasso.

Because of such standouts, cultural evolution can be very fast. Let's say that in a given group the average imitator is only three-quarters as good as the model, but in each round of imitation one person is just a bit better than the model — say 5 percent better. In the next round, that standout is the new model, and the pattern repeats: the average is three-quarters as good as the new model, and one imitator is 5 percent better. By just the seventh round, average performance across the group is a bit better than the first model's. By the twenty-second round, the group's average performance is fully twice as good as the first model's.

Another important aspect of our cultural evolution is that we *Homo ultrasocialis* are able to learn from more than one model at a time. We can observe and interact with several people and sense what each is doing well. And when it's our turn to act, we create something like a weighted average of the best that we've seen. In lab experiments conducted by anthropologist Joe Henrich and psychologist Michael Muthukrishna, participants completed the difficult task of re-creating a target image using unfamiliar software. Their work then served as a model for the next generation. Some participants saw only one model from the previous generation, while others saw five models. After just ten generations, the least skilled person who had five models to draw on performed better than the most skilled person who could only learn from a single model.*

Every year, a real-life demonstration of a group quickly and collectively getting much smarter because of cultural evolution takes place on the campus of

---

* If we return to our numeric example, we can see how much our human ability to mix and match among models helps performance. Let's say mixing and matching boosts the top performer's performance from 5 percent to 7 percent. In that case, the group as a whole is twice as good as the original model not after twenty-two generations, but after only sixteen. And if the performance boost is 10 percent, the group just about doubles its average ability after only eleven rounds.

MIT, where I work. It happens in a course called How to Make (Almost) Anything, which was started in 1998 by Media Lab professor Neil Gershenfeld.

HTMAA lives up to its name. In one semester, students learn to use computer-aided design software. They use laser cutters and 3D scanners and printers. They generate tool paths for milling machines. They each assemble their own small milling machine for home use, then use it for the rest of the semester. They make printed circuit boards, fill them with components, and get them to do something useful. They program embedded devices, network them, and add a lot of LEDs. They create videos and other multimedia to showcase their work, embed this content in web pages, and add them to the course's website.

If that sounds impossible, I agree. I tried to take the course a couple years ago and absolutely couldn't keep up with the pace.* But most of the students can and do, despite often starting the course with little relevant prior knowledge or experience.

How do they accomplish this? First of all, by acting like kindergartners building marshmallow towers: they just jump in and do it. Gershenfeld's "lectures" are a fast-flowing stream of mini explanations and demos; in other words, a bunch of models. Students quickly start making use of those models. They're expected to make something every week and be ready to show off their creation in class and talk about how they built it. There are no pencil-and-paper problem sets, and no exams. There's just the experience of making things under conditions of high observability and low plausible deniability (since everyone knows that anyone can get cold-called in any class to show their work).

As they're learning to be makers, students have a lot of models to draw on. There's Gershenfeld, of course, who talks with students and offers suggestions in every class. There's also a corps of dedicated teaching assistants and lab managers who give tutorials and offer help. These are all great resources, but a big part of HTMAA's brilliance is how it makes every former student a readily available model for the current cohort. The course

---

* My press secretary has come up with many ego-preserving explanations for why I had to drop out of HTMAA. I won't bore you with them.

accomplishes this by requiring that everyone document their work every week (with text, pictures, audio and video, code, CAD files, and so on) and add it to that semester's website.

All those websites are archived and searchable from the course's home page. HTMAA students quickly learn that once they have an idea for their weekly project, the smart first step is to search the archive and see if anyone did something similar in the past. They almost always find several models this way, and are free to incorporate the best elements from them as they begin their own work for the week.

The course's fast pace, weekly iteration cycle, and abundance of models generate huge amounts of learning and rapid cultural evolution. An MIT education is often described as a drink from a fire hose.* This is nowhere more true than in HTMAA, but the course is designed to give the students everything they need not to drown if they're ready, willing, and able to embrace the great geek norm of speed and exercise their human superpower of learning from models. As Gershenfeld said to me, "I think of the course as a pyramid scheme — people who have learned must teach people who are about to learn."

Joe Henrich summarizes what ultimate research has revealed about our species' ability to make remarkably fast progress: "It's our collective brains operating over generations, and not the innate inventive power or creative abilities of individual brains, that explain our species' fancy technologies and massive ecological success." Our *Homo sapiens* label isn't wrong, but it misses the bigger point. We're really *Homo ultrasocialis*.

On the Road and into Space

Modern business geeks are obsessed with speed because they see how it leads to faster learning and fewer liar's clubs. As a result, they're adamantly opposed to slowing down. Facebook's original internal motto was "Move Fast and Break Things." By the middle of the 2010s, however, many inside and outside the tech industry believed that was the wrong sentiment — one

---

* Trust me, it's an accurate description.

that was causing bad outcomes that reverberated far beyond Silicon Valley. The geek community realized that it needed to update its rallying cry. What it settled on was "Move Fast and Fix Things." The fact that the first two words didn't change reveals that to the geeks, speed — iterating quickly, having a fast cadence, being agile — is nonnegotiable. They orient themselves around minimum viable products, ship cycles, and all the offshoots and varieties of agile development: sprints, scrums, kanban, DevOps, and so on. They argue passionately about the details of all of these, but I have yet to hear an argument from any business geek that we should go back to the days of the waterfall methodology and projects with long timelines, low observability, and high plausible deniability.

The Agile Manifesto was about building software, but its principles work just fine for hardware, too. Even huge projects like building a metropolitan subway system can be managed in a fast-cadence, iterative way. The key is to make the projects modular — to break them up into small chunks that create value, that can be objectively assessed, that are visible to everyone, and that can be pieced together to create the final product.

Management researcher Bent Flyvbjerg has studied megaprojects like bullet train networks, undersea tunnels, and the Olympic Games. He's reached the same conclusion as the business geeks who are currently disrupting industry after industry. As Flyvbjerg puts it, "I've researched and consulted on megaprojects for more than thirty years, and I've found that two factors play a critical role in determining whether an organization will meet with success or failure: replicable modularity in design and speed in iteration."

Subway lines suffer from all the problems that affect big projects, and are notoriously slow to build. Copenhagen's City Circle Line took ten years to build, London's Victoria line closer to twenty, and New York's Second Avenue line was approved in 1929 and *partially* opened in 2017.* But under

---

* The forever-unfinished Second Avenue line provided fodder for decades' worth of jokes among New Yorkers. "The Flood," an episode of the TV series *Mad Men* that aired in 2017, is set in 1968. In it, one of the show's main characters is worried that the apartment she's interested in is too far east. Her realtor assures her, "When they finish the Second Avenue subway, this apartment will quadruple in value."

the leadership of civil engineer Manuel Melis Maynar, Madrid was able to add seventy-six stations and more than 130 kilometers of track to its subway system in just eight years by modularizing both station design and construction and tunnel drilling. Instead of having each station be a unique monument to the joys of traveling underground, Madrid Metro under Melis used the same design and construction methods for all of them. Each station thus served as a model for all the later ones, which accelerated cultural evolution (in this case, that meant learning about how to build subway stations and tunnels). Melis also made many models available to tunneling crews by having up to six huge subterranean boring machines operating at the same time. This approach was unprecedented, but Flyvbjerg highlights why it worked so well:

> The tunnel modules were replicated over and over, facilitating positive learning...As an unforeseen benefit, the tunnel-boring teams began to compete with one another, accelerating the pace further. They'd meet in Madrid's tapas bars at night and compare notes on daily progress, making sure their team was ahead, transferring learning in the process. And by having many machines and teams operating at the same time, Melis could also systematically study which performed best and hire them the next time around. More positive learning.

Flyvbjerg's account of Madrid's success shows it's beneficial to ask and answer ultimate questions about our strange species—questions about why we are the way we are. This approach gives us a new way to understand important phenomena like learning curves. Learning happens when we humans can observe generations of models and incorporate their best features. We can also subconsciously mix and match among models. Some of us can even improve on the models we see. So setting up projects to generate lots of models (via modularity) and lots of generations (via fast iteration) is a great way to maximize learning and improvement.

Tesla and SpaceX, two companies associated with Elon Musk, are leaders in the great geek norm of speed. Their achievements are impressive. As we saw earlier in this chapter, since 2012 Tesla has been providing OTA software updates at a fast cadence to its cars as they sit in their owners' driveways and garages at night. In recent years, Tesla Model 3s have received close to twenty annual updates, some of which have been major upgrades or additions to the cars' capabilities. The most famous of these updates, and a demonstration of just how quickly Tesla can iterate and respond to feedback, came over the course of a few days in the spring of 2018.

On May 21, *Consumer Reports* published the results of its Model 3 road test and concluded that it could not give the car the magazine's coveted "recommended" status. The most serious problem encountered during testing was a long stopping distance. *Consumer Reports* wrote, "The Tesla's stopping distance of 152 feet from 60 mph was far worse than any contemporary car we've tested and about 7 feet longer than the stopping distance of a Ford F-150 full-sized pickup." Tesla disputed these results, and Musk tweeted on May 21, "Very strange. Model 3 is designed to have super good stopping distance & others [*sic*] reviewers have confirmed this. If there is vehicle variability, we will figure it out & address. May just be a question of firmware tuning, in which case can be solved by an OTA software update." Four days later, that update was deployed to all Model 3s. *Consumer Reports* retested the car and on May 30 revised its online review to say, "*CR* now recommends the Model 3." Jake Fisher, *CR*'s head of auto testing, said, "To see something updated that quickly is quite remarkable. We've never seen a manufacturer do this in the course of a week."

SpaceX also stands out from the competition. It's the world's only maker of commercially viable reusable rockets, and now carries about two-thirds of all the payload that leaves Earth for space. One of the main reasons SpaceX's market share is so high is that its costs are so low. A 2018 NASA report found that compared to the Ariane 5 rocket developed and launched by France's Arianespace, SpaceX's Falcon 9 was 80 percent cheaper at putting a kilogram of payload into low-Earth orbit.*

---

* Compared to the US Space Shuttle, which was retired in 2011 after a second fatal in-flight accident, SpaceX was 95 percent cheaper at getting a kilogram into low-Earth orbit, and 75 percent cheaper at getting cargo and crew to the International Space Station.

The company's adherence to the great geek norm of speed is visible throughout the development of its newest and biggest rocket, called Starship. This vessel's mission is to take humans to the moon and beyond. Along the way it will also put a lot of communications satellites and other payload into orbit around the Earth. But SpaceX didn't work on Starship by creating a thorough overall plan and then sticking to it. Instead, the company worked like kindergartners in the marshmallow challenge: it started building things, getting feedback on them, and making changes.

The initial plan was for the main body of the Starship spaceship to be made out of a carbon fiber composite, which has an excellent strength-to-weight ratio. In a presentation Musk gave in September of 2018, he showed pictures of a huge, gleaming metal cylinder, called a mandrel, that was serving as a mold. Carbon fiber was wound around the mandrel (like a spider winds its silk around its prey), then soaked in epoxy and heated; the finished part was then separated from the mandrel. Musk's presentation included pictures of one of these parts: a thin-walled hollow black cylinder, thirty feet in diameter, made out of carbon fiber.

Just four months later, however, SpaceX announced that the Starship spaceship would be made out of stainless steel instead of carbon fiber. The company had learned from its experiments with carbon fiber that although the material had some desirable properties, it took a long time to make each part, and more than a third of them had to be scrapped. So the idea of a carbon fiber body was abandoned. Rather than seeing this switch as evidence of a flawed development process, SpaceX viewed it as proof that its process was working just as intended: the company was iterating quickly and incorporating lessons learned, even if these lessons were expensive. As "space enthusiast" Florian Kordina put it on the *Everyday Astronaut* website in May of 2020,

> Everything for Starship is still on the table at this moment. I mean, we are literally seeing them build a factory around a rocket instead of vice versa...

We will see more hardware fail. There will be setbacks. We will probably see explosions! But…not only is it ok to fail, it is halfway expected. This approach promotes learning through prototyping at lower cost and greater speed. Elon has said over and over approximately, "Failure is an option here, if things are not failing, you are not innovating enough."

Kordina was right about future hardware failures and explosions. The eighth Starship spaceship built, labeled SN8, launched successfully but crashed and burned on its attempted landing (there was no loss of life; all SN missions were uncrewed). SN9 suffered a similar fate, landing at about a thirty-degree angle and blowing up. SN10 completed a hard landing but exploded about eight minutes later. SN11's flight took place in heavy fog, so observers couldn't see what happened a little less than six minutes into the flight, when the debris from the rocket started falling on the landing site; analyses revealed that a methane leak in an engine probably caused an explosion. SN12 through SN14 never made it to the launchpad, but SN15 finally completed a successful soft landing (although with a small fire that was extinguished within twenty minutes). SpaceX felt that it had learned what it needed to from these experiments, and announced that its next test flight would be an uncrewed orbital trip around the Earth, featuring all of Starship's main elements: the spaceship itself, a huge booster rocket, and a total of thirty-nine newly developed Raptor engines to propel them.

By the spring of 2021, NASA was impressed enough with progress on Starship and other programs to award SpaceX a $2.9 billion contract to land astronauts on the moon. The company will have some competition in this arena from NASA itself. Since 2011, the space agency has been at work on its own large rocket, called the Space Launch System (SLS). Compared to SpaceX, NASA has developed the SLS in a way that's heavy on up-front planning and low on iteration and experimentation. For example, there have been no test flights of any rockets associated with the SLS. Instead, the program's first flight was an uncrewed trip around the moon involving all of the system's major components: boosters and a core stage (which use engines and other parts originally developed for the Space Shuttle) that provide the power required to escape the Earth's gravity, and an upper stage that propels astronauts and cargo to the moon.

This maiden flight was originally scheduled for 2016. Despite having "no unusual engineering hurdles to leap" (as spaceflight journalist David W. Brown put it), it was delayed twenty-six times before finally launching in November of 2022. It was an expensive flight. In March of 2022, Paul Martin, the inspector general for NASA, testified before Congress. He estimated that the operational costs for each of the first four Artemis launches, which comprise an SLS rocket and Orion spacecraft, would be more than $4 billion. This figure is only a per-mission cost; it does not include any of the tens of billions of dollars spent developing this equipment. If those development costs were amortized across the first ten Artemis missions, the price tag for each would be more like $8 billion. Meanwhile rocket engineer Ian Vorbach, who writes a newsletter about space startups, estimates that early Starship launches will cost $150 to $250 million each.

The vast differences between NASA and SpaceX are well summarized by Musk: "I have this mantra. It's called, *'If a schedule is long, it's wrong. If it's tight, it's right.'* And I just, basically, [go with] recursive improvement on schedule, with feedback loop. 'Did this make it go faster?'" One of the most fundamental things the business geeks have done is increase the clock speed—the pace of iteration and innovation—of the industries they've entered.

Let's condense what we've seen and learned about speed into an ultimate ground rule. As always, we'll start with the general form of the rule: *Shape the ultrasociality of group members so that the group's cultural evolution is as rapid as possible in the desired direction.* For the great geek norm of speed, this ground rule becomes: *To accelerate learning and progress, plan less and iterate more; organize projects around short cycles in which participants show their work, have access to peers and models, deliver to customers, and get feedback.*

These short cycles have one more big benefit: they bewilder your opponents and give you a competitive advantage. To see how big this advantage can be, let's wrap up this chapter with the story of a military maverick who was obsessed with speed.

The Geek Art of War

John Boyd was having trouble getting his peers in the fighter-pilot community to listen to him. So he shot a bunch of them out of the sky.

Boyd has a near-mythic reputation in some military circles. He almost single-handedly turned aerial combat from a poorly understood practice into an artful science of energy management and maneuverability. He then broadened out, considered the entire history of human warfare, and distilled lessons that have become central to the doctrine of the United States and many other countries. Boyd has been called "the most influential military thinker since Sun Tzu wrote *The Art of War* 2,400 years ago."

When he showed up at Nellis Air Force Base in the Nevada desert to attend its Fighter Weapons School (FWS) in 1955, Boyd already had a reputation as an excellent pilot. However, he'd never shot down an enemy plane in combat. He had flown twenty-nine missions in the Korean War, but only as a wingman; he'd never even fired his guns in an actual dogfight. As a result, his ideas about air-to-air combat didn't initially get much of a hearing at Nellis. Fighter pilots esteem wartime kills over all else, and Boyd didn't have any. So even though he performed well enough as a student at FWS to be offered a position as an instructor immediately after graduating, he still wasn't getting the attention he felt he deserved. Boyd didn't just think he was a hotshot pilot—someone with catlike reflexes, eagle eyesight, nerves of steel, and so on. He also felt like he was homing in on an understanding of the first principles of aerial combat.

Because he was so confident in those principles, he offered the other pilots at Nellis a standing bet: the two combatants would fly to a prearranged position and climb to thirty thousand feet, then Boyd's challenger would get in position behind him (which is exactly where a fighter pilot wants to be). If Boyd couldn't reverse their positions and get a simulated kill within forty seconds, he'd pay his adversary $40. He never paid because he never lost. Not to an FWS student. Not to another instructor. And not to any of the navy, marine, or foreign pilots who came through Nellis in the mid- to late 1950s. His reputation spread; he became known as Forty-Second Boyd and Pope John. And people started listening to him.

He talked about how the victor in an aerial dogfight was *not* the pilot who could move through the sky faster—who had the more powerful plane—but instead the one who could iterate faster. As Harry Hillaker, an aircraft designer who worked with Boyd in the 1970s on the F-16 fighter (which is still in use around the world today), put it, Boyd's approach to aerial warfare was based on "'fast transients,' that is, quick changes in speed, altitude, and direction... The idea of 'fast transients' advances the theory that, to win or gain superiority, you must get inside the adversary's time scale." The way to do this is to make skillful use of a plane's capabilities: its energy (either from its engines or in a dive) and its maneuverability.

Boyd was a great orator, famous for his ability to elaborate his ideas at length and harangue anyone who disagreed with him, but he knew that he needed to do more than just talk about how to win a dogfight. He also needed to quantify his ideas. So he worked with air force mathematician Tom Christie and made use of newly available tools called computers to develop energy-maneuverability (E-M) theory. It's hard to overstate how influential this theory has been. As Boyd's biographer Robert Coram put it, "While still a junior officer, John Boyd changed the way every air force in the world flies and fights... After E-M, nothing was ever the same in aviation. E-M was as clear a line of demarcation between the old and the new as was the shift from the Copernican world to the Newtonian world."

Throughout the rest of his career, Boyd continued to pursue the fundamental question of why one combatant wins over another. He broadened his inquiries beyond aerial combat and studied the entire history of warfare. His conclusion was simple: maneuverability is the key to victory. The military doctrine he formulated stressed the importance of "getting inside the adversary's time scale"—being able to spot and seize opportunities more quickly. A plane or tank platoon with this ability keeps the adversary unbalanced and confused. Boyd emphasized that once you're inside the opponent's time scale, your moves can seem random and unpredictable because you're reacting to something they haven't yet seen or understood. As he put it, "We should operate at a faster tempo than our adversaries or inside our adversaries' time scales...Such activity will make us appear ambiguous (non predictable) [and] thereby generate confusion and disorder among our adversaries."

Rather than setting his ideas down in a book, Boyd instead developed a six-hour presentation called "Patterns of Conflict" that he gave on request to groups throughout the US military and federal government. A young congressman from Wyoming named Dick Cheney heard it and was so impressed that he invited Boyd to his office several times. When Iraq invaded Kuwait in August of 1990, Cheney was the secretary of defense. As he reviewed the initial battle plan for Operation Desert Storm, the American-led effort to drive out Iraq, he saw that it did not reflect maneuverist thinking. Instead, it was a standard plan for a conflict of attrition—for going toe-to-toe with the enemy and inflicting such heavy losses on them that they would be forced to surrender.

The US military almost certainly would have won a war of attrition against the Iraqi forces in Kuwait, but Cheney was convinced that a maneuverist plan could do better—could end the conflict faster and with fewer losses. So he called Boyd out of retirement and asked him to work on it. Boyd contributed to the creation of a very different battle plan, one featuring fast and bold moves that would disorient the enemy.

It worked beautifully. Three days before the "official" start of the war, a small group of US Marines ventured deep into enemy territory and struck hard. The Iraqi army mistakenly thought that this attack was the main assault and rushed in reinforcements. Once they arrived many of the Iraqi forces surrendered, since they continued to believe that they were facing a superior force. Approximately fifteen Iraqi divisions surrendered to two marine divisions. The revised Desert Storm battle plan succeeded in "folding the enemy in on himself" (to use Boyd's words). The ensuing war was not one of attrition. It was a rout. Iraqi forces were expelled from Kuwait only four days after the main assault began, and fewer than one hundred US soldiers were killed in action. After the war, Marine Corps commandant Charles Krulak wrote that "the Iraqi army collapsed morally and intellectually under the onslaught of American and Coalition forces. John Boyd was an architect of that victory as surely as if he'd commanded a fighter wing or a maneuver division in the desert."

In his 1991 testimony to Congress after the end of the first Gulf War, Boyd summarized his maneuverist theory, and the competitive advantages of the great geek norm of speed: "Conflict can be viewed as repeated cycles of observing, orienting, deciding, and acting by both sides, and also, I might add, at all levels.* The adversary that can move through these cycles faster gains an inestimable advantage by disrupting his enemy's ability to respond effectively." Business geeks are obsessed with speed because in addition to all of its other benefits—disbanding liar's clubs, mitigating the 90 percent syndrome, and increasing a team's rate of learning and cultural evolution—it also disrupts and bewilders opponents.

Many industrial-era companies simply can't keep up with the geeks. These companies can't update their software as quickly, which becomes a serious disadvantage at a time when software is eating the world. When embarking on product development efforts, industrial-era companies often plan extensively and jockey for status instead of building prototypes as quickly as possible. They behave, in short, like teams of MBAs do on the marshmallow challenge. Their geek competitors, on the other hand, act like kindergartners.

The geeks see the long time scales of many industrial-era companies as a profound vulnerability. The two keys to exploiting it are a faster cadence and high levels of observability. Competitors that can't reduce their vulnerability by adopting the great geek norm of speed risk finding themselves feeling much like one of John Boyd's opponents in a dogfight high over the Nevada desert: bewildered at how quickly their position has deteriorated, and confronting a decisive loss.

Venture capitalist Steve Jurvetson told me flatly that "any company that thinks they're not a software company is not long for this world, because the

---

* This cycle became known as the OODA loop.

agile way we've learned to build software is becoming the agile way we build everything. I sometimes feel like I have a sixth sense. I can see dead companies. They don't know they're dead, but they're dead because they're not responsive enough. And the companies that iterate more quickly will just run circles around them. They're innovating every couple of years on something that you might take seven years to do."

As he left his job, VW Group boss Herbert Diess sounded a bit like Jurvetson. As Bloomberg reported in September of 2022,

On his last day as Volkswagen's chief executive officer, Herbert Diess shared footage from his farewell dinner. The video clip captures the sixty-three-year-old grabbing a microphone, asking his colleagues to gather a little closer and then making a prediction: Other old-guard manufacturers will have trouble with software just as VW has.

"Where we are struggling through," Diess said, "that will be the same for everybody else."

Chapter Summary

Most large projects are finished late, and their problems don't become apparent until their original completion date draws near. This phenomenon is called the "90 percent syndrome."

The "liar's club" is a major cause of the 90 percent syndrome. During a project, members of the liar's club say that they're on time even when they're not, and hope that someone else gets found out first. The liar's club thrives on low observability and high plausible deniability.

To combat the liar's club, the business geeks rely on the norm of speed: iterating quickly and getting feedback from customers. The iteration and feedback are observable, which breaks up the liar's club.

Another benefit of speed is that it accelerates learning. Setting up projects to generate lots of models (via modularity) and lots of generations (via fast iteration) lets us *Homo ultrasocialis* learn faster from one another.

For the geek norm of speed, the ultimate ground rule is: *To accelerate learning and progress, plan less and iterate more; organize projects around short cycles in which participants show their work, have access to peers and models, deliver to customers, and get feedback.*

The geeks see the long time scales of many industrial-era companies as a profound vulnerability. The two keys to exploiting it are a faster cadence and high levels of observability.

Survey for Your Organization

These ten statements can be used to assess how well an organization follows the great geek norm of speed. Respondents reply to each with a number between one and seven, where one means "strongly disagree" and seven means "strongly agree."

1. Many of our recent large projects have experienced significant delays.*
2. We have a short cycle time for delivering something to (internal or external) customers and getting feedback from them.
3. We do not have a culture of experimentation or learning from failure.*
4. Customers are discouraged from requesting changes in the middle of a project.*
5. When a project starts to fall behind schedule, that fact quickly becomes obvious to everyone involved.
6. It's easy for people to see what work others are doing and learn from them.
7. We often make big changes while in the middle of a project.
8. We break big projects up into small, modular pieces that we can finish quickly.
9. We believe that extensive up-front planning is a good way to avoid unpleasant surprises down the line.*
10. When we have a choice between analyzing possible solutions and building something to see if it works, we choose analyzing.*

---

* Scores for these statements need to be reversed. To do this, subtract the respondent's score from eight. For example, if the respondent answered with six, the reversed score would be two.

CHAPTER 7

Openness

A Better Business Model

A good leader can engage in a debate frankly and
thoroughly, knowing that at the end he and the other
side must be closer, and thus emerge stronger. You
don't have that idea when you are arrogant, superfi-
cial, and uninformed.

—Nelson Mandela

Let's wrap up our discussion of the great geek norms by looking at a prom-
inent industrial-era company that wound up with norms so toxic that
they helped drive it out of business. We first came across the accounting firm
Arthur Andersen in chapter 1, when we used it to illustrate what a norm is.
We saw that there was a strong norm of conformity at AA: when prospective
hire Barbara Ley Toffler showed up at one of its offices for a job interview,
everyone was dressed alike even though the formal dress code had been
relaxed. Once she started working there, she realized that conformity was
just part of a bundle of norms at Andersen that provide a clear illustration of
what the business geeks are working so hard to avoid.

In the spring of 1998, after Toffler had been working at the firm for
about three years, she led a discussion of ethics with a group of managers.
These were the employees most directly responsible for conducting audits of
clients' financial statements, which was what AA had been doing for more

than eighty years. As at most professional services firms, managers worked under the supervision of a partner who signed off on the overall audit.

Toffler began by writing on a blackboard the list of stakeholders for an AA manager: "Client, public investor, partner, firm, SEC, community, government, fellow employees, family." She then asked which among them was the most important. After a tense silence and some prompting, one manager volunteered that the partner was their most important stakeholder. Others agreed; no one dissented.

Toffler then asked the obvious follow-up question about ethics: "What if your partner asks you to do something you think is wrong? Would you do it?" After another long silence, someone replied, "I guess I might ask a question. But if he insisted I do it, yes, I would. Partners don't want to hear bad news."

You can almost hear the desperation in Toffler's final question: "But would you tell anyone else?"

"No," came the response. "It could hurt my career."

A few months later, Toffler had her own experience of not standing up to a partner who asked her to do something she felt was wrong. In December of 1998, she was part of a team proposing to help a banking client roll out new policies and training materials to its staff.* Toffler came up with a price of $75,000 for her group's share of the project. The lead partner on the project was infuriated:

"What's this $75,000?" he shouted, reverting to the machine-gun style of speaking he used to keep anyone from sneaking in a contrary word or thought. "What do you mean, $75,000? This is the big time, young lady... You make that $150,000," he ordered. "Back into it."

Toffler did as she was told and padded her fees. The irony was surely not lost on her that the materials she was preparing for the bank were about the

---

* In the late 1990s, this was largely done by distributing binders and CD-ROMs.

importance of corporate ethics. Or that she had been hired by Andersen as the head of its new Ethics and Responsible Business Practices Group.

From Probity to a Federal Probe

Toffler was at AA in the middle of its rapid descent from corporate watchdog through willing accomplice to corporate corpse. Arthur Andersen, the son of Norwegian immigrants, founded his auditing company in Chicago in 1913. Creative, profit-boosting accounting was common at the time, but Andersen was having none of it. According to an often-told story, in 1914 he noticed improper expense accounting at a railroad that was one of his company's largest clients. He pointed the problem out but got no response. So he notified the company's president that he would include the matter in his official auditor's report. The incensed executive traveled to Chicago, burst into Andersen's office, and demanded a retraction. Instead of backing down, Andersen shot back, "There is not enough money in the city of Chicago to induce me to change that report!" The railroad went bankrupt several months later, while the firm of Arthur Andersen thrived on its way to decades of growth.

As late as the 1970s and '80s, the firm's leaders still seemed willing to speak up about what they felt were bad accounting practices, and to walk away from clients who were insufficiently concerned about the risks they were taking. AA partners were outspoken about the correct ways to account for bad debts and depreciating computers, and Andersen dropped most of its savings-and-loan clients because of their willingness to loan money to organizations that probably weren't going to pay it back. When the S&L industry started its slow-motion implosion in the late 1980s, the firm avoided most of the damage.*

By the time of Toffler's conversation with the audit managers, however, things had changed. It's a safe bet that some of the participants in that 1998 meeting had firsthand knowledge that their partners were doing something

---

* But not all of it. In 1993, AA agreed to pay an $82 million fine related to its "negligent" audits of Lincoln Savings and Loan and other institutions.

wrong—that they were engaging in unethical and possibly illegal activities as they went about their work.

In 1997, for example, multiple AA partners were alerted that the Baptist Foundation of Arizona, an Andersen audit client, was running an elaborate Ponzi scheme for the benefit of some of its executives. AA didn't meaningfully investigate any of these claims, and instead offered a series of unqualified (in other words, clean) audits for the foundation. When that organization collapsed, in late 1999, around eleven thousand largely elderly clients were left almost $600 million poorer.

The Baptist Foundation was not an isolated example. Drug distributor McKessonHBOC, another Andersen audit client, had to restate $300 million in earnings from 1998 and 1999. Boston Chicken went bankrupt in 1999 after being forced by the SEC to restate earnings that AA had signed off on earlier in the decade. And if any of the managers participating in Toffler's ethics discussion were working on the Enron audit, they were likely aware how problematic that company's accounting practices were. Enron had set up its first special-purpose entity (SPE) in 1991. Ten years later, SPEs would prove to be instrumental in turning both Enron and AA into nonentities.

In February 2001 a team of twelve AA partners met to discuss the previous year's audit of Enron, a Houston-based energy company that had successfully repositioned itself as a fast-growing exemplar of the "new economy." The partners soon focused on the approximately three thousand SPEs the company had set up. SPEs are legal as long as they meet several criteria for independence, but it was pretty clear that Enron's didn't. For example, at least one of the company's SPEs was controlled by Andrew Fastow, who was then Enron's CFO (in fact, the SPE was named for Fastow's wife and children). An internal AA memo drafted the day after the February meeting engaged in a bit of understatement by calling the accounting around this SPE "aggressive," but saying that nonetheless "the conclusion was reached to retain Enron as a client, citing that it appeared we had the appropriate people and processes in place to serve Enron and manage our engagement risks." The memo also hinted at why it was important to retain this particular client: it was "not unforeseeable" that AA's fees could reach $100 million per year. Arthur Andersen issued an unqualified audit opinion for Enron's 2000 financial statements.

Enron filed for bankruptcy in December 2001, after the full extent of its aggressive accounting came to light. In June 2002 AA was found guilty of obstructing the federal government's pursuit of its defunct client.* Weeks later, in August 2022, Andersen wrote its own obituary, announcing that it would cease auditing public companies.

I was starting my career as a management academic when AA's scandals and disintegration were front-page news. I could hardly believe the accounts I kept reading about the firm's role in one corporate scandal after another. It was as if my hometown hospital had been exposed for running an organ-harvesting ring.

I grew up near Chicago, and had absorbed the image of Andersen as a model of Midwestern probity, rectitude, and solidity. When I was a kid in the 1970s and early '80s AA partners were considered pillars of the community at a time when people still used that phrase unironically.

Those partners were in the same category as doctors: affluent people who deserved their affluence *because they did something important*. Doctors delivered your babies and performed bypass surgery on your uncle. They helped keep the community healthy. AA partners audited companies, kept them honest, and made sure that we could trust their numbers. They helped keep the markets healthy.

Andersen partners had high status. They had made it to the top of a prestigious profession (if not exactly a glamorous one), and they made a good living. They weren't as well compensated as CEOs, but they were respected and perhaps even a little bit feared by CEOs. Both their careers and their company seemed solid as bedrock.

But in its final years Arthur Andersen was routinely giving clean audits to clients with major problems (as long as they were major clients); was silencing internal whistleblowers; was riven by infighting, and was entrenched in what Toffler described as a "fortress mentality that required fighting

---

* In 2005, the US Supreme Court unanimously overturned this conviction, finding that instructions given to the jury were unfair and confusing.

regulation attempts and denying accusations." By the end, the situation was grimly comical. Toffler writes that "AA's 1999 annual report, published as its flawed audits were piling up and shortly before it was dealt a mortal wound by the federal conviction, is a small masterpiece of hypocrisy, stating, 'After all, to be successful in the future, we must hold fast to our core values: Integrity, Respect, Passion for Excellence, One Firm, Stewardship, Personal Growth.'"

The Roads to Perdition

The story of Arthur Andersen brings up a fundamental riddle: *How do companies lose their way so badly?* What happens to cause them to lose their bearings and become toxic to their communities, customers, employees, and owners? Most corporate nosedives aren't as dramatic as AA's, but they're still vexing because the closer we look, the harder it is to pin down their sources. Yes, there are some truly terrible bosses, and they can cause a lot of damage. But the problem at most foundering companies is broader than a single malevolent or incompetent leader. At these organizations there's a miasma of dysfunction that permeates everything. Where does it come from and how does it spread?

We've seen some of the big causes of corporate dysfunction in previous chapters, and they're all present in the decline of Arthur Andersen. For example, partners during the firm's final years were clearly listening to their internal press secretaries justifying the clean audits they were issuing for dirty clients. Even after a few close calls, overconfidence and self-justification were pervasive. Real debate and argumentation were rare, as Toffler saw from her conversation with the managers about ethics. There were a few internal whistleblowers during the firm's final years, but their concerns weren't given much of a hearing. Instead of debating the bad news, the leaders of the firm simply ignored it.

By the 1990s AA had incentives in place that were guaranteed to cause counterproductive behavior. When the firm landed a large consulting engagement, most of the resulting financial rewards were allocated to partners based not on who initiated the contact, put together the materials that convinced the client, or closed the sale, but instead on who ran the office that staffed the project. So if partners from the New York and Los Angeles offices collaborated to sell a big project to a Tokyo-based company, a three-way battle would immediately break out within AA. The New York and LA partners would argue that they should be rewarded for bringing in work, while the Tokyo partner, who was in the strongest bargaining position, would say that they should get most of the rewards since their office would be doing most of the work.

Negotiations among the partners in situations like this were time-consuming and adversarial. Toffler writes in *Final Accounting* (coauthored with reporter Jennifer Reingold), "As consulting became more important to the Firm, in which the only way you could win was by screwing your fellow partner,... Arthur Andersen became a place where people spent a great deal of time in bloody internecine battles that could have been better spent working with clients, pursuing new business, or mentoring young employees." Toffler recalls that after one sales call in 1996, "as another Arthur Andersen consultant from a different group and I rode together to the airport, we weren't excitedly discussing the possibilities for the project. Our minds were whirring madly: Each of us, it seemed, was entirely focused on how to cut the other one out of the deal."

The financial incentives during the final years of AA were bad, but the social ones were even worse. And as we've seen in earlier chapters, social incentives are tremendously important to us *Homo ultrasocialis*. We've also seen that we assess our social position—our status—not in absolute terms (how am I doing?), but relative ones (how am I doing *compared to those around me?*). In *Final Accounting*, Toffler describes an internal status shift within Andersen that caused audit partners to change their behavior and steer the company into danger.

Since 1953, when AA paid $1.2 million* for a thirty-ton Univac I computer, the firm had been doing technology consulting projects for its clients as well as auditing their books. As the corporate world digitized, these projects kept getting bigger and more lucrative. By 1988, consulting was contributing 40 percent of AA's revenue, and probably even more of its profits. In the mid-1990s, Andersen's audit business was growing by a healthy 11

---

* The equivalent of more than $12 million in 2021.

percent a year, but consulting was growing more than twice as fast. The fact that the consulting side of the business made annual transfer payments to the auditing side padded the audit partners' bank accounts, but not their egos.

The rapid growth and increasing power of consulting within the firm left Andersen's audit partners feeling left behind and resentful, even though their standards of living were still high and rising. The wife of one of them summed up their plight with scalpel-sharp wit: "All of these guys have to fly first class and stay in the best hotels. Because they're just accountants."

The formal separation of Andersen Consulting (AC) and Arthur Andersen into separate business units in 1989 didn't fix the problem. In fact, it probably deepened audit partners' feelings of losing status and getting left behind. As Toffler writes,

In the New York offices on the Avenue of the Americas, the groups moved to different floors, so the only interaction we [at AA] had with AC people was in the elevators. You could always tell who was who. For one thing, the Andersen Consulting people dressed better. They just seemed hipper and richer. The same was true of the offices. You didn't need to be a psychic to see which way the money was flowing. You just had to peer out the elevator door. Every Arthur Andersen floor had a forest-green carpet leading to [the firm's standard wooden] doors.* By the time I got to New York, that green carpet had become frayed and sad. It evoked another era, that of bankers' lamps, cigars, and suspenders. But on the AC floors, blond wood and frosted glass conveyed another image—one of modernity and growth. It was a jarring contrast to the stolid secrecy of AA. "If you mistakenly went to the wrong floor, you said, 'Wow, nice offices!'" said a partner who worked in the New York office in the late 1990s. "Then you went back to your own floor and it was like a rabbit warren—a bunch of rat holes with a ratty carpet. It was ugly!"

---

* All of AA's offices throughout the eighty-four countries where the firm did business had the same solid wood doors. Together they projected an impression of conformity. And not of openness.

The gaps between AA and AC led to bitter infighting over revenue sharing and control of the firm, culminating in an arbitration ruling in 2000 that allowed Andersen Consulting to leave the firm entirely and become the company now known as Accenture. Even before this breakup, though, AA had formed its own consulting practice and worked to grow it as quickly as possible. As a result, audit partners became even less likely to challenge their clients' questionable accounting, since doing so could jeopardize lucrative consulting projects.

Departments of Defensiveness

Press secretaries, overconfidence, bad financial incentives, and status anxiety all contributed to AA's dysfunctions and downfall, but they're not the whole story. We also need to understand something else, something deeper about why so many organizations wind up with norms so rotten that they cause a professional ethicist like Toffler to behave unethically.

To see why this happens, let's go all the way back to Quibi, the spectacularly unsuccessful media startup we looked at in chapter 1. Here's a summary of what happened there: an arrogant, out-of-touch member of Hollywood's old guard doesn't listen to advice or evidence, micromanages, and ignores reality.

Now here's another summary: an experienced, passionate executive with an excellent track record takes charge of an important effort, works relentlessly to succeed, stays true to his vision, and radiates optimism.

That first phrasing is a good description of Quibi with the benefit of hindsight. But the second one is a pretty good description of the venture at its launch. It's also a description that would make a lot of us feel good about its chances for success. We might even want to be part of it as an employee or investor (and Quibi had no trouble attracting either). That second description is a classic business success narrative. Which is exactly what makes it so scary.

We owe that shift in phrasing to Chris Argyris, who I think is the all-time most underappreciated scholar of organizations. When I was a very junior professor at Harvard he was a very senior one, and I learned a lot from him. His work was popular in some quarters in the 1970s and '80s, but has now largely faded from view. This is a shame, because Argyris did what I think is the best work in the history of business research to help answer two fundamental questions: *Why do organizations lose their way? Why are they so hard to correct when they do?*

The heart of Argyris's answer is found in those two descriptions of Quibi. One of his great contributions was to show why guidelines for running a company that seem smart and sensible are instead so often a recipe for chronic dysfunction. Argyris called such guidelines a "theory in use." We'd call them norms, since they're behaviors that everyone in an organization expects from each other. He identified a theory in use at many of the industrial-era companies he studied, and labeled it Model 1.* Its norms include:

1. Be in unilateral control over others.
2. Strive to win and minimize losing.
3. Suppress negative feelings.

In other words, put someone in charge and have clear lines of authority and responsibility. Work hard toward victory and don't concede defeat. Stay positive.

Who could argue with any of that? Maybe that's not the right playbook for teaching preschoolers or rehearsing an avant-garde play at a collectivist theater troupe, but it sure looks right, or at least close to right, for getting things done in the business world, no?

With thunderclap simplicity, Argyris said *no*. And then he explained why. The core problem, which crops up over and over again in all kinds of ways, is that Model 1 produces defensive reasoning — reasoning designed to protect the status quo. And the status quo covers many things: people's jobs and reputations; the original goals of an effort or design of a product; the size, influence, and importance of one group or division; a big decision made by the boss; the company's current offerings; and so on.

---

* Argyris's labels for things were often...a little dry?

"Strive to win and minimize losing" is very close to "Dig in your heels and don't ever admit you're wrong, or that another idea is better," and also "Keep growing your head count and budget." "Suppress negative feelings" easily turns into "Shut down argumentation, disagreement, and debate." "Be in unilateral control over others" becomes indistinguishable from "Don't tolerate any dissent, and don't give others much freedom or autonomy"; it also lends itself to "Involve yourself in as many activities and decisions as possible."

Model 1, in short, is a recipe for the dysfunctions we've examined in this book: excess bureaucracy, sclerosis, chronic delays, decisions that ignore evidence, cultures of silence, and debased ethics. These are the fruits of Model 1. While not inevitable, they are likely—the default outcomes we should expect under Model 1's norms. The examples, case studies, and statistics we've looked at so far support that uncomfortable conclusion. Model 1 strangles and squelches the things that the business geeks are adamant about. It creates corporate cultures that are the opposite of freewheeling, fast-moving, evidence-driven, egalitarian, argumentative, and autonomous.*

Argyris didn't ground his ideas in ultimate research about us ultrasocial human beings. He couldn't; most of that research didn't yet exist when he was conceptualizing his breakthrough ideas. But now that we can rely on all the ultimate work about modular minds and press secretaries; justificatory versus argumentative reasoning; status seeking; dominance and prestige leaders; liar's clubs; observability and plausible deniability; cultural evolution; and other topics we've looked at, we can see that he was way ahead of his time.

In his book *Reasons and Rationalizations: The Limits to Organizational Knowledge,* Argyris laid out how defensiveness leads to the kind of culture Toffler experienced—and became part of—at Arthur Andersen. As you read Argyris's words below, be on the lookout for the press secretary, self-deception, low observability, high plausible deniability, and liar's clubs. They're all there.

---

* Model 1 isn't explicitly about moving slowly. But it might as well be, since, as we saw in chapter 6, the great geek norm of speed depends on autonomy and openly acknowledging problems, both of which run counter to Model 1.

The characteristics of a defensive reasoning mind-set include the following:

The objective is to protect and defend actor(s) or supra-individual units such as groups, inter-groups, and organizations...

Transparency is avoided in the service of protecting the self and denying that one is protecting the self.

Self-deception is denied by cover-up. In order for the cover-up to work, it too must be covered up.

It's easy to see how this could play out: An Andersen audit partner starts engaging in defensive reasoning in order to protect the relationship with a lucrative client. This means suppressing some inconvenient truths (*are these accounting practices really legitimate?*). The partner's press secretary is happy to assist here by drafting internal memos saying something like, "We have the appropriate people and processes in place to serve the client and manage our engagement risks"—exactly the kind of self-justifying language that showed up in internal AA memos about Enron. In a few early meetings, managers involved with the engagement bring up evidence or arguments that the client's accounting is suspect. The defensive partner doesn't like these contributions and has several options for shutting them down—everything from "Let's all be on the same team here," to "Hey, what's with all the negativity?," to "Do you know how much this client is worth?" Everyone on the engagement quickly gets the message that stressing problems and standing up for proper accounting practices is a career-limiting move.

As a result, a liar's club quickly forms. But instead of confronting a boss's question, *Are you on time?*, the members of this club confront the internal question, *Are you going to speak up?* There's no direct personal cost to staying silent, while the costs of speaking up are clearly high. The people involved assess and compare these costs quickly and effortlessly, and most of them stay silent. This is the self-interested thing to do, whether or not it's noble or moral or in the best interests of the company, the client, or society.

But it's not enough to just suppress open discussion about one client's accounting practices. For continued success, the defensive parties also have to suppress any discussion about suppression itself. Under Model 1, it's important to squelch comments like, "Hey, you know we never talk about all the accounting scandals we've been part of recently," and "Why can't we talk about the fact that there are things we can't talk about here?" and so on. As Argyris puts it:

> Defensive reasoning thrives in contexts where the defensive features cannot be legitimately challenged. One consequence of this is that not only are issues undiscussable, but that undiscussability is itself undiscussable...
>
> This results in ultra-stable systems that are self-sealing and anti-corrective. Human beings report that they are helpless to make any changes because they do not know what to do, and because, as victims, they could not act to reverse the ultra-stable anti-learning state of their universe.

We've got a name for these ultrastable, self-sealing, anticorrective systems: they're called Nash equilibria. As we've seen with everything from toilet paper shopping during a pandemic to bureaucracy to liar's clubs, Nash equilibria—situations where no one can benefit by going rogue—are remarkably stable, whether or not they're "good" or "beneficial." Game theory shows us how Model 1 creates a particular kind of equilibrium: a disheartening prisoner's dilemma characterized by topics that are important but undiscussable (like the widespread unethical behavior of Arthur Andersen's final years), and also the fact that the undiscussables are themselves undiscussable. Late in the firm's life, AA's equilibrium of defensiveness and undiscussability was ultra-stable, self-sealing, and anticorrective to the point that a partner was comfortable openly berating and demeaning Toffler and ordering her, a professional ethicist, to do clearly unethical things like double her fees. Which she did.

I've occasionally bumped into those undiscussables myself. When I was starting out as a professor at Harvard Business School, we junior faculty got invited to the first of two meetings for deciding which job candidates, if any, to hire for the following year (the second meeting, where final decisions were made, was reserved for senior faculty). When I first started attending these meetings, I offered my opinions and occasionally disagreed with my senior colleagues — the ones who would later be deciding whether I got to keep my job. Eventually my mentor pulled me into his office and said, "Shut up in there."* Good advice. I took it.

What he didn't need to tell me was, "And don't speak up at the next meeting to give some kind of *J'accuse* speech where you say that senior faculty are so defensive that they don't want their opinions about who to hire challenged by junior faculty." I knew that topic was undiscussable. And that the broader topic of intrafaculty undiscussability was undiscussable, and so on. I internally labeled the discussions in those meetings (and a few others) as no-go zones and kept my mouth shut. When I imagine being in a job where I'd have to do that throughout the day, every day, instead of just a few times a year, I feel despair coming close.

Once you're aware of Model 1 you start to see it all over the place in accounts of lousy corporate cultures. These stories often include two features of defensive reasoning: emphasizing winning and suppressing negativity. Industrial-era stalwart General Electric, for example, was famous for doing both. Longtime CEO Jack Welch's 2005 book, written with his journalist wife, Suzy Welch, and billed as "the ultimate business how-to," was titled *Winning.*† His successor, Jeffrey Immelt, kept up the relentless emphasis on victory. As journalists Thomas Gryta and Ted Mann write in *Lights Out,* their book about GE's decline, "Under Immelt, there had been a buzzy, vague, optimistic spin that not only often failed to hold up under scrutiny but had eroded GE's credibility with Wall Street and its workers alike." That buzzy, vague optimism had a dark side: "Immelt rarely folded his hand, even when some of his lieutenants thought he should. To him, leadership was perseverance in the face of doubt. And opposition to that approach wasn't just disagreement but something worse. To Immelt, naysaying in these situations was a form of betrayal."

Gyrta and Mann give a tight summary of how Model 1 created lasting damage at GE: "Even if it was never delivered explicitly, the lesson sunk in, down

* I think those were his exact words.
† Another Jack Welch book was the not-super-sciency *Straight from the Gut.*

through the levels of the company. There was no market for hard truths or bad news. Not as far as the guy at the top was concerned." The same was clearly true in the final years of Arthur Andersen, a hierarchical, top-down organization whose audit partners were in competition with each other and desperate for "wins" that would let them gain status vis-à-vis their consulting peers.

Model 1 doesn't take hold only at older companies. When the going gets rocky, even leaders at young tech companies based in Silicon Valley fall back on defensive reasoning that stresses victory and refuses to countenance failure. In June of 2022, as Facebook's parent company, Meta, was confronting sharply slowing growth and increased competition, chief product officer Chris Cox wrote in a memo, "I have to underscore that we are in serious times here and the headwinds are fierce. We need to execute flawlessly." In a seminar I attended, psychologist Amy Edmondson deftly summarized the main consequence of this kind of communication: "All this does is guarantee that he won't hear any bad news" about less-than-flawless execution.

Open for Business

Earlier in this book we heard Jeff Bezos's vivid description of what happens to what he calls Day 2 companies: "Day 2 is stasis. Followed by irrelevance. Followed by excruciating, painful decline." Now we see that Model 1 is a major contributor to Day 2. The business geeks fight back against both by embracing a norm of openness, which we can define as *sharing information and being receptive to arguments, reevaluations, and changes in direction.* This norm is the opposite of the defensiveness, clinging to the status quo, and undiscussables chronicled by Argyris.

We've already seen several examples of how openness is practiced at geek companies. Let's revisit some of them, and show how they combat the key elements of Model 1: assuming unilateral control, striving to win and minimizing losing or failing, suppressing negativity, and creating undiscussable topics.

Not assuming unilateral control: In chapter 1 we came across the acronym HiPPO, which stands for "highest-paid person's opinion." Among the geeks,

HiPPO has become shorthand for anyone (but especially a credentialed, experienced expert) who doesn't like having their judgment questioned. HiPPOs seek unilateral control over all kinds of things, from the look and feel of a web page to the decision to launch a new product. As we saw in chapter 4, the great geek norm of science is all about *not* giving the final word to HiPPOs (no matter how big they are and how wide they can open their mouths), and instead getting them to produce evidence and argue about its interpretation. A/B testing, which originated at Google and has spread to countless other companies, is one way to do this. It takes unilateral control away from designers and forces them to justify their decisions like everyone else has to: with evidence and supporting arguments.

In chapter 5, on the great geek norm of ownership, we saw how Jeff Bezos, who "makes ordinary control freaks look like stoned hippies," realized that he had to give up a great deal of control if he wanted to prevent Amazon from becoming a bureaucratic mess. The company replaced its centralized, tightly controlled innovation process with a radically decentralized one characterized by two-pizza teams and (later) single-threaded leaders. As part of his work to get Microsoft back on track, Satya Nadella made a similarly large and bold move: he took away unilateral ownership and control of core resources like data and code throughout the company, and made them available to all who wanted to work with them.

Even when decisions need to be made by a senior leader, the business geeks don't want to make them unilaterally. Carl Bass told me that when he became CEO of the design software company Autodesk in 2006, "I still had this old-fashioned idea that being an executive leader meant that you make really important decisions. By the time I left, I made almost no important decisions. I mean that very seriously; I probably made one every two years. And to make them, I'd say to a roomful of people, 'I'm going to make the call, but first I want to hear all your opinions, all right?'" At Google, Eric Schmidt also gave up even trying to appear that he was in unilateral control. "We had a list of running issues that we'd debate," he told me. "We had a rule that we didn't want consensus. We wanted the best idea. The way you get it is you involve everyone in the conversation, especially the people who don't normally talk. The goal is to listen until we find the best idea, which can come from anywhere. That's part of how you build an agile culture. That's how you can see around rocks, because somebody can see around the rock."

Not striving to win and minimizing losing or failing: In most aerospace companies, losing an important piece of equipment is not acceptable. But as we saw in chapter 1, Planet CEO Will Marshall has a different philosophy. His company designs communications satellites with low cost and high redundancy, so that "if only 80 or 90 percent of them work, we'll be great with that." In chapter 6 we learned that as SpaceX develops its novel rockets, it emphasizes learning rapidly instead of getting the design right from the start. Several versions of its Starship rocket exploded as they attempted to land. Elon Musk and his colleagues would have preferred them to alight flawlessly, but when they didn't, SpaceX didn't change its approach.* Nor did the company stick to its original plan to make the Starship rocket out of carbon fiber. When experience showed that this manufacturing method was too unreliable and expensive, SpaceX simply walked away from it.

Amazon draws a distinction between "one-way doors," or decisions that are difficult to reverse, and "two-way doors," which aren't. Making the wrong choice at a two-way door is seen as an acceptable cost of moving fast and taking ownership. As we saw in chapter 1, when Ardine Williams was hesitating before making a change she considered important, a senior colleague asked if it were a one- or two-way door. "He asked me, 'What happens if this change you're proposing is a mess?' And I said 'Well, we turn it off.' He said, 'How long will that take?' And I said, 'Less than twenty-four hours.' He said, 'I'm back to where I started, Ardine. Push the button.'" Amazon, in short, made failing at two-way doors part of the company's culture.

Not suppressing negativity: Williams recalled that even though the change she was making was a two-way door, it was "probably one of the hardest things I've done in my career personally," because it flew in the face of what

---

* Remember, no one died: these were uncrewed flights.

she was used to: cross-functional processes, management review committees, elaborate decision loops, and other trappings of bureaucracy. Her trepidation highlights that the geek way asks people to do uncomfortable things: take action and responsibility, argue with their superiors, do things that might fail visibly, bring up sensitive topics, expose their ideas to negative feedback from others, and so on.

Companies practicing Model 1 work to minimize discomfort and other negative feelings. Geek companies don't. We've seen that Netflix, for example, requires executives to "farm for dissent" before making big moves. Actively asking your colleagues to find fault with your idea is no fun (at least for most of us), but Netflix doesn't care; it believes that its executives have enough grit and resilience to handle the resulting negativity. Argyris agreed. In his view, high-performing companies credit their people with "a high capacity for self-reflection and self-examination without becoming so upset that they lose their effectiveness."*

The great geek norm of science can't work without this capacity. We saw in chapter 4 how science is, as Robert Trivers puts it, "based on a series of increasingly sophisticated and remorseless anti-deceit and anti-self-deception mechanisms." Science distinguishes between rival hypotheses. It tells which idea is better. I speak from ample personal experience when I say that when your idea is found lacking—when the evidence doesn't support it, or someone convincingly argues against it—negative emotions ensue. But geek companies recognize that we can handle them. As Ben Horowitz says, "With Marc [Andreessen] and me, even after eighteen years, he upsets me almost every day by finding something wrong in my thinking, and I do the same for him. It works." They're friends and business partners, despite the upsets that come with argumentation.

---

* Argyris had a wonderful ability to call you out on your shortcomings without humiliating you or making you feel bad. In one of our discussions I told him I'd send him some relevant research. I didn't. The next time we got together he calmly and kindly said something to me like "If we're going to work together I need you to do the things you say you're going to do." From then on, I did.

Not having undiscussable topics: Recall Andreessen's insight from chapter 4: "[At] a lot of companies, . . . people have trepidations about speaking truth to power. And a lot of what I've always found the really wise and smart leaders are trying to do is they're trying to actually find the people in the organization who will actually talk back. . . There are other organizations where that doesn't work at all, and I would recommend getting out of those as fast as possible." As he put it in a 2022 tweet: "The most serious problem facing any organization is the one that cannot be discussed."

As we saw in the previous chapter, the agile development movement was born early this century out of the frustration with how software was being written. The success of agile is largely owing to its ability to eliminate undiscussables. In many large efforts, a liar's club spontaneously and tacitly forms, and the crucial question "Who's falling behind?" becomes undiscussable, as does the fact that the liar's club exists in the first place. The great geek norm of speed, as practiced in agile development, disbands the liar's club by increasing observability and decreasing plausible deniability. By making everyone's progress (or lack of it) visible and unignorable, agile approaches reduce the chances of a death spiral of undiscussability, undiscussable undiscussability, and so on.

Geek leaders can also reduce undiscussability simply by asking for feedback and receiving it appropriately. Remember that we *Homo ultrasocialis,* like members of other social species, are innately reluctant to challenge dominant individuals. So the ideas and pronouncements of people high on the organization chart tend to go unchallenged. That tendency can change, though, if the bosses ask for feedback instead of praise, and if they respond to it with openness (interest, curiosity, gratitude) instead of defensiveness (hostility, dismissiveness, threats). In chapter 1, I wrote how I saw HubSpot CEO Brian Halligan respond with authentic openness to negative feedback from a new hire in a large meeting. It's a strong testament to HubSpot's geek culture that I was the only one in the room who found their interaction at all surprising.

As these examples show, openness has many dimensions. It means being willing to confront the possibility that your idea is wrong, that your project is not going well, or that your judgment is off. It also entails responding without hostility or scorn to challenges, and without pulling rank when the challenges come from someone less prestigious or lower on the org chart. It's about creating a psychologically safe environment instead of a threatening one. Openness means admitting that your can't-miss product idea has in fact missed. It also means being willing to experiment, iterate, fail, and learn instead of preparing and planning in an attempt to avoid anything going wrong, ever. An essential aspect of openness is being willing to let go: to let people and projects move ahead without your involvement, sign-off, or blessing. And openness is about discussing even uncomfortable topics.

The Pivotal Importance of Failures

Over my career I've spent a lot of time both in Silicon Valley companies and at companies in "the rest of the economy." The most striking difference between them is how much more open the former are. In the part of the business world that pioneered the geek way and still follows it more deeply than anywhere else, Model 1 behaviors are relatively scarce.

One of my favorite questions to ask someone about their professional life is, "Is it okay to disagree with your boss in a meeting?" People who work at geek companies often seem puzzled by the question. Their answer usually is, "That's my job." A big part of their job, as they see it, is to help advance an effort or make an important decision in the face of uncertainty. Both of those require debate. As we saw in chapter 4, argumentation is critical for good outcomes.

At industrial-era companies, on the other hand, my question about disagreeing with the boss is often met with silence, deflection, or a nervous laugh. At a lot of places, low-ranking employees in meetings are there to listen and learn, not to talk back. Hierarchies are alive and well, and argumentation is close to insubordination. A little while back I was talking about the geek way with an editor at a well-known book publisher. I told him the story about attending a meeting at HubSpot where a new employee openly disagreed with the CEO. He said, "Wow. If that had happened here, that kid would forever be known as the new hire who talked back in an editorial meeting." He didn't say that this would not help the "kid's" reputation at work; he didn't need to.

While the strong norm at Model 1 companies is to "strive to win and minimize losing," geek companies realize that those two are actually incompatible—that winning in the long run necessitates conducting experiments, taking risks, and placing bets, not all of which are going to succeed. The business geeks don't enjoy the failures they experience, but they know that trying to never fail is a dead end. A culture that minimizes losses is, they believe, a culture that becomes conservative, slow-moving, and hesitant. In other words, it becomes what Jeff Bezos calls a Day 2 culture.

To head off Day 2, Bezos and Amazon have long stressed and celebrated trying things instead of notching victories. Throughout its history, Amazon has handed out big used sneakers as Just Do It awards, given to people who come up with an idea that's outside the scope of their job. JDI ideas don't have to be successful; they don't even have to be implemented. They just have to show initiative and a "bias for action" instead of a mania for "winning." More than twenty years after these awards were launched, Bezos continued to emphasize that Amazon did not follow Model 1's norms. In his 2018 shareholder letter, he stressed that the company was not trying to minimize losing: "As a company grows, everything needs to scale, including the size of your failed experiments. If the size of your failures isn't growing, you're not going to be inventing at a size that can actually move the needle. Amazon will be experimenting at the right scale for a company of our size if we occasionally have multibillion-dollar failures."*

Business geeks realize that sometimes their company's entire go-to-market strategy is a failure. This can happen for all kinds of reasons: a critical technology doesn't work as planned, customers don't want what founders thought they wanted, a recession hits, and so on. Instead of doggedly pursuing their initial vision, geeks remain open to the idea of a pivot—a reorientation

---

* As I write in early 2023, it appears that Amazon's Alexa, a countertop piece of hardware that users interact with via voice, might be one of those failures. Investigations revealed that Alexa was a "colossal failure" in the market and that the hardware division of which Alexa was a part was losing approximately $10 billion per year.

of the entire company. YouTube, for example, started in 2005 as a video dating site. That business didn't take off, but its founders realized that they had developed a valuable capability: they could receive videos in many formats from all over the Internet, standardize them, and present them to a global audience. That capability remains at the core of a business that had more than 2.5 billion users by late 2022. Other well-known pivots include Twitter, which started out as a resource for finding podcasts; Instagram, originally a location-based game called *Burbn;* Slack, also born out of an unpopular game; and Pinterest, which was originally a mobile shopping app. Not all pivots are successful, of course, but the business geeks have realized that pivoting—being open to the idea that what you're trying to do as a company just isn't working and needs to change—is a smarter move than refusing to admit that your original idea was wrong and running an organization into the ground.

Pied Piper, the fictional company at the center of the HBO sitcom *Silicon Valley,* went through a few pivots. Its original product was a music-finding app. It then got into video compression algorithms, then made servers, and eventually came up with AI software powerful enough to unlock all the world's secrets.* Many geeks I know watched *Silicon Valley* avidly (a couple even contributed to it) and thought it was hilarious. Their reaction tells us something about the geek way because, as comedian Rick Reynolds put it, "Only the truth is funny." A big reason the business geek community laughed so much at the show was that it got a lot right about the kinds of companies they were familiar with. In particular, it conveyed the great geek norm of openness.

Pied Piper was one incessant argument, punctuated by periods of writing code. Its employees showed little deference to Richard Hendricks, the company's beleaguered CEO. The software developers Bertram Guilfoyle and Dinesh Chugtai respected Hendricks's technical abilities and realized he was the final decision maker about company strategy, but they felt gloriously free to disagree with him visibly, at great length, and with frequent vulgarity. Even Hendricks's devoted chief of staff, Jared Dunn, argued with him at important junctures. Hendricks didn't find any of this unacceptable.

---

* The employees at Pied Piper decided to shut down this dangerous technology.

He didn't demand respect, try to unilaterally control his team, suppress negativity when things weren't going well, or engage in many other classic Model 1 behaviors. Instead, he tried to guide what everyone was arguing about, listen to them, and make the decisions that were incumbent on him as CEO. Hendricks and Pied Piper made plenty of mistakes, and *Silicon Valley* poked fun at that region's self-regard and hypocrisy. But the show also accurately reflected that corporate cultures in the geek watering hole that is Silicon Valley are fundamentally more open than those in most of the rest of the business world.

How to Keep a Good Thing Going

Yamini Rangan didn't watch *Silicon Valley* because, as she told me, "it was too close to home." Rangan had built her career in West Coast tech companies, and the show reminded her of work instead of taking her mind off it. Her work life changed in 2019, when she was approached by an American company that was geographically far away from the Valley, yet culturally quite close. It was HubSpot, the Cambridge-based maker of marketing software we've already encountered in these pages.

Rangan was intrigued by HubSpot, but as she put it, "I told myself that I wouldn't work for an East Coast company. I'd worked for one a long time back, and I didn't like the travel and the constant going back and forth and not being in the physical headquarters of the company." However, she was interested enough to speak with Brian Halligan, who encouraged her to take a look at the company's Culture Code. This was a presentation, posted online for the first time in 2013, that served the same purpose for HubSpot that the culture deck did for Netflix. Rangan told me that the Culture Code "was written in a way where if I were at my best and I put my best thoughts in terms of building a culture for a company, it would've gotten to 80 percent of what the deck said. If I had started a company, this is what I would have actually put in. And I just found myself thinking about how authentic it would be to join a place where the values are so aligned. The values of humility and adaptability and transparency—every one of those values spoke to me."

Rangan traveled to Massachusetts to talk with HubSpotters. "I was struck by how every single person that I spoke with that day—and it was from nine to five—every single person was humble," she said. "They had this desire to drive excellence, and curiosity, and need to learn. They were more real, more humble, more curious, in more of a growth mindset than I had seen."

Like most geek companies, HubSpot tries to hire people with these characteristics. But as we've seen repeatedly, individual mindsets can easily get overwhelmed by the social environment: Arthur Andersen's formerly upright audit partners started engaging in unethical business practices when they began to feel left behind by the growth in consulting; Microsoft hired people who moved fast, innovated, and built great products, but when the company's culture changed they started scheming and sabotaging each other. So the fact that Rangan found HubSpotters to be humble and open instead of defensive doesn't just suggest to me that the company had a great recruiting process. It also suggests something more powerful: that HubSpot actually had in place the norms of openness described in its Culture Code.

Rangan joined HubSpot as its chief customer officer in January of 2020 and took over from Halligan as the company's CEO in September of 2021. Her time at the top at HubSpot has been marked by deep change and uncertainty: the COVID pandemic forced the company to adopt fully remote and then hybrid work, and its stock price plummeted as investors soured on technology companies. Between September 1, 2021, and December 1, 2022, HubSpot's market capitalization shrank by more than half. I asked Rangan what effect all these challenges had on HubSpot's culture. She answered that they increased the importance of openness:

With the macroeconomic environment changing, and with the market volatility that is happening, sometimes we as a leadership team don't know what trajectory we're on. Is what we see in August going to continue, or what we see in September going to continue? Being transparent in a time of uncertainty calls for knowing that you're wrong sometimes. I'll tell you that I'm uncertain about this, which means next month I might have to change my response because things have changed. So I think being transparent in a time of certainty and business as usual is quite different than being transparent in a time of great uncertainty. And the only way you can do that is to be vulnerable and say, I don't know, I honestly don't know.

Throughout our conversation, the concepts of vulnerability, transparency, authenticity, and humility—concepts that are signs of weakness in organizations following Model 1's defensive norms—kept coming up. When I asked Rangan for a specific behavior that she modeled for HubSpotters, she talked about sharing her performance review.

> One of the things that I did in a director-plus meeting seven or eight months ago, is I shared my performance review with them. The board had given me a performance review and I said, here, based on all the board feedback and based on the feedback that you all have given me, here are the things that I did okay at, and here are all the things that I need to improve, and here's kind of my plan of how I'm going to be improving on those areas. I then heard that a bunch of leaders did the same thing.
>
> This is something that I've done in multiple places to show leaders "your behaviors are exceptionally important." Especially now, because transparency during a time of uncertainty is exceptionally hard. Doing things now that show a level of authenticity and vulnerability is helpful. It gets everybody around you to naturally say, Okay, what do *I* do? How do I do that?

Rangan is being savvy at two levels here. The first is taking advantage of the fact that we *Homo ultrasocialis* mimic high-status people both consciously and unconsciously. If the CEO shares her performance review, it's a behavior that is likely to spread. The second level is being deliberate about what kinds of behaviors to model. Rangan doesn't just share the best parts of her review. That would be a classic Model 1 behavior (where everyone *strives to win and minimizes losing* and tries to *remain in unilateral control*). She instead shares the whole thing, warts and all. That's an authentic move. It shows she's humble, and willing to be vulnerable and transparent. It signals openness in several ways, and defensiveness not at all.

When Rangan started her career in high tech, it was Model 1 all the time. Her first boss cautioned her to never show vulnerability:

> When I joined the tech industry, in sales, my first boss said to me, "Here's your quota; good luck. Do more than men, drink less than men, and never show your weakness." That was literally what she said to me. And I tried to follow that! Especially the not showing weakness part of it, especially in the first ten years of my career.
>
> I had two kids at home. It was incredibly difficult trying to manage two kids and fly around and all of that. But I would never talk about the challenges of having two kids under three and trying to be in tech and not sleeping enough, because that was a weakness.
>
> And I found out that I was just losing myself. I stopped recognizing who I was. I'm authentic, I'm warm, I think I'm humble, and I have a growth mindset. For the first ten years in tech, being in sales and being an engineer, I had to train myself not to do any of that stuff. And it didn't serve me well.
>
> So at some point I just thought, "I gotta be who I am." And I don't care how far I go in my career, but I'm just going to be who I am. I'm going to talk about the things that I failed at. I'm going to talk about how difficult it is as a woman to rise up in tech and how difficult it is to manage all of this. I'm going to talk about imposter syndrome, which I still have. I was just tired of following the "do more work and don't show weakness" playbook. I'm not afraid to do more work, but I wanted to find places where I could be myself.

Rangan found such a place at HubSpot. Under her leadership, the company has continued to work on its culture of openness. By the end of 2022, the HubSpot Culture Code was on its thirty-third revision. It continued to underpin a company that many people wanted to work at. HubSpot came in second among large US companies in Glassdoor's Best Places to Work awards for 2022, and Comparably, another site for employee reviews, named Rangan the Best CEO for Women.

The Life-Changing Magic of Common Knowledge

HubSpot's openness extends to some of the company's most sensitive information. After the company went public, in 2014, it took the unusual step of designating all of its employees—not just top executives—as insiders with access to important financial information. As the Culture Code puts it,

> Everyone has equal access to the same data. This is important because better data leads to better insights...
> Examples of things we share and discuss:
> - Financials (forecasts, balance sheet, P&L, etc.)
> - Our diversity goals (and shortcomings)
> - Management meeting decks
> - Answers from our "Ask Me Anything" sessions

Many other geek companies also share information in ways that seem extreme. In 1998, Reed Hastings started handing out and discussing Netflix's quarterly financial statements with all employees (in the company's parking lot, which was the only space big enough) and posting a document outlining the company's strategy on a bulletin board next to the copy machine. These practices continued even after Netflix went public. The company's "strategy bets" document is posted prominently on its Intranet, and as Hastings puts it, "All financial results, as well as just about any information that Netflix competitors would love to get their hands on, has been available to all of our employees."*

As these examples show, the business geeks tend toward "radical transparency," a phrase coined in 2001 to describe putting even sensitive information

---

* In 2021, a former Netflix engineer was found guilty of insider trading after passing on privileged information about company performance to an outsider who used it to trade stock.

in front of as many eyeballs as possible. Ray Dalio, the founder of the hedge fund Bridgewater Associates, was a passionate advocate of this approach even before it had a name. From Bridgewater's start in 1975, he worked to build its capacity to do things like record all meetings and make them universally searchable and accessible within the company. He also believed that employees' reputations—covering everything from how attentive and inspiring they were to how well they were able to communicate and think strategically—should be quantified and shown to everyone. So people at Bridgewater are now required to frequently give each other numerical feedback after meetings and other interactions, using an iPad app called Dot Collector. Everyone's aggregated dot scores are always visible to everyone else in the company.

What's going on here? Why is there this mania among so many business geeks to share—if not overshare—information? It's easy to identify risks that come with radical transparency: facilitating insider trading, letting the competition know what you're up to, exposing internal problems, making people uncomfortable as their weaknesses are made public, and so on. Are the benefits really worth it?

Many geeks believe that they are. To see why, let's revisit a well-known story about a town that let an uncomfortable situation continue far too long.

The folktale of the emperor's new clothes is over a thousand years old, and variations of it exist in many cultures. The version we know best comes from Hans Christian Andersen's nineteenth-century collection of Danish tales. It relates how swindlers came to the country's capital city and promoted themselves as weavers of gorgeous textiles with a unique property: they could only be seen by intelligent people who were fit for their positions. The emperor heard about these wondrous fabrics and sent a succession of ministers to examine them. Of course there was nothing for them to examine—there was no actual cloth—but each minister worried that the weavers might be telling the truth, in which case he was seeing nothing because he was stupid or unfit. If that were true, the minister would surely be disgraced and lose his job. To avoid that possibility, all the ministers sent to inspect the "textiles" praised them lavishly.

After the swindlers had pocketed several payments from the emperor they declared that his new clothes were ready. They asked him to disrobe and then dressed him in his new, imaginary finery while all onlookers vocally admired its great beauty and elegance.* The emperor then walked in procession through the city so that everyone could see and praise his raiment. All adults joined in, since none of them wanted to be seen as stupid or unfit. One small child, however, didn't maintain the charade. "But he hasn't got anything on!" he yelled out loud. This broke the spell, and soon the whole town was agreeing, "He hasn't got anything on!"

The tale of the emperor's new clothes highlights the major importance of the apparently minor difference between *mutual knowledge* and *common knowledge*. Mutual knowledge is the stuff that everybody knows. The fact that the emperor had no clothes on as he paraded down the street was mutual knowledge for the city's inhabitants. But they didn't all know that everybody else also knew the same thing. Because of the clever lie told by the swindling "tailors," all of the cityfolk thought that there was at least some chance that other people—the intelligent and fit ones—could in fact see the emperor's clothes even though they themselves could not. So to avoid the risk of appearing stupid and unfit, they all stayed quiet.

Because of the confusion sown by the swindlers, in short, the emperor's state of undress wasn't common knowledge. Common knowledge is the stuff that everybody knows, and that everybody knows everybody else also knows, and that everybody knows that everybody else knows that everybody else knows, and so on. When the child shouted out the truth, he wasn't saying anything anyone didn't already know, but he was converting mutual knowledge to common knowledge. Everybody suddenly knew that everybody else was seeing the same thing that they were seeing, and the spell was broken.

As this folktale shows, common knowledge has an odd, almost supernatural power to get a group of people to change their behavior in ways that appear coordinated but aren't. My favorite demonstration of this

---

* In some versions of the story the emperor is permitted a bit of dignity: instead of disrobing completely, he strips down to his underwear.

phenomenon comes from a logic puzzle that exists in many versions dating back at least as far as the 1960s. One version is set on the fictional Bad Breath Island.*

It's a small place where everyone knows everyone else. It's also a high-IQ place. It's common knowledge that the inhabitants of this island are all logical, clear thinkers. What *isn't* common knowledge is who has bad breath, since that uncomfortable topic is never discussed in any way by anyone. In fact, bad breath is considered so shameful that if anyone knows for sure that they have it, they will jump in a canoe in the middle of the night and paddle away, never to return. Like most of us, the inhabitants of Bad Breath Island can't smell their own breath accurately, even though they can smell everyone else's perfectly well. So they walk around knowing who else has bad breath, but not knowing if they have it themselves, and never ever discussing this taboo subject.

Every once in a while, a completely truthful alien shows up and tells them things. (The fact that the alien is completely truthful is common knowledge.) One day, the alien appears, waits patiently for all the islanders to gather, says, "At least one of you on this island has bad breath," and then disappears.

The alien didn't tell the islanders anything they didn't already know. They can smell, after all. They can tell if their neighbors have bad breath or not. And for a few days after the alien's visit, nothing changes. But on the seventh morning after the alien's visit, everyone wakes up to find that the seven people with bad breath left the island during the night. No one is surprised. With a new, shared awareness that halitosis has been eradicated once and for all on Bad Breath Island, they all go home and unpack the suitcases they'd prepared in case they needed to paddle away that night.

What happened here? How could the alien's announcement have led to this result, and how are the islanders remaining on the seventh day so sure they don't have bad breath themselves?

---

* Another version is a bit spicier: it revolves not around people with bad breath, but instead cheating husbands who get executed if their wives find out.

To start to see how, think about the only case in which the alien's announcement could actually have provided new information to anyone. This is the case in which there's only one person with bad breath on the island. That person — let's call him Sven — had a functioning sense of smell and interacted with all the other islanders, and knew that no one else had bad breath. But Sven couldn't tell how his own breath smelled. He knew, then, that either no one on the island had bad breath, or only he did. And since the truthful alien's announcement eliminated the possibility that no one else had bad breath, Sven concluded that he, and he alone, had it. So Sven paddled away in shame, that very night.

Now think about all the other islanders in this case. They all knew that Sven had bad breath. And prior to the alien's visit, there were only two mutually exclusive possibilities: either only Sven had bad breath, or two people did (Sven *and themselves*). All these islanders breathed a huge (nonsmelly) sigh of relief when they got up the morning after the alien's visit and saw that Sven, their logical, smelly-breathed neighbor, had paddled away. Why? Because this fact reveals which of their two possibilities is reality: it's the one where only one person has bad breath. And that person correctly self-identified and left. Everyone else therefore knew that they didn't have to slink away in shame, so went home and unpacked their bags.

The same logic works when the number of people with bad breath is greater than one. If there are two, for example, both of them know that there are two possibilities: one bad-breathed islander, or two. When they get up on the first morning after the alien's visit and see that no one has paddled away in the night (as would be the case if there were one person with bad breath on the island), they are forced to conclude that the correct number is two, and that they are one of the two. So they independently both decide to paddle away that night. The rest of the islanders — who knew that either two or three people had bad breath — breathe sighs of relief when they get up on the second morning and learn that the true number was two. These folk unpack their suitcases and get on with their lives until the alien's next visit. And so on and so on, up to and past our starting case of seven bad-breathed islanders.

This example is (more than a) little contrived, but like the tale of the emperor's new clothes it shows us how creating common knowledge can quickly and deeply change a situation. Common knowledge increases observability, and gives everybody assurance that everyone has observed the same thing. It eliminates plausible deniability, both externally and internally, and so makes both deception and self-deception much more difficult. Common knowledge often forces people to confront realities they'd rather avoid. Once the alien visitor spoke, it was only a matter of time until all the bad-breathed islanders left.

Common knowledge is organizational truth serum in a lot of ways, which is why the business geeks are so fond of it. They work to ensure that important information is not just mutual knowledge, but also common knowledge.

The business geeks take that extra step because people and groups behave differently when no one can convince themselves or anyone else of things that are contradicted by common knowledge. A manager at Bridgewater won't spend a lot of time talking about how important it is to do the right thing if everyone at the company can see that the manager's peer-assigned "managerial courage" score is low. Team members working on an agile project can't tell themselves that they're not falling behind, or that everyone else is equally late, or that no one knows how late they really are, if they're the only team whose cards aren't yet in the Done column of the kanban board. No one on the iPhone camera team at Apple will keep arguing against giving consumers the ability to preview the blurry background of portraits if the whole team is there watching the demo showing how powerful that feature is. The business geeks emphasize common knowledge—it's part of their toolkit for radical transparency—because they recognize what a powerful weapon it is against self-deception, liar's clubs, and situations where the emperor has no clothes.

Why We Comply

I think that openness is important for one final reason. It holds a special place among the great geek norms because it establishes a critical form of community policing—when it's functioning well, openness turns everyone into guardians of an organization's culture. This community policing reduces the risk that the culture will get warped over time or hijacked. As philosopher Dan Williams writes about one aspect of openness,

> A good argument for strong norms of free expression is not that it leads to truth, but that it's a form of system design that protects against the harms produced by small but well-organised groups that impose self-serving orthodoxies and taboos on the broader population. When that happens, you can't challenge the orthodoxies without risking social punishment. By upholding norms in favour of free expression, however, you lower the scope & costs of such punishment.

The audit partners at Arthur Andersen were a small but well-organized group within the company. They imposed a self-serving orthodoxy of growth at any cost, and a taboo on speaking up against unethical behavior. The orthodoxy and the taboo were harmful to the organization and ran directly counter to its stated values. But because AA didn't have strong norms of free expression (Toffler learned, for example, that managers at the firm were extremely reluctant to speak out or speak up against partners), the partners went unchallenged.

Part of the reason is that AA managers were worried about getting fired, or at least getting a bad performance review, if they blew the whistle on their boss's unethical behavior. But that's not the whole reason. I believe that it's not even the most important one. After all, Toffler didn't work directly for the partner who ordered her to double what she was charging a client. He didn't have the authority to fire her; he may not even have been part of her performance review. So then why did she acquiesce to him?

The puzzle deepens because before her stint at Andersen, Toffler had devoted her career to studying and improving business ethics, and considered herself to be willing to speak out and speak truth to power. Her one-word description of herself was "debunker." After her first year teaching at Harvard Business School, her students gave her a spray can they'd labeled as

Bullshit Repellent. Yet after just a few years of working at Andersen, she found herself, as she recalled, "fighting with my colleagues, as willing to steal a client as anyone else in the Firm, overseeing work that often was shaped more by time and fee constraints than by thoughtful expertise." She didn't just give in one time to one unethical request; she instead became someone willing to cross the line over and over. Shortly after she left Andersen, Toffler had lunch with a CEO with whom she had worked throughout her career. As she tells it, he was straight with her:

> "You were selling us stuff you didn't think we needed [when you were at AA]." Then he summed it all up with one sentence. "Barbara, this is not the you I used to know," he said. I had to agree with him. This was not the me I used to know.

What force was powerful enough to make her unrecognizable even to herself? In his argument for a norm of openness quoted a few paragraphs earlier, philosopher Dan Williams identifies it precisely: it's the risk of social punishment.

That seems both vague and insufficient, doesn't it? How could something as lightweight as "social punishment" be strong enough to get a professional ethicist to become unrecognizably unethical to herself and others after just a few years? It's easy to see how some changes in circumstance would be transformational. If Toffler had been sent off to fight in the trenches of World War I, say, or inducted into a ruthless drug cartel, she might well have become a very different person. But she joined an auditing firm. She moved from one white-collar job to another, nothing more. And yet something about the norms she encountered at Andersen, and the social punishment she knew she would face if she didn't follow them, changed her into "not the me I used to know."

To understand how this happened, and to wrap up our ultimate exploration of us *Homo ultrasocialis,* let's look not just at the norm of openness, but at norms in general. As we've discussed, norms are the behaviors that a community expects of its members. Our reputations depend on how well we follow our communities' norms. These reputations are maintained, spread, and updated in a distributed and highly effective way: by gossip.

"Gossip" has negative connotations, and also sexist ones: it's been used as a dismissive label for something women are prone to do. But it's actually something we all do. Anthropologist Robin Dunbar and his colleagues sampled free-flowing conversations in many locations and found that on average 65 percent of time was devoted to social topics—gossip, in other words—and only 35 percent to everything else: politics, sports, music and culture, and technical topics.* There was no large difference in how much men and women gossiped.

We *Homo ultrasocialis* use gossip to share and spread information about how well group members are following norms. My colleagues and I in business academia spend a lot of time talking about who has good ideas, who does their fair share of work on a project, who takes more credit than they deserve, who's scrupulous with their claims and their data, and perhaps most fundamentally who is just plain old "smart." Like all humans, we gossip about things that matter to us, and that we actually do need to be concerned about.

This gossip creates our reputation and standing in the group. It's like we all have a display over our heads showing our gossip-generated "norm scores": our ratings for how well we follow the group's code of conduct. Does Andy plagiarize? Does he skip meetings? Is he verbally abusive? Does he shirk the work, yet crave the spotlight? When he gets involved in a project does it speed up or slow down? My overhead display shows my scores on these and many other measures to members of my community. Other members "see" those scores and act accordingly. They also update these scores with their gossip about me. I, of course, do the same for them.

When norms are violated, the community punishes the violator. How? By subjecting the offender to social exclusion, which is tremendously painful and upsetting to us *Homo ultrasocialis*. Remember, throughout most of our

---

* These conversations all took place in Europe. Research on gossip among non-European people shows that the percentage of time devoted to gossip is even higher than the 65 percent that Dunbar observed.

history as a species individuals needed to be part of a group to survive. To help ensure our survival, then, evolution designed us to want to be part of a group. Part of this design is a strong aversion to anything that feels like exile or ostracism or exclusion. Being snubbed, getting the cold shoulder, having a lively conversation die down as soon as you enter a room, being kicked out: all of these feel truly lousy. Evolution designed us so that social exclusion *hurts,* because that exclusion is such a killer for members of our species.

Neuroscientist Matthew Lieberman tells the story about an experiment he and psychologist Naomi Eisenberger ran where they subjected unsuspecting people to social exclusion while in an fMRI machine that precisely tracked their brain activity. When they got out of the machine, the strength of their reactions was surprising. As Lieberman writes, subjects "would spontaneously start talking to us about what had just happened to them. They were genuinely angry or sad about what they had gone through."

A bigger surprise, though, came as the experimenters were analyzing the fMRI data they'd collected. At some point they looked over at the computer of a colleague who was analyzing data from an fMRI study of reactions to physical pain. As Lieberman recalls, "Looking at the screens, side by side, without knowing which was an analysis of physical pain and which was an analysis of social pain, you wouldn't have been able to tell the difference." Physical pain and social pain are so closely related that Tylenol actually helps with both. Compared to a control group, people who took a daily dose of 1,000 milligrams of Tylenol started reporting significantly less social pain after a bit more than a week.

Social punishment is universal across human groups because it's so effective. You don't need to designate an enforcer to go around beating people up every time they violate a norm. All you need is a group of humans who have collectively decided what the norms are. Gossip, reputations, and social pain will take care of things from there. As Lieberman puts it, "Our sensitivity to social rejection is so central to our well-being that our brains treat it like a painful event, whether the instance of social rejection matters or not."

The ultimate definition of a norm, then, is that it's any behavior where noncompliance leads to punishment via social rejection. We've been debating for a long time what holds human groups together. Some take the exalted view that what unites us is what we love. If, as St. Augustine said in *The City of God*, "a people is an assemblage of reasonable beings bound together by a common agreement as to the objects of their love, then, in order to discover the character of any people, we have only to observe what they love." The flip side, as expressed by the playwright Anton Chekhov, is that "love, friendship, respect do not unite people as much as common hatred for something." Ultimate research suggests a very different way to look at the issue: whether we love the people around us or hate them, what unites them and us into a coherent group is what we've collectively decided to punish with painful social rejection—with the threat or reality of ostracism from the group. A big part of what unites us, in other words, is our norms.

Over and over we've seen how norms overwhelm individual differences and cause most if not all people in a group to behave the same way. Norms were instrumental in causing Princeton seminarians to be unhelpful, Kenyan TB patients to be altruistic, and employees at companies including Amazon and Microsoft to change from acting like cogs in the giant machinery of bureaucracy to acting like empowered owners.

At Google and plenty of other geek companies, a newly hired designer who said something like, "There's no need to A/B test this change—I know that users will like it better," would probably have a colleague or boss explain the norm to them with a "That's not the way we do things around here" conversation. If the designer didn't listen, they'd start experiencing ostracism and other kinds of social pain: not getting invited to meetings, not having a lot of people to eat lunch with, not getting consulted very often, not getting included in projects, and eventually not having a job there anymore.

Similarly, managers at Amazon who engage in the ancient bureaucratic art of trying to impede someone else's progress are violating the company's norm of ownership. They get known as "blockers," and tend not to last long. I can only imagine what would happen to a software engineer at Tesla who suggested that the company use the waterfall approach to developing software to write the code for its next car, or the head of a rocket development program at

SpaceX who insisted that the team stick with the first design it came up with no matter what testing revealed. Both of those hypotheticals would be violations of the great geek norm of speed that's in place at the two companies.

One of the craziest things about our norm psychology is how flexible it is. There are a few moral absolutes that are consistent across all human groups. Nowhere is it okay, for example, to randomly murder members of your in-group. Outside of these absolutes, though, there's seemingly infinite variety. People in hunter-gatherer bands don't have clearly defined roles. People in kingdoms generally do. The Dutch tend to be quite direct, while the Japanese don't. Some groups continue to defer to the judgment of elders and experts; others have embraced the scientific method. AA managers were extremely reluctant to disagree with their partners, while HubSpotters feel very much at ease disagreeing with their CEO. Because they embrace norms of science, ownership, speed, and openness, geek businesses are fast-moving, freewheeling, egalitarian, evidence-driven, autonomous, and argumentative. Most industrial-era business cultures aren't. Our norm psychology can easily accommodate any of these options.

Self-Correcting Organizations

Arthur Andersen's defensive and unethical norms were distasteful to Toffler, but she generally followed them. As she writes, "One of the powerful personal lessons of my Arthur Andersen experience is that, despite my self-image as a debunker, my frequent battles with my bosses, and an occasional outbreak of 'my way,' I basically went along with the culture...If you hang around a place long enough, you inevitably start to act like most of the people around you." When her colleagues were behaving badly, they expected her to behave badly, too—and she did. Norms sure are strong.

Luckily, this applies to healthy norms like openness as well as unhealthy defensive ones. If you join a company where openness is the norm—where important information like managers' scores and project status are common knowledge, where failures don't doom careers, where leaders are willing to show vulnerability, and where free expression is common—you're basically going to go along with this culture. You'll pick up on the norms in place around you and start following them, because that's what we *Homo ultrasocialis* are designed to do. You're going to become more comfortable sharing, taking risks, and speaking up.

You'll also start speaking out about norm violations and other bad behavior if that's what you see your peers doing. In other words, you'll join the ongoing community policing that keeps the company's culture on track. This is why openness holds a special place among the great geek norms: it's a distributed self-correction mechanism.

Organizations with defensive norms lack this kind of distributed capacity for self-correction. As a result, they can get badly off track; a huge gap can open up between what they say about themselves and what they actually do. AA's 1999 annual report, which described "our core values: Integrity, Respect, Passion for Excellence, One Firm, Stewardship, Personal Growth," reads in hindsight like a bad joke. But the gulf between the firm's words and its actions was anything but a joke—and by that point the gulf was undiscussable. The business geeks keep working on the norm of openness—despite the challenges it brings and the constant work it entails—because they don't want to get to that point. In order to remain true to themselves and maintain their norms of science, ownership, and speed, they need to remain open.

To close out this book, let's use what we've learned about a great geek norm to create a fourth and final ultimate ground rule. The general form of the rule is: *Shape the ultrasociality of group members so that the group's cultural evolution is as rapid as possible in the desired direction.* For the norm of openness, which holds a special place because it acts as the guardian of the other norms, the ground rule becomes: *Welcome challenges to the status quo and increase common knowledge in order to combat defensiveness and undiscussable topics.* It's the best way to keep the geek way going strong.

Chapter Summary

Many companies have "Model 1" norms: be in unilateral control over others; strive to win and minimize losing; suppress negative feelings. These sound sensible, but they're actually corrosive because they create a culture of defensiveness and undiscussability.

Model 1 strangles and squelches the things that the business geeks are adamant about. It creates corporate cultures that are the opposite of freewheeling, fast-moving, evidence-driven, egalitarian, argumentative, and autonomous.

The business geeks avoid defensiveness by embracing a norm of openness, which we can define as *sharing information and being receptive to arguments, reevaluations, and changes in direction.*

The geeks realize that the two goals of "strive to win and minimize losing" are incompatible — that in the long run, winning necessitates conducting experiments, taking risks, and placing bets, not all of which are going to succeed.

Common knowledge (an extreme form of information sharing) is organizational truth serum.

For the geek norm of openness, the ultimate ground rule is: *Welcome challenges to the status quo and increase common knowledge in order to combat defensiveness and undiscussable topics.*

The ultimate definition of a norm is that it's any behavior where noncompliance leads to punishment via social rejection.

Openness holds a special place among the great geek norms: it's a distributed self-correction mechanism.

Survey for Your Organization

These ten statements can be used to assess how well an organization follows the great geek norm of openness. Respondents reply to each with a number between one and seven, where one means "strongly disagree" and seven means "strongly agree."

1. Senior leaders here are willing to be vulnerable and admit that they were wrong or that they don't know the answer.
2. Managers and executives here don't want to hear any bad news.*
3. Managers and executives here expect to be obeyed without question.*
4. We emphasize winning and suppress negativity.*
5. There are lots of taboo topics here.*
6. People here frequently challenge the status quo and speak up when they disagree with a course of action.
7. Being associated with a failed effort does not harm your career at this company.
8. When people disagree with each other here, they do so respectfully.
9. People here rarely admit that someone else has caused them to change their mind or follow a different course of action.*
10. People here think their colleagues can handle candid feedback and constructive criticism.

---

* Scores for these statements need to be reversed. To do this, subtract the respondent's score from eight. For example, if the respondent answered with six, the reversed score would be two.

Four Geek Mantras

Science: Argue about evidence.

Ownership: Align, then unleash.

Speed: Iterate with feedback.

Openness: Reflect, don't defend.

Conclusion

Vitality, If Not Immortality

it's no use worrying about Time
but we did have a few tricks up our sleeves
— *Frank O'Hara*

None of the business geeks I spoke to for this book think they've discovered the corporate fountain of youth. They don't think that their companies — or anyone else's — have figured out how to be permanently successful. Not once did I hear anything like "We've got this figured out. We'll be permanently on top." Silicon Valley's leaders aren't known as a particularly humble bunch, but when I talk with them I don't hear a lot of arrogance about the long-term future of their companies.

There are two big reasons why the business geeks don't believe in immortal businesses. The first is that innovation and competition are a one-two punch that can knock out anyone. Say, for example, that a startup truthfully announces tomorrow that it's built a working industrial-strength quantum computer. This would shake things up, since most of the digital infrastructure that we've built up around the world to ensure privacy and security would be instantly obsolete. E-commerce, financial services, communications, and other large industries would be shaken to their core. What's more, progress in AI, optimization, simulation, and several other fundamental aspects of computing would experience a, well, quantum leap forward. Incumbents in these areas would be in for a tough time.

TikTok, an online platform for sharing short videos, is a lesser innovation than quantum computing. But its rapid growth probably has some folk at Meta—the parent company of both Facebook and Whats-App—worried. Those two social media platforms both had global scale and strong network effects, and they both allowed users to post videos. So how much room could there be for yet another video-sharing service? Plenty, as it turns out. TikTok was launched in 2016; by 2021 it had more than 650 million users around the world and was, as the *Wall Street Journal* put it, "the most popular app in the world." The lesson from TikTok's rapid incursion into Meta's territory is that incumbency provides a lot of advantages, but no guarantees. The only guarantee is that someone out there is working on something that has the potential to disrupt you.

That disruption becomes a lot easier if incumbents succumb to any of the classic organizational dysfunctions. The second reason that the business geeks don't believe in corporate immortality, and I believe the bigger one, is that those dysfunctions just keep reappearing. They're as hard to kill as the boogeyman terrorizing kids in a horror film. They continue to haunt even the kinds of companies that have pioneered the geek way. Recent events show that Internet-era tech firms and their leaders are not immune to the self-inflicted harms that plagued companies throughout the industrial era.

Overconfidence at the top is alive and well in Silicon Valley. As we saw in chapter 4, overconfidence is "the most 'pervasive and potentially catastrophic' of all the cognitive biases to which human beings fall victim." The great geek norm of science is supposed to blunt its effects by making everyone—even the CEO—follow the evidence and stress-test their ideas via debate. But that norm appears to have been set aside as Mark Zuckerberg directed the company he founded to pursue the "metaverse."

That company used to be called Facebook. It changed its name to Meta in late 2021 to show how serious it was about the metaverse, an online environment whose "defining characteristic," according to Zuckerberg, "is that you really feel like you're present with other people or in another place. You might look at documents, you might look at a website, but in the future you're going to be *in* it." His company had been working on creating this feeling of presence for years—and spending a lot of money on it—before the company changed its name. By one estimate, Meta's annualized meta-verse investment was $15 billion by the end of 2022.

To many observers, the company didn't have much to show for all this effort and investment. The first big consumer application for the metaverse was *Horizon Worlds,* which was released in December of 2021. It was a 3D virtual reality application in which participants could create environments and interact with each other. But it didn't draw many participants. Internal Meta documents revealed that by October of 2022, *Horizon* had fewer than two hundred thousand users each month.

It wasn't even very popular among the people working on it. Vishal Shah, the company's VP of Metaverse, wrote memos to the *Horizon* team saying, "We don't spend that much time in *Horizon*," and asking, "Why is that? Why don't we love the product we've built so much that we use it all the time?"

An answer came from Adi Robertson, a reporter for the tech news web-site *The Verge.* She reviewed Meta's top-of-the-line Quest Pro, a virtual real-ity headset used to navigate the metaverse. Robertson felt "consistently nauseated" using the device in its default mode, but even after she solved that problem she found that Workrooms, the main application intended for business use, was "one of the worst apps I've ever used." She described how hard it was to set up a virtual meeting with colleagues: "Even after a full year of availability, the Workrooms experience is...like spinning a roulette wheel designed by Franz Kafka, where the prize for winning is a fancy Zoom meeting."

Zuckerberg's vision for the metaverse wasn't shared by many of his employees. A poll conducted in May of 2022 found that less than 60 percent of Meta's workforce understood the strategy that caused the company to change its name. Some people evidently felt that in the face of real business challenges like the rise of TikTok and other competitors and slowing growth, their CEO's obsession with the metaverse was a costly distraction. The *New York Times* reported that some Meta employees referred to metaverse proj-ects with the dismissive acronym MMH, which stood for "make Mark happy."

In October of 2022 Meta shareholder Brad Gerstner wrote an open letter to Zuckerberg calling the company's investment in the metaverse "supersized and terrifying, even by Silicon Valley standards" and asking him to halve it. But Meta's CEO doesn't have to listen to Gerstner, other investors, or even its board of directors. Zuckerberg holds the majority of his company's voting shares, which means that there are few institutional checks on his confidence that the path he's set for his company is the right one.

There are even fewer checks on Elon Musk at Twitter, since he owns that company outright. His actions with respect to it have been characterized by great confidence that he could get what he wanted, even when what he wanted was not to actually own it once he'd agreed to buy it. After signing a contract to acquire Twitter for approximately $44 billion in April of 2022, he tried to back out of the deal, claiming that he was misled. Twitter sued to get him to actually follow through on his commitment. Shortly before the trial was to start, Musk reagreed to the purchase, and on October 27 he became the company's owner.

His first major change to the business, launched soon after he walked into Twitter headquarters carrying a sink (to help let the fact that he owned the place "sink in"), was to try to get more of its users to pay for it. In 2009 Twitter had begun verifying accounts of celebrities, politicians, and others who were likely to be impersonated. Once verified, users got a blue badge containing a white check mark added to their profiles; this became known (inaccurately) as a "blue check." In later years, verification was expanded at no charge to other notable people, and to organizations like companies and public health agencies.

Musk decided to upend Twitter's verification system. Just a couple weeks after taking over as "chief twit," Musk announced that the blue check would come with a $20 per month charge. In a Twitter exchange with author Stephen King, he lowered it to $8. The resulting "Twitter Blue" service launched on November 9, available to anyone with an Apple ID, a phone number, and the willingness to pay $7.99 per month. That money didn't buy verification; it instead apparently bought freedom from verification. Fake blue-check accounts for George W. Bush and Tony Blair posted nostalgia for the Iraq

War. A fake Twitter Blue account for drug company Eli Lilly announced that insulin was now free. The *Washington Post* set up fake blue-check accounts for comedian Blaire Erskine and senator Ed Markey (with their permission). On November 11, Markey sent a letter to Musk pointing out his fake account and noting, "Apparently, due to Twitter's lax verification practices and apparent need for cash, anyone could pay $8.00 and impersonate someone on your platform. Selling the truth is dangerous and unacceptable."

By the time Markey's letter was sent, Twitter had already paused new Twitter Blue sign-ups "to help address impersonation issues" (as an internal company message put it). But both the company's reputation and its revenues had been damaged by the fiasco. On November 11, the giant ad agency Omnicom recommended that its clients "pause activity on Twitter in the short term" because of "potentially serious implications." Companies including Pfizer, General Mills, VW, and General Motors had already decided to pull ads from Twitter; they were apparently unperturbed by Musk's tweeted threat to "thermonuclear name and shame" advertisers who boycotted the platform. Since Twitter got about 90 percent of its revenue from ads, that threat seemed ill-advised. In fact, his whole initial Twitter Blue plan did. Musk tweeted that Blue customers would see half as many ads, but an analysis showed, as the *Washington Post* put it, that Twitter's "top 1 percent of U.S. users—who are in turn the ones most likely to shell out $8—earn the service more than $40 each month in [advertising] revenue." Every Twitter Blue subscription that halved that $40 while bringing in only $8 would be a revenue killer.

We the Problem

There's a problem facing all companies, geek or not, that's even deeper and more pervasive than overconfident leaders making bad decisions. It's us. It's all of us. It's that we want what we want, and our wants get misaligned with the goals of organizations that we're part of. As we've seen, we create liar's clubs and elaborate bureaucracies. We form coalitions that fight for turf, then fight to keep it. We act defensively and try to be in unilateral control.

We work hard to ignore reality when reality makes us look bad. We punish those who violate norms, even if those norms—like staying silent about unethical practices—are harmful to the organization.

Our companies often don't want us to do these things, but "company" is a very remote and abstract concept to us *Homo ultrasocialis*. Self-image, social rank, prestige, and reputation, meanwhile, are as concrete and enticing to us as a delicious, calorie-rich meal. And status losses and social exclusion are as painful as a toothache or a broken heart.

So there's always a deep tension between organizations and the people who populate them. An organization wants its members to pursue its goals, while the members themselves want to pursue *their* goals. Anthropologist Joe Henrich thinks this tension has been around as long as we modern humans have. As he writes, "History suggests that all prosocial institutions age and eventually collapse at the hands of self-interest . . . That is, although it may take a long time, individuals and coalitions eventually figure out how to beat or manipulate the system to their own ends, and these techniques spread and slowly corrode any prosocial effects."

"Cooperative enterprise" is a good synonym for "prosocial institution," and a company is very much a cooperative enterprise. Henrich's insight gives us reason to expect that all companies will in some way, at some point, experience the age-old tension between their goals and those of individuals and coalitions.

This tension has absolutely cropped up at Silicon Valley tech companies. In September of 2020, Brian Armstrong, the CEO of the cryptocurrency exchange Coinbase, wrote a blog post about a gap he perceived between his company's goals and the interests of some employees.

It has become common for Silicon Valley companies to engage in a wide variety of social activism, even those unrelated to what the company does, and there are certainly employees who really want this in the company they work for . . .

While I think these efforts are well intentioned, they have the potential to destroy a lot of value at most companies, both by being a

distraction, and by creating internal division...I believe most
employees don't want to work in these divisive environments. They
want to work on a winning team that is united and making progress
toward an important mission.

So, wrote Armstrong in an attempt to realign Coinbase's workforce with its goals,

We won't:

- Debate causes or political candidates internally that are unrelated to work
- Expect the company to represent our personal beliefs externally
- Assume negative intent, or not have each others [*sic*] back
- Take on activism outside of our core mission at work

The leadership of Kraken, another cryptocurrency company, and Basecamp, a twenty-year-old maker of collaboration software, made similar public announcements around the same time. Public reaction to them was intense, and often negative. The changes also caused internal turbulence. More than one-third of Basecamp's sixty employees, for example, announced their intention to leave the company. However, in a tweet posted almost a year after his post, Armstrong maintained that he made the right decision. "We have a much more aligned company now, where we can focus on getting work done toward our mission. And it has allowed us to hire some of the best talent from organizations where employees are fed up with politics, infighting, and distraction."

Cultural flashpoints change over time, but bureaucracy is ageless. It's the oldest and most common way that "individuals and coalitions eventually figure out how to beat or manipulate the system to their own ends." As we saw in chapter 5, bureaucracy causes companies to become sclerotic, uncompetitive messes. Today's tech giants have solved many hard problems, but the gravity-like pull of bureaucratization still bedevils them.

In its early years Facebook was in the eyes of many an archetypal Internet-era company, one that stayed lean and moved fast. But as it aged and became Meta, it bulked up and slowed down. By 2021 it was being described by *New York Times* technology columnist Kevin Roose as a "lumbering bureaucracy." Its growth and valuation soared during the COVID pandemic, but as the lockdowns eased and people around the world returned to in-person interactions, it became clear that Meta had become far too large. In layoffs announced in late 2022 and 2023, the company cut about a quarter of its workforce.

In letters and all-hands meetings accompanying these reductions, Zuckerberg stressed that they weren't just about reducing costs—they were also intended to dismantle the bureaucracy that had been built up. He stressed that the job cuts would "force us to find ways to be scrappier and get things done more efficiently" by trimming "environments or projects where there are too many cooks in the kitchen, which is just a kind of common complaint that I hear over and over again across the whole company." By 2023 Meta's CEO had come to understand bureaucracy's self-perpetuating nature: "As we add different groups, our product teams naturally hire more roles to handle all the interactions with those other groups."

Even at Amazon, a company that enshrined the principle of "bias for action" and stresses the great geek norm of ownership more than any other large organization I'm familiar with, bureaucracy creeps in. Journalist Brad Stone wrote two books about Amazon and its founder, Jeff Bezos. In the second book, *Amazon Unbound,* Stone tells how, as the company grew, Bezos had to intervene periodically to keep his organization lean, focused on his goals, and in Day 1 mode. In 2017, for example, he issued a "span of control" directive mandating that managers take on more direct reports instead of adding more layers to the org chart. According to Stone, this "war against the bureaucracy" caused huge internal turmoil. But it worked. Head-count growth decreased, margins improved, and net income more than doubled in 2018.

But the "giant machinery operated by dwarves" keeps reassembling itself. By 2021, the tech news website *The Information* was reporting that

Andy Jassy, Bezos's successor as CEO, was confronted with creeping bureaucracy both in the company's advertising business and at AWS, where "more paperwork and stricter management styles" kept cropping up.

As all these examples show, the geek way is not effortlessly self-sustaining. Its advocates stressed to me how much work it takes to maintain strong norms of science, ownership, speed, and openness, and how even when they're in place the classic dysfunctions can still creep in. But these norms are still worth pursuing, and fighting for. During a conversation I had with Carl Bass, the former CEO of Autodesk and a mentor to many of Silicon Valley's younger leaders, we came up with my favorite explanation why.

Carl and I are both middle-aged. We agreed that because of our better diets, more regular exercise, and other lifestyle improvements, we are healthier than our fathers were at the same age. Those improvements aren't going to make us immortal, but they are definitely going to help us live longer, healthier lives.

They can also help us keep up with younger folk. As *Outside* magazine puts it, these days "aging professional athletes compete—and win—for decades longer than before." This is not solely because of paleo diets, cryogenic baths, steroids, or any other single factor. It's instead because of innovations in many different areas—nutrition, training, sports medicine, and so on—that are now being brought together to enable longer periods of peak performance.

The geek way is a similar bundle of innovations. The great geek norms of science, ownership, speed, and openness help a company perform at a high level and compete successfully. These same norms also help a company sustain strong performance over time. For how long? That's a crucial question, but one that we just don't know the answer to yet. The geek way is too new. We don't yet know how much it extends the healthy life span of a company, or how long it can be sustained in the face of the dysfunctions that have been around as long as organizations have.

I also don't know where the next cohort of large, innovative, fast-growing, customer- and investor-delighting companies is going to come from. But I do know that they're not going to be following the industrial-era business playbook, because that playbook just doesn't work as well as the geek way.

In the preceding chapters we've seen why this is. Companies following the old playbook rely heavily on the opinions and judgments of experts. While they're listening to experts, however, the experts are listening to their mental press secretary modules. And the job of our press secretaries is not to get to the truth or perceive reality correctly. It's instead to distort reality to make us feel good about ourselves so we can look good to others. Experts are no better than the rest of us at ignoring their press secretaries and seeing things objectively. So we can't just rely on them. Instead, we have to make them (and everyone else) produce a lot of evidence and engage in a lot of argumentation. These two activities are at the heart of science, the best process we've ever come up with for being less wrong over time.

The thoroughly planned-out big projects common to industrial-era companies are going to keep going off track because they spawn liar's clubs. The people involved in these efforts habitually deceive others and themselves about how much progress they're making. By the time these deceptions come to light, it's often too late to get a project done on time. The only sure way to break up the liar's clubs is to stop all the planning and start building in a way that ensures high observability and low plausible deniability. The agile development methods invented and embraced by the geeks do this. These methods also deliver two other major benefits: they let us natural copycats learn more quickly, and they bewilder the competition. Companies that use pre-agile methods can't tap into these benefits.

Because of their belief in the importance of coordination, communication, cross-functional processes, and control, companies following the old playbook become more bureaucratic and sclerotic over time. Work that should be done quickly gets bogged down, good ideas get blocked, and internal politics play an ever-larger role in important decisions. All this happens for the ultimate reason that we ultrasocial human beings like status in all of its forms. Highly coordinated work gives us plenty of places to obtain it, and then resist letting go of it. Realizing this, the business geeks have worked to create environments in which people and teams are simultaneously autonomous and aligned. They have great freedom to act independently—with as few interfaces as possible—and they also know how their work fits into the overall goals and strategy of the company.

As a result of their emphasis on Model 1's norms—striving to win, minimizing losing, being in unilateral control, and suppressing negativity—companies following the industrial-era playbook become defensive. Their people refuse to give an inch or concede a point. They preserve the status quo, stick with things that aren't working, and discourage honest conversations. The fact that they're doing all these things becomes undiscussable, as does the fact that the undiscussables exist. People coming into such companies quickly pick up on their norms, and help perpetuate them. Because the business geeks want very different norms, they work on openness instead of defensiveness. They seek honest feedback, lean in to difficult conversations, acknowledge and try to learn from failures, and pivot when necessary.

Companies that grew up during the industrial era have to throw away that era's playbook if they want to stand a chance when the geeks come to town. The idea that companies following the old playbook can fight back effectively against the geek way by doing a major reorganization, embracing a bold new strategy, or shuffling the leadership is laughable. Incumbents did all of these things over the past twenty years; they didn't halt the disruption, or even slow it down much. The industrial-era playbook yields companies that move too slowly, are wrong too often, miss too many important developments, don't learn and improve quickly enough, and fail to give their people the autonomy, empowerment, purpose, and voice that they want and deserve. These are insurmountable handicaps once competitors start adopting the geek way.

Chapter Summary

None of the business geeks I spoke to for this book think they've discovered the corporate fountain of youth. They don't think that their companies—or anyone else's—have figured out how to be permanently successful.

There's a problem facing all companies. It's that we humans want what we want, and our wants get misaligned with the goals of organizations that we're part of. We create liar's clubs and elaborate bureaucracies. We form coalitions that fight for turf, then fight to keep it. We act defensively and try to be in unilateral control. We work hard to ignore reality when reality makes us look bad. We punish those who violate norms, even if those norms—like not speaking up about unethical practices—are harmful to the organization.

There's always a deep tension between organizations and the people that make them up. An organization wants its members to pursue its goals, while the members themselves want to pursue *their* goals. Today's tech giants have solved many hard problems, but the gravity-like pull of bureaucratization still bedevils them.

The geek way is not effortlessly self-sustaining. Its advocates stressed to me how much work it takes to maintain strong norms of science, ownership, speed, and openness, and how, even when they're in place, the classic dysfunctions can still creep in.

I don't know where the next cohort of large, innovative, fast-growing, customer- and investor-delighting companies is going to come from. But I do know that they're not going to be following the industrial-era business playbook, because that playbook just doesn't work as well as the geek way.

Companies that grew up during the industrial era have to throw away that era's playbook if they want to stand a chance when the geeks come to town.

Acknowledgments

Writing this book felt like a lonely effort. Writing these acknowledgments makes me realize how wrong that feeling is.

Three people deserve special gratitude for putting up with me as I flailed around trying to figure things out. First is my literary agent and consigliere Rafe Sagalyn, who kept finding encouraging ways to say "no." Rafe was steadfast in his belief that there was an important book to be written about the geek way and that I was the person to write it. He was just as adamant, though, that the first twenty or so drafts of my book proposal weren't getting the job done.

When I finally had something that wasn't embarrassing gibberish Rafe showed it to a few editors including Pronoy Sarkar at Little, Brown. Pronoy is more direct than Rafe. As he agreed to buy the book he said to me (as near as I can recall), "You're not going to write the book described in this proposal. You're going to write a better, bigger book." I said back something like, "I'm looking forward to working with you," while thinking of a much shorter response that also ended in "you." But Pronoy was right. We followed the geek way ourselves as we worked together — iterating, arguing, and trying not to be defensive — and wound up with a better, bigger book.

The third person who guided me was my great friend Erez Yoeli, an economist, game theorist, deep thinker, and coauthor of the stellar book *Hidden Games*. Erez and I started talking about us weirdo humans soon after we met and have never stopped. He pushed and clarified my thinking, taught me a ton, and always asked the right questions. Combinations of Rafe, Pronoy, and Erez have been with this book from its start. If you came across something you liked in these pages, chances are excellent that one of them is responsible for it.

I interviewed a bunch of alpha geeks throughout this project, and I'm grateful to all of them. The preceding pages contain quotes from my conversations with (in alphabetical order) Nikesh Arora, Carl Bass, Patrick Collison, Sam Corcos, Liane Hornsey, Drew Houston, Steve Jurvetson, Vinod Khosla, James Manyika, Will Marshall, Satya Nadella, Yamini Rangan, Eric Schmidt, Sebastian Thrun, Hal Varian, and Ardine Williams. Don Sull shared data from his fascinating "Culture 500" project with me, which was generous far beyond normal professional courtesy. Reid Hoffman took our conversation one big step further by offering to write a foreword; I don't quite know how to thank him.

As hazy ideas get turned into a nonfiction book, the "nonfiction" part becomes more and more important. Facts have to be checked, claims supported, data wrangled, and so on. I discovered a while back that the MBA students at MIT Sloan are fantastic colleagues for these tasks and worked with three teams of them: first Roni Grader and Isaac Rahamin, then Roni and Shahar Kidron Shamir, then Roy Reinhorn and Ziv Heimlich Shtacher. They put up with a lot: tight deadlines, sometimes laborious assignments, and an author (me) who alternated between being maddeningly vague ("Find out if America's market capitalization is getting younger") and maddeningly precise ("Shrink the font for the y-axis label one point"). They worked with competence, enthusiasm, and good cheer. And they needed very little encouragement to embrace the geek way and start productively arguing with me.

I bounced ideas and manuscript drafts off many people, and each of the resulting conversations helped me see some aspect of the book better. I want to thank Andrew Anagnost, Sinan Aral, Matt Beane, Erik Brynjolfsson, Thomas Buberl, Ed and Leslie Fine, Carter Gaffney, Adam Grant, Nancy Haller, Maika Hemphill, Carole Hooven, Karen Karniol-Tambour, Vanya Koonce, Ruth Luscombe, David McAfee, James Milin, Michael Muthukrishna, Krizia Quarta, Daniel Rock, Jonathan Ruane, Amy Shepherd, Mustafa Suleyman, David Verrill, and Katherine Zarrella. I know I've forgotten some people who should be on this list, and I'm sorry.

I also want to apologize for the errors found in these pages. They're the only part of the book that I take full credit for.

Notes

Introduction: The Misunderstood Revolution

4   **"a fool or crazy person"**: Tom Chatfield, "Social Media, Doctor Who, and the Rise of the Geeks," *BBC Future*, August 4, 2013, www.bbc.com/future/article/20130805-the-unstoppable -rise-of-the-geeks.

6   **"limitations of muscle power"**: Erik Brynjolfsson and Andrew McAfee, *The Second Machine Age: Work, Progress, and Prosperity in a Time of Brilliant Technologies* (New York: W. W. Norton, 2016), loc. 82–101, Kindle.

6   **"the most influential recent business book"**: "Harvard Business School Risks Going from Great to Good," *The Economist*, May 4, 2017, www.economist.com/business/2017/05/04/harvard -business-school-risks-going-from-great-to-good.

6   **"the pinup boys of the Davos crowd"**: John Thornhill, "When Artificial Intelligence Is Bad News for the Boss," *Financial Times*, June 13, 2017, www.ft.com/content/14588e62-4f88-11e7 -bfb8-997009366969.

7   **In 2018 GE was delisted:** Matt Phillips, "G.E. Dropped from the Dow After More Than a Century," *New York Times*, June 19, 2018, www.nytimes.com/2018/06/19/business/dealbook/general -electric-dow-jones.html.

7   **US newspaper advertising revenues declined:** Derek Thompson, "The Print Apocalypse and How to Survive It," *The Atlantic*, November 3, 2016, www.theatlantic.com/business/archive /2016/11/the-print-apocalypse-and-how-to-survive-it/506429/.

7   **Magazines didn't fare much better:** Kaly Hays, "Magazines' Ad Revenue Continues Decline Despite Some Audience Growth," *Women's Wear Daily*, July 22, 2019, https://wwd.com/feature /magazines-ad-revenue-continues-decline-despite-some-audience-growth-1203224173/.

7   **revenues from recorded music fell:** Paul Resnikoff, "U.S. Recorded Music Revenues 46 Percent Lower," *Digital Music News*, June 15, 2021, www.digitalmusicnews.com/2021/06/15/us-recorded -music-revenues-46-percent-lower/.

7   **"a problem of definition":** Ben Thompson, "Sequoia and Productive Capital," *Stratechery*, October 27, 2021, https://stratechery.com/2021/sequoia-productive-capital/?utm_source=pocket_mylist.

8   **2010 interview with Bill Gates:** Mary Riddell, "Bill Gates: Do I Fly First Class? No, I Have My Own Plane," *Irish Independent*, October 10, 2010, www.independent.ie/business/technology /bill-gates-do-i-fly-first-class-no-i-have-my-own-plane-26691821.html.

8   **"willing to be misunderstood":** John Cook, "Amazon's Bezos on Innovation," *GeekWire*, June 7, 2011, www.geekwire.com/2011/amazons-bezos-innovation/.

11   **long PowerPoint presentation:** "Netflix Culture: Freedom & Responsibility," *Slideshare*, August 1, 2009, www.slideshare.net/reed2001/culture-1798664.

Notes

11 **viewed more than 17 million times:** "Netflix Culture," *Slideshare.*

11 **what Facebook COO Sheryl Sandberg said:** Nancy Hass, "Netflix Founder Reed Hastings: *House of Cards* and *Arrested Development*," *GQ,* January 29, 2013, www.gq.com/story/netflix -founder-reed-hastings-house-of-cards-arrested-development.

11 **asked Hastings to join Facebook's board:** Hass, "Netflix Founder Reed Hastings."

11 **"My main job today":** Henry Blodget, "Jeff Bezos on Profits, Failure, and Making Big Bets," *Business Insider,* December 13, 2014, www.businessinsider.com/amazons-jeff-bezos-on-profits -failure-succession-big-bets-2014-12.

12 **"We both went to Montessori school":** Peter Sims, "The Montessori Mafia," *Wall Street Journal,* April 5, 2011, www.wsj.com/articles/BL-IMB-2034.

13 **"master of his acts":** "Maria Montessori Quotes," American Montessori Society, accessed February 13, 2023, https://amshq.org/About-Montessori/History-of-Montessori/Who-Was-Maria -Montessori/Maria-Montessori-Quotes.

13 **Bezos was also a Montessori kid:** Sims, "Montessori Mafia."

14 **a study published in *Science*:** Angeline Lillard and Nicole Else-Quest, "Evaluating Montessori Education," *Science,* vol. 313, no. 5795 (2006), 1893–94, https://doi.org/10.1126/science.1132362.

15 **how many started off in Montessori schools:** Josh Lerner, "How Do Innovators Think?," *Harvard Business Review,* September 28, 2009, https://hbr.org/2009/09/how-do-innovators-think.

15 **"constantly asking questions":** "What Do Researchers at Harvard Think About Montessori?," *KM School,* accessed February 13, 2023, www.kmschool.org/edu-faq/what-do-researchers-at -harvard-think-about-montessori/.

16 **"Education should aim at destroying free will":** "Johann Gottlieb Fichte," *Wikiquote,* Wikimedia Foundation, accessed February 13, 2023, https://en.wikiquote.org/wiki/Talk:Johann _Gottlieb_Fichte#:~:text=20.,their%20schoolmasters%20would%20have%20wished.

17 **"The great majority of business scholars":** Gad Saad, *Evolutionary Psychology in the Business Sciences* (Heidelberg: Springer, 2011), https://epdf.pub/queue/evolutionary-psychology-in-the -business-sciences.html.

17 **"except in the light of evolution":** Theodosius Dobzhansky, "Nothing in Biology Makes Sense Except in the Light of Evolution," *American Biology Teacher,* vol. 35, no. 3 (1973), 125–29, https://doi.org/10.2307/4444260.

17 **"Evolution didn't stop at the neck":** Ashutosh Jogalekar, "Why Prejudice Alone Doesn't Explain the Gender Gap in Science," *Scientific American,* April 22, 2014, https://blogs.scientific american.com/the-curious-wavefunction/why-prejudice-alone-doesnt-explain-the-gender -gap-in-science/.

17 **Daniel Dennett wrote:** Daniel Dennett, *Darwin's Dangerous Idea* (New York: Simon & Schuster, 1995), 21.

20 **sound even better than a Stradivarius:** Claudia Fritz, Joseph Curtin, Jacques Poitevineau, and Fan-Chia Tao, "Listener Evaluations of New and Old Italian Violins," *Proceedings of the National Academy of Sciences,* vol. 114, no. 21 (2017), 5395–5400, https://doi.org/10.1073/pnas .1619443114.

21 **"voracious consumers of theory":** Dina Gerdeman and Clayton M. Christensen, "What Job Would Consumers Want to Hire a Product to Do? Other," *Working Knowledge,* accessed February 13, 2023, https://hbswk.hbs.edu/item/clay-christensen-the-theory-of-jobs-to-be-done.

21 **childbed fever:** Ignaz Semmelweis, *Etiology, Concept, and Prophylaxis of Childbed Fever,* trans. K. Codell Carter (Madison: University of Wisconsin Press, 1983), 142–43.

21 **Word got around:** Semmelweis, *Etiology,* 69.

22 **"life seemed worthless":** Manya Magnus, *Essential Readings in Infectious Disease Epidemiology* (Sudbury, MA: Jones and Bartlett, 2009), www.google.com/books/edition/Essential_Readings _in_Infectious_Disease/gxub4qxc9j4C?hl=en&gbpv=1&dq=%22made+me+so+miserable+that +life+seemed+worthless%22&pg=PA7&printsec=frontcover.

22 **In April, the maternal mortality rate:** Semmelweis, *Etiology,* 142–43.

23 **committed to a Viennese asylum:** K. Codell Carter and Barbara R. Carter, *Childbed Fever: A Scientific Biography of Ignaz Semmelweis* (New Brunswick, NJ: Transaction Publishers, 2005), 76–78.

24 ***global* average maternal mortality rate:** "Maternal Mortality Ratio," *Our World in Data,* accessed February 15, 2023, https://ourworldindata.org/grapher/maternal-mortality?tab=chart.

25 **turned away from the idea of miasmas:** Thomas Schlich, "Asepsis and Bacteriology: A Realignment of Surgery and Laboratory Science," *Medical History,* vol. 56, no. 3 (2012), 308–34, https:// doi.org/10.1017/mdh.2012.22.

Chapter 1: The Fourfold Path to Geekdom

29 **Breakthrough Award:** Rachel Hoover and Michael Braukus, "NASA's LCROSS Wins 2010 *Popular Mechanics* Breakthrough Award," *NASA,* accessed February 13, 2023, www.nasa.gov /centers/ames/news/releases/2010/10-86AR.html.

29 **Planet now scans the Earth every day:** "Satellite Imagery Analytics," *Planet,* accessed February 13, 2023, www.planet.com/products/planet-imagery/#:-:text=Planet%20operates%20more%20 than%20200,understanding%20of%20changing%20ground%20conditions.

31 **growing at about 40 percent per year:** Jordan Novet, "Amazon's Cloud Revenue Growth Rate Continues to Slow Down in Q3, Now Up 39%," *VentureBeat,* October 23, 2014, https:// venturebeat.com/business/aws-revenue-3q14/.

34 **Doug Bowman, had had enough:** Douglas Bowman, "Goodbye, Google," *StopDesign* (blog), March 20, 2009, https://stopdesign.com/archive/2009/03/20/goodbye-google.html.

34 **"The roots of good design":** "A Selection of Quotes," *Paul Rand,* accessed February 13, 2023, www.paulrand.design/writing/quotes.html.

35 **showed one version of a search results page:** Brian Christian, "The A/B Test: Inside the Technology That's Changing the Rules of Business," *Wired,* April 25, 2012, www.wired.com/2012/04 /ff-abtesting/.

35 **"we don't want high-level executives discussing":** Michael Luca and Max H. Bazerman, "Want to Make Better Decisions? Start Experimenting," *MIT Sloan Management Review,* June 4, 2020, https://sloanreview.mit.edu/article/want-to-make-better-decisions-start-experimenting/.

35 **an additional $200 million:** Alex Hern, "Why Google Has 200m Reasons to Put Engineers over Designers," *The Guardian,* February 5, 2014, www.theguardian.com/technology/2014 /feb/05/why-google-engineers-designers.

35 **"Most websites suck":** Christian, "A/B Test."

35 **Google still employs professional designers:** Jenny Brewer, "How Google Went from Being a Tech Company to a Design Company," *It's Nice That* (blog), March 8, 2022, www.itsnicethat .com/articles/google-visual-design-summit-creative-industry-080322.

37 **Glassdoor started publishing a list:** "Best Places to Work 2020," *Glassdoor,* accessed February 14, 2023, www.glassdoor.com/Award/Best-Places-to-Work-2020-LST_KQ0,24.htm.

38 **"sea of golf shirts":** Barbara Ley Toffler and Jennifer Reingold, *Final Accounting: Ambition, Greed, and the Fall of Arthur Andersen* (New York: Crown, 2004), 369–72.

38 **"overcustomizing your office":** Toffler and Reingold, *Final Accounting,* 695.

40 **Katzenberg flew across the country:** Kim Masters, "How Leonard Nimoy Was Convinced to

Join the First *Star Trek* Movie," *Hollywood Reporter,* February 27, 2015, www.hollywoodreporter .com/news/general-news/how-leonard-nimoy-was-convinced-778379/.

40 **it had climbed to number 1:** Don Hahn, *Waking Sleeping Beauty* (Burbank, CA: Stone Circle Pictures / Walt Disney Studios Motion Pictures, 2009).

40 **acquired by NBCUniversal:** Benjamin Wallace, "Is Anyone Watching Quibi? The Streaming Platform Raised $1.75 Billion and Secured a Roster of A-List Talent, but It Can't Get Audiences to Notice," *Vulture,* July 6, 2020, www.vulture.com/2020/07/is-anyone-watching-quibi.html.

41 **Quibi, which Katzenberg unveiled:** "Quibi," Wikipedia, last modified January 22, 2023, https://en.wikipedia.org/wiki/Quibi.

41 **Hollywood A-listers:** Brian Heater, "The Short, Strange Life of Quibi," *TechCrunch,* October 23, 2020, https://techcrunch.com/2020/10/23/the-short-strange-life-of-quibi/.

41 **how many times the app was downloaded:** "Quibi," Wikipedia.

41 **number 3 in the Apple app store:** Sarah Perez, "Quibi Gains 300k Launch Day Downloads, Hits No. 3 on App Store," *TechCrunch,* April 7, 2020, https://techcrunch.com/2020/04/07/quibi -gains-300k-launch-day-downloads-hits-no-3-on-app-store/.

41 **1.7 million downloads in the first week:** "Quibi Reaches 1.7m Downloads in the First Week," *BBC News,* April 13, 2020, www.bbc.com/news/technology-52275692.

41 **"Yep, Quibi Is Bad":** Kathryn VanArendonk, "Yep, Quibi Is Bad," *Vulture,* April 24, 2020, www.vulture.com/2020/04/the-bites-are-quick-and-bad.html.

42 **"I attribute everything":** Nicole Sperling, "Jeffrey Katzenberg Blames Pandemic for Quibi's Rough Start," *New York Times,* May 11, 2020. www.nytimes.com/2020/05/11/business/media /jeffrey-katzenberg-quibi-coronavirus.html.

42 **TikTok, for example:** Adario Strange, "Netflix's New Short Video Strategy Aims to Succeed Where Quibi Failed," *Quartz,* November 9, 2021, https://qz.com/2086948/netflixs-new-short -video-strategy-could-prove-quibi-was-right.

42 **puzzling shortcomings:** Wallace, "Is Anyone Watching Quibi?"

42 **Whitman took a 10 percent pay cut:** Todd Spangler, "Quibi Says Senior Execs Taking 10% Pay Cut, Denies It's Making Layoffs," *Variety,* June 2, 2020, https://variety.com/2020/digital/news /quibi-pay-cuts-layoffs-katzenberg-whitman-1234624653/.

42 **company's target of 7.4 million:** Allie Gemmill, "How Is Quibi Doing? New Report Shows App May Miss a Subscriber Goal," *Collider,* June 15, 2020, https://collider.com/quibi-subcriber -goal-report-new-details/.

42 **"exploring several strategic options":** Amol Sharma, Benjamin Mullin, and Cara Lombardo, "Quibi Explores Strategic Options Including Possible Sale," *Wall Street Journal,* September 21, 2020, www.wsj.com/articles/quibi-explores-strategic-options-including-a-possible-sale-11600707806.

42 **the Quibi experiment was ending:** Dominic Patten, "Quibi's Jeffrey Katzenberg and Meg Whitman Detail 'Clear-Eyed' Decision to Shut It Down," *Deadline,* October 22, 2020, https:// deadline.com/2020/10/quibi-shuts-down-jeffrey-katzenberg-meg-whitman-interview-exclusive -1234601254/.

43 **A postmortem in the *Wall Street Journal:*** Benjamin Mullin and Lillian Rizzo, "Quibi Was Sup-posed to Revolutionize Hollywood. Here's Why It Failed," *Wall Street Journal,* accessed Febru-ary 14, 2023, www.wsj.com/articles/quibi-was-supposed-to-revolutionize-hollywood-heres-why -it-failed-11604343850?mod=hp_lead_pos5.

43 **returned most remaining cash:** Todd Spangler, "Roku Acquires Global Rights to 75-Plus Quibi Shows, Will Stream Them for Free," *Variety,* January 8, 2021, https://variety.com/2021 /digital/news/roku-acquires-quibi-shows-free-streaming-1234881238/.

43   **On December 1:** Dominic Patten and Dade Hayes, "Quibi Officially Fades to Black, as Projected When Founders Announced Shutdown in October—Update," *Deadline*, December 1, 2020, https://deadline.com/2020/12/quibi-fades-to-black-december-1-jeffery-katzenberg-meg -whitman-1234602207/

43   **these rights were sold:** Spangler, "Roku Acquires Global Rights."

44   **"native to, and only for, the phone":** Josef Adalian, "Quibi Is Finally Here. Wait, What's Quibi?," *Vulture,* April 6, 2020, www.vulture.com/article/what-is-quibi-explained.html.

44   **declined to comment on the record:** Josef Adalian, "Quibi Is for Mobile Streaming and Mobile Streaming Only," *Vulture,* April 6, 2020, www.vulture.com/2020/04/quibi-mobile-phone-app -streaming-tv.html.

44   **"such a cocky pitch environment":** Wallace, "Is Anyone Watching Quibi?"

44   **Katzenberg's certainty was core:** Wallace, "Is Anyone Watching Quibi?"

44   **"an incredible lack of knowledge":** Wallace, "Is Anyone Watching Quibi?"

44   **"I say, 'Where's your data?' ":** Wallace, "Is Anyone Watching Quibi?"

44   **"I don't pretend to know":** Kim Masters, " 'A Bottomless Need to Win': How Quibi's Implosion Shapes Katzenberg's Legacy and Future," *Hollywood Reporter,* August 24, 2021, www .hollywoodreporter.com/business/business-news/a-bottomless-need-to-win-how-quibis -implosion-shapes-katzenbergs-legacy-and-future-4083520/.

44   **Omakase:** Wallace, "Is Anyone Watching Quibi?"

45   **"quinoa-based doggy snack":** Wallace, "Is Anyone Watching Quibi?"

45   **"almost a beta":** Dade Hayes, "Jeffrey Katzenberg: Quibi Hit Covid-19 'Cement Wall,' but Slow Start Is Like a 'Beta' Allowing a Chance to Regroup," *Deadline,* June 19, 2020, https://deadline .com/2020/06/jeffrey-katzenberg-quibi-hit-cement-wall-covid-19-but-slow-start-is-like-a -beta-launch-1202963453/.

45   **a tweet on April 6:** Benedict Evans (@benedictevans), Twitter, April 6, 2020, 4:41 a.m., https:// twitter.com/benedictevans/status/1247081959962050561.

46   **"everything from casting to wardrobe":** JP Mangalindan, "Quibi Leaders' $1.7 Billion Failure Is a Story of Self-Sabotage," *Businessweek,* Bloomberg, November 11, 2020, www.bloomberg.com/news /features/2020-11-11/what-went-wrong-at-quibi-jeffrey-katzenberg-meg-whitman-and-self-sabotage.

46   **his points of comparison:** Wallace, "Is Anyone Watching Quibi?"

46   **"Take the worst parts of Hollywood":** Mangalindan, "Quibi Leaders' $1.7 Billion Failure."

46   **more than fifty-five years old:** Wallace, "Is Anyone Watching Quibi?"

46   **a brilliant summary:** Wallace, "Is Anyone Watching Quibi?"

47   **"mediocre job":** Michelle Conlin, "Netflix: Flex to the Max," *Businessweek,* Bloomberg, September 24, 2007, www.bloomberg.com/news/articles/2007-09-23/netflix-flex-to-the-max.

47   **mailed DVDs to their own houses:** Christopher McFadden, "The Fascinating History of Netflix," *Interesting Engineering,* July 4, 2020, https://interestingengineering.com/culture/the -fascinating-history-of-netflix.

48   **Streaming on Netflix started in 2007:** McFadden, "Fascinating History."

48   **all the downstream Internet traffic:** Todd Spangler, "Netflix Bandwidth Consumption Eclipsed by Web Media Streaming Applications," *Variety,* September 12, 2019, https://variety.com /2019/digital/news/netflix-loses-title-top-downstream-bandwidth-application-1203330313/.

48   **"is the Albanian army going to take over the world":** Dawn Chmielewski, "How Netflix's Reed Hastings Rewrote the Hollywood Script," *Forbes,* September 7, 2020, www.forbes.com /sites/dawnchmielewski/2020/09/07/how-netflixs-reed-hastings-rewrote-the-hollywood -script/?sh=210bb11e15df.

48 **second only to HBO:** Joe Otterson, "*Game of Thrones,* HBO Top Total Emmy Wins," *Variety,* September 23, 2019, https://variety.com/2019/tv/awards/netflix-hbo-2019-emmys-awards-game-of-thrones-1203341183/.

48 **took the lead in nominations:** Christopher Rosen, "HBO Thoroughly Defeated Netflix at the Emmy Awards," *Vanity Fair,* September 21, 2020, www.vanityfair.com/hollywood/2020/09/hbo-netflix-emmys-2020.

48 **nearly fifty-year-old record:** Stephen Battaglio, "Emmys 2021: Netflix Tops HBO with 44 Wins," *Los Angeles Times,* September 19, 2021, www.latimes.com/entertainment-arts/business/story/2021-09-19/emmys-2021-television-awards-scorecard-netflix-queens-gambit.

48 **"one-inch-tall barrier of subtitles":** Nicole Sperling, "From *Call My Agent!* to Hollywood Career," *New York Times,* July 30, 2021, www.nytimes.com/2021/07/30/movies/camille-cottin-call-my-agent-stillwater.html.

48 **platform's most popular show:** Carmen Chin, "*Squid Game* Soars to the Number One Spot on Netflix in the US," *NME,* September 23, 2021, www.nme.com/en_asia/news/tv/squid-game-soars-to-the-number-one-spot-on-netflix-in-the-us-3053012.

48 **almost a hundred other countries:** Joe Flint and Kimberly Chin, "Netflix Reports Jump in Users, Calls *Squid Game* Its Most Popular Show Ever," *Wall Street Journal,* October 19, 2021, www.wsj.com/articles/netflix-adds-more-users-than-it-predicted-boosted-by-squid-game-11634674211.

49 **media columnist Ben Smith:** Ben Smith, "The Week Old Hollywood Finally, Actually Died," *New York Times,* August 16, 2020, www.nytimes.com/2020/08/16/business/media/hollywood-studios-firings-streaming.html.

49 **$47 billion loss:** James B. Stewart, "Was This $100 Billion Deal the Worst Merger Ever?" *New York Times,* November 19, 2022, https://www.nytimes.com/2022/11/19/business/media/att-time-warner-deal.html.

50 **Netflix was particularly hard hit:** Steve Inskeep and Bobby Allyn, "Netflix Is Losing Subscribers for the First Time in a Decade," NPR, April 21, 2022, www.npr.org/2022/04/21/1093977684/netflix-is-losing-subscribers-for-the-first-time-in-a-decade.

50 **"I wouldn't bet against Netflix":** Maureen Dowd, "Ted Sarandos Talks About That Stock Drop, Backing Dave Chappelle, and Hollywood Schadenfreude," *New York Times,* May 31, 2022, www.nytimes.com/2022/05/28/style/ted-sarandos-netflix.html.

50 **"probably a seventy-thirty mix":** Tim Wu, "Netflix's Secret Special Algorithm Is a Human," *The New Yorker,* January 27, 2015, www.newyorker.com/business/currency/hollywoods-big-data-big-deal.

51 **As designer Joshua Porter put it:** Joshua Porter, "The Freedom of Fast Iterations: How Netflix Designs a Winning Web Site," *UIE,* March 25, 2016, https://articles.uie.com/fast_iterations/.

51 **"Greed" Hastings:** Greg Sandoval, "Netflix's Lost Year: The Inside Story of the Price-Hike Train Wreck," *CNET,* July 11, 2012, www.cnet.com/tech/services-and-software/netflixs-lost-year-the-inside-story-of-the-price-hike-train-wreck/.

51 **"Qwikster sounds like a lot of things":** Jason Gilbert, "Qwikster Goes Qwikly: A Look Back at a Netflix Mistake," *HuffPost,* December 7, 2017, www.huffpost.com/entry/qwikster-netflix-mistake_n_1003367.

52 **Elmo smoking a joint:** Greg Kumparak, "The Guy Behind the Qwikster Twitter Account Realizes What He Has, Wants a Mountain of Cash," *TechCrunch,* September 20, 2011, https://techcrunch.com/2011/09/19/the-guy-behind-the-qwikster-twitter-account-realizes-what-he-has-wants-a-mountain-of-cash/.

52 **odd, amateurish video:** "Netflix CEO Reed Hastings Apologizes for Mishandling the Change to Qwikster," YouTube video, 2011, www.youtube.com/watch?v=7tWK0tW1fig.

52 **parodied on *Saturday Night Live:*** "Netflix Apology," *Saturday Night Live,* aired October 1, 2011, YouTube video, uploaded September 18, 2013, www.youtube.com/watch?v=0eAXW-zkGlM.

52 ***Fortune*'s Businessperson of the Year:** Michael V. Copeland, "Reed Hastings: Leader of the Pack," *Fortune,* November 18, 2010, https://fortune.com/2010/11/18/reed-hastings-leader-of -the-pack/.

52 **"Qwikster was a dumb idea":** Gilbert, "Qwikster Goes Qwikly."

52 **Man so much to plan:** Jay Yarow, "Guy Behind Qwikster Account Wants 'Bank,' Will Probably Get Nothing," *Business Insider,* September 20, 2011, https://businessinsider.com/qwikster-account -negotiations-2011-9).

52 **"I knew it was going to be a disaster":** Reed Hastings and Erin Meyer, *No Rules Rules: Netflix and the Culture of Reinvention* (New York: Penguin Press, 2020), 141.

53 **"Socializing is a type of farming for dissent":** Hastings and Meyer, *No Rules Rules,* 144.

54 **"We are focused on streaming":** Hastings and Meyer, *No Rules Rules,* 147.

54 **As Schendel put it:** Hastings and Meyer, *No Rules Rules,* 147.

55 **"I'm just some researcher":** Hastings and Meyer, *No Rules Rules,* 148.

56 **"at Netflix we have pockets":** Hastings and Meyer, *No Rules Rules,* 270.

56 **"innovation, speed, and flexibility":** Hastings and Meyer, *No Rules Rules,* 271.

Chapter 2: Dialed In

62 **As Warren Buffett famously put it:** "In the Short-Run, the Market Is a Voting Machine, but in the Long-Run, the Market Is a Weighing Machine," *Quote Investigator,* January 17, 2020, https:// quoteinvestigator.com/2020/01/09/market/.

63 **The tech-heavy Nasdaq:** Dan Caplinger, "Just How Badly Did Stock Markets Perform in 2022?," *Nasdaq,* December 30, 2022, www.nasdaq.com/articles/just-how-badly-did-stock-markets -perform-in-2022.

67 **Big Nine cultural values:** Donald Sull, Charles Sull, and Andrew Chamberlain, "Measuring Culture in Leading Companies," *MIT Sloan Management Review,* June 24, 2019, https://sloanreview .mit.edu/projects/measuring-culture-in-leading-companies/.

69 **Women make up only a third:** Sam Daley, "Women in Tech Statistics Show the Industry Has a Long Way to Go," *Built In,* March 31, 2021, https://builtin.com/women-tech/women-in-tech -workplace-statistics.

69 **improved by only one percentage point:** Sara Harrison, "Five Years of Tech Diversity Reports—and Little Progress," *Wired,* October 1, 2019, www.wired.com/story/five-years-tech -diversity-reports-little-progress/.

69 **A 2021 analysis by Bloomberg:** Jeff Green, Katherine Chiglinsky, and Cedric Sam, "Billionaire CEOs Elon Musk, Warren Buffett Resist Offering Worker Race Data," Bloomberg, March 21, 2022, www.bloomberg.com/graphics/diversity-equality-in-american-business/#xj4y7vzkg.

72 **"first ranking of its kind":** Daniel Roth, "Behind the Top Attractors: How We Discovered the World's Best Hirers and Keepers of Talent," LinkedIn, June 20, 2016, www.linkedin.com/pulse /behind-top-attractors-how-we-discovered-worlds-best-hirers-roth/.

72 **Journalist Suzy Welch highlighted:** Suzy Welch, "LinkedIn Looked at Billions of Actions to See Who Is Winning the Talent Wars. Here's What I Learned," LinkedIn, June 20, 2016, www .linkedin.com/pulse/linkedin-looked-billions-actions-see-who-winning-talent-suzy-welch /?trk=prof-post.

72 **based on seven pillars:** "Top Companies 2022: The 50 Best Workplaces to Grow Your Career in the U.S.," LinkedIn, April 6, 2022, https://www.linkedin.com/pulse/top-companies-2022-50 -best-workplaces-grow-your-career-us-/.

73 **"Tech companies have raised the bar":** Welch, "LinkedIn Looked at Billions of Actions."

73 **achieving enough female and minority representation:** Green et al., "Billionaire CEOs."

75 **often attributed to the writer Dorothy Parker:** "This Is Not a Novel to Be Tossed Aside Lightly. It Should Be Thrown with Great Force," *Quote Investigator,* September 19, 2021, https:// quoteinvestigator.com/2013/03/26/great-force/#:~:text=From%20a%20review%20by%20 Dorothy,of%20the%20Algonquin%20Round%20Table.

75 *Harvard Business Review* **survey:** Gary Hamel and Michele Zanini, "What We Learned About Bureaucracy from 7,000 *HBR* Readers," *Harvard Business Review,* August 10, 2017, https://hbr.org/2017/08/what-we-learned-about-bureaucracy-from-7000-hbr-readers.

75 **biggest barriers to innovation:** Scott Kirsner, "The Biggest Obstacles to Innovation in Large Companies," *Harvard Business Review,* June 30, 2018, https://hbr.org/2018/07/the-biggest -obstacles-to-innovation-in-large-companies.

75 **"90 percent syndrome":** David N. Ford and John D. Sterman, "The Liar's Club: Concealing Rework in Concurrent Development," *Concurrent Engineering,* vol. 11, no. 3 (2003), 211–19, https://doi.org/10.1177/106329303038028.

75 **essentially no correlation:** Donald Sull, Stefano Turconi, and Charles Sull, "When It Comes to Culture, Does Your Company Walk the Talk?," July 21, 2020, https://sloanreview.mit.edu /article/when-it-comes-to-culture-does-your-company-walk-the-talk/.

75 **no more than half of employees:** Jim Harter, "Obsolete Annual Reviews: Gallup's Advice," *Gallup,* September 28, 2015, www.gallup.com/workplace/236567/obsolete-annual-reviews -gallup-advice.aspx.

75 **sometimes less than 10 percent:** Art Johnson, "Aligning an Organization Requires an Effective Leader," *The Business Journals,* September 12, 2014, www.bizjournals.com/bizjournals/how-to /growth-strategies/2014/09/aligning-organization-requires-effective-leader.html.

76 **forty-seven hours:** Lydia Saad, "The '40-Hour' Workweek Is Actually Longer—by Seven Hours," *Gallup,* August 29, 2014, https://news.gallup.com/poll/175286/hour-workweek-actually -longer-seven-hours.aspx.

76 **as they do asleep:** Jeffrey M. Jones, "In U.S., 40% Get Less Than Recommended Amount of Sleep," *Gallup,* December 19, 2013, https://news.gallup.com/poll/166553/less-recommended -amount-sleep.aspx#:~:text=Americans%20currently%20average%206.8%20hours,nine%20hours %20sleep%20for%20adults.

76 **as much time with their coworkers:** Esteban Ortiz-Ospina, "Who Do We Spend Time with Across Our Lifetime?," *Our World in Data,* December 11, 2020, https://ourworldindata.org/time -with-others-lifetime#from-adolescence-to-old-age-who-do-we-spend-our-time-with.

76 **Fully 70 percent said they would keep working:** Isabel V. Sawhill and Christopher Pulliam, "Money Alone Doesn't Buy Happiness, Work Does," *Brookings,* November 5, 2018, www .brookings.edu/blog/up-front/2018/11/05/money-alone-doesnt-buy-happiness-work-does/.

76 **Social scientist Arthur Brooks:** Arthur C. Brooks, "The Secret to Happiness at Work," *The Atlantic,* September 2, 2021, www.theatlantic.com/family/archive/2021/09/dream-job-values -happiness/619951/.

77 **"confounded by culture":** Boris Groysberg, Jeremiah Lee, Jesse Price, and J. Yo-Jud Cheng, "The Leader's Guide to Corporate Culture," *Harvard Business Review,* January–February 2018, https://hbr.org/2018/01/the-leaders-guide-to-corporate-culture.

77 **"You're going to have a culture anyways":** Dharmesh Shah, "Culture Code: Building a Company You Love," LinkedIn, March 20, 2013, www.linkedin.com/pulse/20130320171133-658789 -culture-code-building-a-company-you-love/.

Chapter 3: Ultra and Ultimate

79 **adult chimps and orangutans:** Esther Herrmann, Josep Call, Hernàndez-Lloreda María Victoria, Brian Hare, and Michael Tomasello, "Humans Have Evolved Specialized Skills of Social Cognition: The Cultural Intelligence Hypothesis," *Science,* vol. 317, no. 5843 (2007), 1360–66, https://doi.org/10.1126/science.1146282.

81 **started to cook at least some of their food:** Ann Gibbons, "The Evolution of Diet," *National Geographic Magazine,* accessed February 13, 2023, www.nationalgeographic.com/foodfeatures /evolution-of-diet/.

81 **cooking food became universal:** Graham Lawton, "Every Human Culture Includes Cooking— This Is How It Began," *NewScientist,* November 2, 2016, www.newscientist.com/article/mg23 230980-600-every-human-culture-includes-cooking-this-is-how-it-began/.

81 **"their experience shows":** Richard Wrangham, *Catching Fire* (New York: Basic Books, 2009), 32.

81 **There's debate:** Ann Gibbons, "The Evolution of Diet," *National Geographic,* https://www .nationalgeographic.com/foodfeatures/evolution-of-diet/.

82 **"obligate dependence":** Richard Wrangham and Rachel Carmody, "Human Adaptation to the Control of Fire," *Evolutionary Anthropology: Issues, News, and Reviews,* vol. 19, no. 5 (2010), 187–99, https://doi.org/10.1002/evan.20275.

82 **If evolution made us:** L. V. Anderson, "Who Mastered Fire?," *Slate,* October 5, 2012, https:// slate.com/technology/2012/10/who-invented-fire-when-did-people-start-cooking.html.

82 **"primarily raw":** "Lenny Kravitz Credits His Rockstar Physique & Energy at 56 to His Vegan Diet," *Peaceful Dumpling* (blog), October 7, 2020, www.peacefuldumpling.com/lenny-kravitz -vegan-diet.

82 **that they don't know:** "How Did the Sentinelese Not Know How to Make Fire?," *Reddit,* accessed February 13, 2023, www.reddit.com/r/AskAnthropology/comments/1qwuxg/how _did_the_sentinelese_not_know_how_to_make_fire/.

83 **culture-possessing animals:** Carolyn Beans, "Can Animal Culture Drive Evolution?," *Proceedings of the National Academy of Sciences,* vol. 114, no. 30 (2017), 7734–37, https://doi.org/10.1073 /pnas.1709475114.

83 **"pinnacle of chimpanzee culture":** Steve Stewart-Williams and Michael Shermer, *The Ape That Understood the Universe: How the Mind and Culture Evolve* (Cambridge: Cambridge University Press, 2021), loc. 19, Kindle.

83 **but they don't build on:** Gillian L. Vale, Nicola McGuigan, Emily Burdett, Susan P. Lambeth, Amanda Lucas, Bruce Rawlings, Steven J. Schapiro, Stuart K. Watson, and Andrew Whiten, "Why Do Chimpanzees Have Diverse Behavioral Repertoires Yet Lack More Complex Cultures? Invention and Social Information Use in a Cumulative Task," *Evolution and Human Behavior,* vol. 42, no. 3 (2021), 247–58, https://doi.org/10.1016/j.evolhumbehav.2020.11.003.

83 **"By 'culture' I mean the large body":** Joseph Patrick Henrich, *The Secret of Our Success: How Culture Is Driving Human Evolution, Domesticating Our Species, and Making Us Smarter* (Princeton, NJ: Princeton University Press, 2016), loc. 3, Kindle.

83 **using a long stick like a spear:** "Orangutan from Borneo Photographed Using a Spear Tool to Fish," *Primatology.net,* https://primatology.wordpress.com/2008/04/29/orangutan-photographed -using-tool-as-spear-to-fish/.

84 **"two chimpanzees carrying a log together":** Jonathan Haidt, *The Righteous Mind: Why Good People Are Divided by Politics and Religion* (New York: Pantheon, 2012), loc. 237, Kindle.

84 **70 million combatants:** T. A. Hughes and John Graham Royde-Smith, "World War II," *Britannica*, February 2, 2023, www.britannica.com/event/World-War-II.

84 **nineteen thousand years to reach Proxima Centauri:** Matt Williams, "How Long Would It Take to Travel to the Nearest Star?," *Universe Today*, January 26, 2016, www.universetoday .com/15403/how-long-would-it-take-to-travel-to-the-nearest-star/#:~:text=In%20short%2C %20at%20a%20maximum,be%20over%202%2C700%20human%20generations.

85 **"the only object in the known universe":** David Deutsch, "After Billions of Years of Monotony, the Universe Is Waking Up," TED video, 2019, www.ted.com/talks/david_deutsch_after _billions_of_years_of_monotony_the_universe_is_waking_up/transcript?language=en.

85 **more than 80 percent of China's population:** "Urban Population (% of Total Population)— China," *World Bank*, accessed February 13, 2023, https://data.worldbank.org/indicator/SP.URB .TOTL.IN.ZS?locations=CN.

85 **In 1970, 10 percent of all births:** Riley Griffin, "Almost Half of U.S. Births Happen Outside Marriage, Signaling Cultural Shift," Bloomberg, October 17, 2018, www.bloomberg.com/news /articles/2018-10-17/almost-half-of-u-s-births-happen-outside-marriage-signaling-cultural -shift?leadSource=uverify+wall.

85 **In 1945, a bit over 11 percent:** Bastian Herre, Esteban Ortiz-Ospina, and Max Roser, "Democracy," *Our World in Data*, accessed February 14, 2023, https://ourworldindata.org/democracy.

86 **"major evolutionary transitions":** Eörs Szathmáry and John Maynard Smith, "The Major Evolutionary Transitions," *Nature*, vol. 374, no. 6519 (1995), 227–32, https://doi.org/10.1038 /374227a0.

86 **development of chromosomes:** Jennifer S. Teichert, Florian M. Kruse, and Oliver Trapp, "Direct Prebiotic Pathway to DNA Nucleosides," *Angewandte Chemie International Edition*, vol. 58, no. 29 (2019), 9944–47, https://doi.org/10.1002/anie.201903400.

86 **appearance of cells with nuclei:** "Eukaryotic Cells," in Geoffrey M. Cooper, *The Cell: A Molecular Approach*, 2nd ed. (Oxford: Oxford University Press, 2000).

86 **dawn of multicellular organisms:** "Ancient Origins of Multicellular Life," *Nature Communications*, vol. 533, no. 7 (2016), 441–41, https://doi.org/10.1038/533441b.

86 **emergence of social insects:** Phillip Barden and Michael S. Engel, "Fossil Social Insects," *Encyclopedia of Social Insects* (2019), 1–21, https://doi.org/10.1007/978-3-319-90306-4_45-1.

86 **"fantastically successful":** Joan E. Strassmann and David C. Queller, "Insect Societies as Divided Organisms: The Complexities of Purpose and Cross-Purpose," in *In the Light of Evolution: Volume I: Adaptation and Complex Design*, John C. Avise and Francisco J. Ayala, editors (Washington, DC: National Academies Press, 2007), 154–64.

87 **one of the most famous experiments:** John M. Darley and C. Daniel Batson, *From Jerusalem to Jericho: A Study of Situational and Dispositional Variables in Helping Behavior* (Princeton, NJ: Darley, 1973), 100–108.

90 **1864 article in *Reformed Presbyterian*:** *The Reformed Presbyterian*, January 1855 through July 1858, 1862–76. United Kingdom: n.p., 1864.

92 **For a TB treatment program in Kenya:** Erez Yoeli, Jon Rathauser, Syon P. Bhanot, Maureen K. Kimenye, Eunice Mailu, Enos Masini, Philip Owiti, and David Rand, "Digital Health Support in Treatment for Tuberculosis," *New England Journal of Medicine*, vol. 381, no. 10 (2019), 986–87, https://doi.org/10.1056/nejmc1806550.

95 **"everybody has plans until they get hit":** "Everybody Has Plans Until They Get Hit for the

First Time," *Quote Investigator,* accessed February 13, 2023, https://quoteinvestigator .com/2021/08/25/plans-hit/.

95 **"On Aims and Methods of Ethology":** Nikolaas Tinbergen, "On Aims and Methods of Ethology," *Zeitschrift für Tierpsychologie,* vol. 20, no. 4 (1963), 410–33, https://doi.org/10.1111/j.1439 -0310.1963.tb01161.x.

97 **"List of Cognitive Biases":** "List of Cognitive Biases," Wikipedia, accessed February 13, 2023, https://en.wikipedia.org/wiki/List_of_cognitive_biases.

97 **"Judgment Under Uncertainty":** Amos Tversky and Daniel Kahneman, "Judgment Under Uncertainty: Heuristics and Biases," *Science,* vol. 185, no. 4157 (1974), 1124–31, https://doi .org/10.1126/science.185.4157.1124.

99 **"Nobody is ever going to invent an ethics class":** "Business Ethics," *Jonathan Haidt* (blog), accessed February 13, 2023, https://jonathanhaidt.com/business-ethics/.

Chapter 4: Science

103 **2007 Stanford podcast:** "Winners Don't Take All," podcast, Center for Social Innovation, Stanford Graduate School of Business, July 29, 2007, https://podcasts.apple.com/us/podcast /winners-dont-take-all/id385633199?i=1000085430490.

105 **"Overconfidence has been called":** Scott Plous, *The Psychology of Judgment and Decision Making* (Philadelphia: Temple University Press, 1993).

105 **"The list [of examples of the confirmation bias]":** Hugo Mercier and Dan Sperber, *The Enigma of Reason* (Cambridge, MA: Harvard University Press, 2018), Kindle.

105 **"new formula for Coke":** Mura Dominko, "This Is the Biggest Mistake Coca-Cola Has Ever Made, Say Experts," *Eat This Not That* (blog), February 13, 2021, www.eatthis.com/news -biggest-coca-cola-mistake-ever/.

106 **"one of the easiest [decisions]":** Constance L. Hays, *The Real Thing: Truth and Power at the Coca-Cola Company* (New York: Random House, 2004), 116.

106 **secretly conducted taste tests:** Hays, *Real Thing,* 116.

106 **eight thousand such calls a day:** Christopher Klein, "Why Coca-Cola's 'New Coke' Flopped," *History,* March 13, 2020, www.history.com/news/why-coca-cola-new-coke-flopped.

106 **Old Cola Drinkers of America:** Klein, "Why Coca-Cola's 'New Coke' Flopped."

106 **"taken away my freedom of choice":** Phil Edwards, "New Coke Debuted 30 Years Ago. Here's Why It Was a Sugary Fiasco," *Vox,* April 23, 2015, www.vox.com/2015/4/23/8472539/new -coke-cola-wars.

106 **At least one lawsuit was filed:** Klein, "Why Coca-Cola's 'New Coke' Flopped."

106 **selling the vintage stuff for $50 per case:** Steve Strauss, "The Very, Very Worst Business Decision in the History of Bad Business Decisions," *Zenbusiness* (blog), December 1, 2021, www.zenbusiness .com/blog/the-very-very-worst-business-decision-in-the-history-of-bad-business-decisions/.

106 **Even Fidel Castro weighed in:** Mark Pendergrast, *For God, Country, and Coca-Cola: The Definitive History of the Great American Soft Drink and the Company That Makes It,* 2nd ed. (New York: Basic Books, 2004), 362.

107 **"we are sorry":** Strauss, "The Very, Very Worst Business Decision."

107 **"after meeting every Friday afternoon":** Daniel Kahneman, *Thinking, Fast and Slow* (New York: Farrar, Straus and Giroux, 2011), loc. 245, Kindle.

108 **"He fell silent":** Kahneman, *Thinking,* loc. 246, Kindle.

109 **"The statistics that Seymour provided":** Kahneman, *Thinking,* loc. 247, Kindle.

109 **"We should have quit":** Kahneman, *Thinking,* loc. 247, Kindle.

109 **In his 2020 book, *The Knowledge Machine:*** Michael Strevens, *The Knowledge Machine: How Irrationality Created Modern Science* (New York: Liveright, 2020).

109 **Robert Kurzban and Athena Aktipis:** Strauss, "The Very, Very Worst Business Decision."

110 **confidence is, in fact, sexy:** Norman P. Li, Jose C. Yong, Ming Hong Tsai, Mark H. Lai, Amy J. Lim, and Joshua M. Ackerman, "Confidence Is Sexy and It Can Be Trained: Examining Male Social Confidence in Initial, Opposite-Sex Interactions," *Journal of Personality,* vol. 88, no. 6 (2020), 1235–51, https://doi.org/10.1111/jopy.12568.

110 **"We must have perseverance":** "Marie Curie the Scientist," *Marie Curie,* accessed February 14, 2023, www.mariecurie.org.uk/who/our-history/marie-curie-the-scientist#:~:text=Marie%20 Curie%20quotes,this%20thing%20must%20be%20attained.%22.

110 **"If you have no confidence in self":** Susan Ratcliffe, ed., *Oxford Essential Quotations* (Oxford: Oxford University Press, 2016).

110 **"you can have a lot of fun":** Joe Namath (@RealJoeNamath), " 'When you have confidence, you can have a lot of fun. And when you have fun, you can do amazing things.' -Thought for the day #Jets #Alabama," Twitter, June 3, 2011, 12:20 p.m., https://twitter.com/RealJoeNamath/status /76684619944169472.

110 **David Mamet's 1987 film:** "*House of Games* Script—Dialogue Transcript," *Drew's Script-O-Rama,* accessed February 14, 2023, www.script-o-rama.com/movie_scripts/h/house -of-games-script-transcript.html.

110 **Robert Trivers argues:** Robert Trivers, "The Elements of a Scientific Theory of Self-Deception," *Annals of the New York Academy of Sciences,* vol. 907, no. 1 (2006), 114–31, https://doi.org /10.1111/j.1749-6632.2000.tb06619.x.

111 **"This entire counterintuitive arrangement":** Robert Trivers, *The Folly of Fools: The Logic of Deceit and Self-Deception in Human Life* (New York: Basic Books, 2014), loc. 9, Kindle.

111 **At one company studied:** Seth Stephens-Davidowitz, *Everybody Lies: What the Internet Can Tell Us About Who We Really Are* (New York: Bloomsbury Publishing, 2018), loc. 107–8, Kindle.

111 **Middle-aged adults:** Trivers, *Folly of Fools,* loc. 143, Kindle.

111 **researchers manipulated photos:** Trivers, *Folly of Fools,* loc. 25, Kindle.

111 **In one particularly devilish study:** Trivers, *Folly of Fools,* loc. 16, Kindle.

112 **"Because of the way evolution operates":** Robert Kurzban, *Why Everyone (Else) Is a Hypocrite: Evolution and the Modular Mind* (Princeton, NJ: Princeton University Press, 2010), 9–22.

113 **clever experimental design:** Joseph E. Ledoux, Donald H. Wilson, and Michael S. Gazzaniga, "A Divided Mind: Observations on the Conscious Properties of the Separated Hemispheres," *Annals of Neurology,* vol. 2, no. 5 (1977), 417–21, https://doi.org/10.1002/ana.410020513.

114 **"no such thing as 'the patient'":** Kurzban, *Why Everyone (Else) Is a Hypocrite,* 9–10.

117 **"a win doesn't feel as good":** Andre Agassi, *Open: An Autobiography* (New York: Alfred A. Knopf, 2009).

117 **some people who lie very infrequently:** Kim B. Serota, Timothy R. Levine, and Tony Docan-Morgan, "Unpacking Variation in Lie Prevalence: Prolific Liars, Bad Lie Days, or Both?," *Communication Monographs,* vol. 89, no. 3 (2021), 307–31, https://doi.org/10.1080/03637751.2021 .1985153.

118 **"a reasonable plan":** Kahneman, *Thinking,* loc. 246, Kindle.

119 **"The most politically knowledgeable individuals":** Michael Hannon, "Are Knowledgeable Voters Better Voters?," *Politics, Philosophy & Economics,* vol. 21, no. 1 (2022), 29–54, https://doi .org/10.1177/1470594x211065080.

120 **write a story about themselves:** Sonya Sachdeva, Rumen Iliev, and Douglas L. Medin, "Sinning

Saints and Saintly Sinners," *Psychological Science,* vol. 20, no. 4 (2009), 523–28, https://doi .org/10.1111/j.1467-9280.2009.02326.x.

122 **"iron rule of explanation":** Strevens, *Knowledge Machine,* loc. 96, Kindle.

123 **Looking back, Schally reflected:** Strevens, *Knowledge Machine,* loc. 34, Kindle.

123 **"All of their need to win":** Strevens, *Knowledge Machine,* loc. 98, Kindle.

125 **"more likely to reject their own bad reasons":** Mercier and Sperber, *Enigma of Reason,* loc. 233, Kindle.

125 **"solitary reasoning is biased and lazy":** Mercier and Sperber, *Enigma of Reason,* loc. 11, Kindle.

126 **"a sublimated essence":** Hays, *Real Thing,* 114.

127 **"It wasn't only about the taste":** Hays, *Real Thing,* 120.

128 **"test literally everything":** Stephens-Davidowitz, *Everybody Lies,* loc. 217, Kindle.

129 **"preview the blur":** Joel M. Podolny and Hansen T. Morten, "How Apple Is Organized for Innovation," *Harvard Business Review,* November–December 2020, https://hbr.org/2020/11 /how-apple-is-organized-for-innovation.

129 **"one of the coolest camera features":** Holland Patrick, "You're Not Using iPhone Portrait Mode Correctly: Here's How to Fix That," *CNET,* May 30, 2021, www.cnet.com/tech/mobile /youre-not-using-iphone-portrait-mode-correctly-heres-how-to-fix/.

130 **"a very gregarious business":** Robert J. Sternberg and Janet E. Davidson, *Creative Insight: The Social Dimension of a Solitary Moment* (Cambridge, MA: MIT Press, 1996), 329–63.

130 **Horowitz was not pleased:** Ben Horowitz, *The Hard Thing About Hard Things* (New York: HarperBusiness, 2014), loc. 13–14, Kindle.

131 **"More shocking, Marc and I eventually became friends":** Horowitz, *Hard Thing,* loc. 14, Kindle.

131 **In a 2016 interview:** Tim Ferriss, "Marc Andreessen (#163)," *The Tim Ferris Show,* podcast, accessed February 14, 2023, https://tim.blog/2018/01/01/the-tim-ferriss-show-transcripts-marc -andreessen/.

133 **dates to the mid-1960s:** Edgar H. Schein and Warren G. Bennis, *Personal and Organizational Change Through Group Methods: The Laboratory Approach* (New York: Wiley, 1965).

134 **men are generally more assertive than women:** Scott Barry Kaufman, "Taking Sex Differences in Personality Seriously," *Scientific American,* December 12, 2019, https://blogs.scientificamerican .com/beautiful-minds/taking-sex-differences-in-personality-seriously/.

134 **neuroatypical people:** Xin Wei, Jennifer W. Yu, Paul Shattuck, Mary McCracken, and Jose Blackorby, "Science, Technology, Engineering, and Mathematics (STEM) Participation Among College Students with an Autism Spectrum Disorder," *Journal of Autism and Developmental Disorders,* vol. 43, no. 7 (2012), 1539–46, https://doi.org/10.1007/s10803-012-1700-z.

134 **eighty thousand improvements and bug fixes:** Noam Cohen, "After Years of Abusive E-mails, the Creator of Linux Steps Aside," *The New Yorker,* September 19, 2018, www.newyorker.com /science/elements/after-years-of-abusive-e-mails-the-creator-of-linux-steps-aside.

135 **"Just kill yourself now":** Jon Gold, "Torvalds to Bad Security Devs: 'Kill Yourself Now,'" *Network World,* March 8, 2012, www.networkworld.com/article/2186639/torvalds-to-bad-security -devs---kill-yourself-now-.html.

135 **"Linus, you're one of the worst offenders":** Sage Sharp, email, July 15, 2013, www.spinics.net /lists/stable/msg14037.html.

135 **"I curse when there isn't any argument":** Linus Torvalds, email, July 15, 2013, https://lkml .org/lkml/2013/7/15/446.

135 **would no longer be a Linux kernel developer:** Sage Sharp, "Closing a Door," *Sage Sharp* (blog), September 14, 2019, https://sage.thesharps.us/2015/10/05/closing-a-door/.

136 **confronted by *The New Yorker:*** Cohen, "After Years of Abusive E-mails."

136 **"I had really been ignoring":** Michael Grothaus, "Linux Creator Linus Torvalds Apologizes for Being a Dick All These Years," *Fast Company,* September 17, 2018, www.fastcompany .com/90237651/linux-creator-linus-torvalds-apologizes-for-being-a-dick-all-these-years.

137 **shareholders of Computer Associates:** Ariana Eunjung Cha, "Judge Cuts Execs' $1-Billion Stock Bonus in Half," *Los Angeles Times,* November 10, 1999, www.latimes.com/archives /la-xpm-1999-nov-10-fi-31864-story.html.

137 **booked a lot of the revenue:** Alex Berenson, "A Software Company Runs out of Tricks; the Past May Haunt Computer Associates," *New York Times,* April 29, 2001, www.nytimes.com/2001 /04/29/business/a-software-company-runs-out-of-tricks-the-past-may-haunt-computer-associates .html.

137 **"thirty-five-day month":** "How Serious Was the Fraud at Computer Associates?," *Knowledge at Wharton,* accessed February 14, 2023, https://knowledge.wharton.upenn.edu/article/how-serious -was-the-fraud-at-computer-associates/#:~:text=They%20paid%20more%20than%20they,once %20the%20practices%20were%20revealed.

137 **SEC filed securities fraud charges:** "SEC Files Securities Fraud Charges Against Computer Associates International, Inc., Former CEO Sanjay Kumar, and Two Other Former Company Executives," SEC, accessed February 14, 2023, www.sec.gov/news/press/2004-134.htm.

137 **Kumar, who had been Computer Associates' CEO:** Michael J. de la Merced, "Ex-Leader of Computer Associates Gets 12-Year Sentence and Fine," *New York Times,* November 3, 2006, www.nytimes.com/2006/11/03/technology/03computer.html.

137 **hard-charging sales culture:** Randall Smith, "Copying Wells Fargo, Banks Try Hard Sell," *Wall Street Journal,* February 28, 2011, www.wsj.com/articles/SB1000142405274870443030457 6170702480420980.

137 **12,000 new products:** Bethany McLean, "How Wells Fargo's Cutthroat Corporate Culture Allegedly Drove Bankers to Fraud," *Vanity Fair,* May 31, 2017, www.vanityfair.com/news/2017 /05/wells-fargo-corporate-culture-fraud.

138 **3.5 million fake accounts:** Kevin McCoy, "Wells Fargo Review Finds 1.4m More Potentially Unauthorized Accounts," *USA Today,* August 31, 2017, www.usatoday.com/story/money/2017 /08/31/wells-fargo-review-finds-1-4-m-more-unauthorized-accounts/619794001/.

138 **more than $2.5 billion in fines:** "Attorney General Shapiro Announces $575 Million 50-State Settlement with Wells Fargo Bank for Opening Unauthorized Accounts and Charging Consumers for Unnecessary Auto Insurance, Mortgage Fees," Pennsylvania Office of Attorney General, December 28, 2018, www.attorneygeneral.gov/taking-action/attorney-general-shapiro-announces -575-million-50-state-settlement-with-wells-fargo-bank-for-opening-unauthorized-accounts -and-charging-consumers-for-unnecessary-auto-insurance-mortgage-fees/.

138 **"when a measure becomes a target":** Michael F Stumborg, Timothy D. Blasius, Steven J. Full, and Christine A. Hughes, "Goodhart's Law: Recognizing and Mitigating the Manipulation of Measures in Analysis," *CNA,* September 2022, www.cna.org/reports/2022/09/goodharts-law #:~:text=Goodhart%27s%20Law%20states%20that%20%E2%80%9Cwhen,order%20to %20receive%20the%20reward.

138 **tweeted a photo of himself:** Patrick Collison (@patrickc), "Hit our engagement metrics this weekend! 😂," Twitter, June 23, 2019, 8:33 p.m., https://twitter.com/patrickc/status/1142953801 969573889?lang=en.

139 **"OKRs and compensation":** John E. Doerr, *Measure What Matters: How Google, Bono, and the Gates Foundation Rock the World with OKRs* (New York: Portfolio/Penguin, 2018), loc. 181–82, Kindle.

140 **"A zealous anchorwoman":** Nicholas Negroponte, *Being Digital* (New York: Alfred A. Knopf, 1996).

141 **"you will be drawn to science itself":** Trivers, *Folly of Fools,* loc. 303, Kindle.

141 **"The study of books":** Michel de Montaigne, *Essays,* trans. Charles Cotton (1686), https://hyperessays.net/essays/on-the-art-of-discussion/.

142 **chaos engineering:** Scott Carey, "What Is Chaos Monkey? Chaos Engineering Explained," *InfoWorld,* May 13, 2020, www.infoworld.com/article/3543233/what-is-chaos-monkey-chaos-engineering-explained.html.

Chapter 5: Ownership

145 **discussed on the CIA's website:** "The Art of Simple Sabotage," Central Intelligence Agency, April 1, 2019, www.cia.gov/stories/story/the-art-of-simple-sabotage/.

146 **"The consultants were available now":** Reed Hastings and Erin Meyer, *No Rules Rules: Netflix and the Culture of Reinvention* (New York: Penguin Press, 2020), 66 –67.

147 **"specific form of organization":** Bert Rockman, "Bureaucracy," *Britannica,* accessed January 6, 2023, www.britannica.com/topic/bureaucracy.

147 **"However many people complain":** "Max Weber Quotations," *QuoteTab,* accessed February 15, 2023, www.quotetab.com/quotes/by-max-weber.

147 **survey on bureaucracy:** Gary Hamel and Michele Zanini, "What We Learned About Bureaucracy from 7,000 *HBR* Readers," *Harvard Business Review,* August 10, 2017, https://hbr.org/2017/08/what-we-learned-about-bureaucracy-from-7000-hbr-readers.

147 **18 percent of the workforce:** Jena McGregor, "Zappos Says 18 Percent of the Company Has Left Following Its Radical 'No Bosses' Approach," *Washington Post,* January 14, 2016, https://www.washingtonpost.com/news/on-leadership/wp/2016/01/14/zappos-says-18-percent-of-the-company-has-left-following-its-radical-no-bosses-approach/.

147 **"quietly backed away":** Aimee Groth, "Zappos Has Quietly Backed Away from Holacracy," *Quartz,* January 29, 2020, https://qz.com/work/1776841/zappos-has-quietly-backed-away-from-holacracy.

148 **"promiscuous distribution":** Lawrence H. Summers, "Why Americans Don't Trust Government," *Washington Post,* May 26, 2016, www.washingtonpost.com/news/wonk/wp/2016/05/26/why-americans-dont-trust-government/.

148 **vetocracies:** Ezra Klein, "Francis Fukuyama: America Is in 'One of the Most Severe Political Crises I Have Experienced,'" *Vox,* October 26, 2016, www.vox.com/2016/10/26/13352946/francis-fukuyama-ezra-klein.

148 **40 percent faster than the American economy:** "Reg Stats," Regulatory Studies Center, Trachtenberg School of Public Policy and Public Administration, Columbian College of Arts and Sciences, George Washington University, accessed February 15, 2023, https://regulatorystudies.columbian.gwu.edu/reg-stats.

148 **relatively minor repairs:** Summers, "Why Americans Don't Trust Government."

149 **buying Ferrari outright:** Angus MacKenzie, "What if Ford Had Bought Ferrari?," *Motor Trend,* June 16, 2008, www.motortrend.com/features/what-if-ford-had-bought-ferrari-1895/. Accessed March 16, 2023.

149 **3 percent of Ford's profits:** "Ford Co. Attains Record Earnings," *New York Times,* February 5, 1964, www.nytimes.com/1964/02/05/ford-co-attains-record-earnings.html#:~:text=Ford%20Motor%20Company%20registered%20record,equal%20to%20%244.42%20a%20share.

Notes

150 **Enzo Ferrari's personal secretary:** Luca Ciferri, "Story Reveals Why Enzo Ferrari Said No to Ford," *Automotive News,* August 31, 1998, www.autonews.com/article/19980831/ANA/808310794 /story-reveals-why-enzo-ferrari-said-no-to-ford.

150 **"giant machinery operated by dwarves":** "Honoré de Balzac," *Wikiquote,* Wikimedia Foundation, January 9, 2023, https://en.wikiquote.org/wiki/Honor%C3%A9_de_Balzac.

151 **displaying their formidability:** Brian Barth, "The Secrets of Chicken Flocks' Pecking Order," *Modern Farmer,* October 18, 2018, https://modernfarmer.com/2016/03/pecking-order/.

151 **"driven by a multitude of desires":** Will Storr, *The Status Game: On Human Life and How to Play It* (London: William Collins, 2022), 5.

152 **70 percent chose a higher-status job:** Storr, *Status Game,* 26.

152 **"there was no point":** Storr, *Status Game,* 89.

152 **"esteem given by others":** Storr, *Status Game,* 89.

152 **Whitehall studies:** M. G. Marmot, Geoffrey Rose, M. Shipley, and P. J. S. Hamilton, "Employment Grade and Coronary Heart Disease in British Civil Servants," *Journal of Epidemiology & Community Health,* vol. 32, no. 4 (1978), 244–49, https://doi.org/10.1136/jech.32.4.244.

152 **"It was the new position":** Storr, *Status Game,* 17.

152 **"objective indicators of low social status":** Storr, *Status Game,* 17–18.

153 **"Suicide is encouraged":** Jason Manning, *Suicide: The Social Causes of Self-Destruction* (Charlottesville: University of Virginia Press, 2020), 728.

153 **"as real as oxygen or water":** Storr, *Status Game,* 19.

153 **"exceedingly accurate":** C. Anderson, J. A. D. Hildreth, and L. Howland, "Is the Desire for Status a Fundamental Human Motive? A Review of the Empirical Literature," *Psychological Bulletin,* March 16, 2015.

153 **shifted his low tones:** Stanford W. Gregory and Stephen Webster, "A Nonverbal Signal in Voices of Interview Partners Effectively Predicts Communication Accommodation and Social Status Perceptions," *Journal of Personality and Social Psychology,* vol. 70, no. 6 (1996), 1231–40, https://doi.org/10.1037/0022-3514.70.6.1231.

154 **"I had to learn the hard way":** Christopher Boehm, *Hierarchy in the Forest: The Evolution of Egalitarian Behavior* (Cambridge, MA: Harvard University Press, 2001), 16.

154 **formidability:** Aaron Sell, John Tooby, and Leda Cosmides, "Formidability and the Logic of Human Anger," *Proceedings of the National Academy of Sciences,* vol. 106, no. 35 (2009), 15073–78, https://doi.org/10.1073/pnas.0904312106.

154 **"the most ferocious fighter":** "Mike Tyson? Sonny Liston? Who Is the Scariest Boxer Ever?" *Sky Sports,* November 12, 2015, https://www.skysports.com/boxing/news/12184/10045648/mike -tyson-sonny-liston-who-is-the-scariest-boxer-ever#:~:text=Mike%20Tyson%20(50%2D6 %2DKO44)&text=Perhaps%20the%20most%20ferocious%20fighter,it%20he%20was%20 intimidation%20personified.

156 **"seized through brute force":** Storr, *Status Game,* 328.

157 **retired four-star general Bill Creech:** Bill Creech, *The Five Pillars of TQM: How to Make Total Quality Management Work for You* (New York: Truman Talley / Dutton, 1994), 387.

157 **management scholar Ruthanne Huising:** Ruthanne Huising, "Moving off the Map: How Knowledge of Organizational Operations Empowers and Alienates," *Organization Science,* vol. 30, no. 5 (2019), 1054–75, https://doi.org/10.1287/orsc.2018.1277.

158 **"Show me the incentive":** "The Psychology of Human Misjudgement—Charlie Munger Full Speech," YouTube video, uploaded July 12, 2020, https://youtu.be/Jv7sLrON7QY.

158 **von Stauffenberg principle:** Aharon Liebersohn, *World Wide Agora* (self-pub., Lulu.com, 2006).

159 **Bill Gates wrote a memo:** Bill Gates, "The Internet Tidal Wave," memorandum, May 26, 1995, U.S. Department of Justice, accessed March 1, 2023, www.justice.gov/sites/default/files/atr /legacy/2006/03/03/20.pdf.

159 **almost $620 billion:** Ashleigh Macro, "Apple Beats Microsoft as Most Valuable Public Company in History," *Macworld*, August 21, 2012, www.macworld.com/article/669851/apple-beats -microsoft-as-most-valuable-public-company-in-history.html.

159 **spent well over $80 billion:** Lionel Sujay Vailshery, "Microsoft's Expenditure on Research and Development from 2002 to 2022," *Statista*, July 28, 2022, www.statista.com/statistics/267806 /expenditure-on-research-and-development-by-the-microsoft-corporation/.

159 **2012 *Vanity Fair* article:** Kurt Eichenwald, "Microsoft's Lost Decade," *Vanity Fair*, July 24, 2012, www.vanityfair.com/news/business/2012/08/microsoft-lost-mojo-steve-ballmer.

160 **"The developer concluded":** Eichenwald, "Microsoft's Lost Decade."

161 **"People realized":** Eichenwald, "Microsoft's Lost Decade."

161 **"Marc Turkel":** Eichenwald, "Microsoft's Lost Decade."

162 **In 2011 Microsoft made its bad situation:** Stephen Miller, " 'Stack Ranking' Ends at Microsoft, Generating Heated Debate," *SHRM*, November 20, 2013, www.shrm.org/resourcesandtools /hr-topics/compensation/pages/stack-ranking-microsoft.aspx.

162 **"every current and former":** Eichenwald, "Microsoft's Lost Decade."

162 **Microsoft engineer Brian Cody:** Eichenwald, "Microsoft's Lost Decade."

162 **"People responsible for features":** Eichenwald, "Microsoft's Lost Decade."

163 **"people planned their days":** Eichenwald, "Microsoft's Lost Decade."

163 **"Whenever I had a question":** Eichenwald, "Microsoft's Lost Decade."

163 **"I wanted to build a team":** Eichenwald, "Microsoft's Lost Decade."

164 **full-blown stampedes:** Sky News Australia, "Stunning Toilet Paper Feeding Frenzy Caught on Camera," YouTube video, March 10, 2020, https://youtu.be/df6K9qMr67w.

164 **Amazon and other sites clamped down on it:** Mary Jo Daley and Tom Killion, "Amazon Is Playing Whack-a-Mole with Coronavirus Price Gouging, and It's Harming Pennsylvanians," *Philadelphia Inquirer*, April 13, 2020, www.inquirer.com/opinion/commentary/coronavirus -covid-price-gouging-amazon-online-retail-toilet-paper-20200413.html.

164 **Walmart's CEO went on the *Today* show:** Sharon Terlep, "Americans Have Too Much Toilet Paper. Finally, Sales Slow," *Wall Street Journal*, April 13, 2021, www.wsj.com/articles/americans -have-too-much-toilet-paper-it-is-catching-up-to-companies-11618306200.

164 **"pockets of lower than normal availability":** Lisa Baertlein and Melissa Fares, "Panic Buying of Toilet Paper Hits U.S. Stores Again with New Pandemic Restrictions," *Reuters*, November 20, 2020, www.reuters.com/article/us-health-coronavirus-toiletpaper/panic-buying-of-toilet-paper -hits-u-s-stores-again-with-new-pandemic-restrictions-idUSKBN2802W3.

167 **sychronized business processes:** David A Garvin, "Leveraging Processes for Strategic Advantage," *Harvard Business Review*, September–October 1995, https://hbr.org/1995/09/leveraging -processes-for-strategic-advantage.

168 **The 2016 letter opens with an explanation:** Amazon Staff [Jeff Bezos], "2016 Letter to Shareholders," *About Amazon*, April 17, 2017, www.aboutamazon.com/news/company-news/2016 -letter-to-shareholders.

169 **"unencumbered by competing responsibilities":** Colin Bryar and Bill Carr, *Working Backwards* (London: Pan Macmillan, 2022), 54.

170 **"Amazon is hundreds":** Benedict Evans, "The Amazon Machine," *Benedict Evans* (blog), February 4, 2021, www.ben-evans.com/benedictevans/2017/12/12/the-amazon-machine.

171 **"cross-functional projects"**: Bryar and Carr, *Working Backwards*, 72.

171 **"eliminate communication, not encourage it"**: Bryar and Carr, *Working Backwards*, 72.

172 **"At the next Quarterly Business Review"**: Hastings and Meyer, *No Rules Rules*, 63.

173 **a management process called V2MOM**: Marc Benioff, "Create Strategic Company Alignment with a V2MOM," *The 360 Blog*, Salesforce.com, December 5, 2022, www.salesforce.com/blog /how-to-create-alignment-within-your-company/.

173 **"When I was at Oracle"**: Marc R. Benioff and Carlye Adler, *Behind the Cloud: The Untold Story of How Salesforce.com Went from Idea to Billion-Dollar Company—and Revolutionized an Industry* (San Francisco: Jossey-Bass, 2010), 225.

174 **presented it to Benioff**: Eugene Kim, "These Are the Five Questions Salesforce Asks Itself Before Every Big Decision," *Business Insider*, February 15, 2023, www.businessinsider.com/salesforce -v2mom-process-2015-2.

174 **"we've expanded the scope"**: Benioff, "Create Strategic Company Alignment."

175 **"the biggest secret of Salesforce.com"**: Benioff and Adler, *Behind the Cloud*, 225.

175 **"a mere 7 percent of employees"**: Art Johnson, "Aligning an Organization Requires an Effective Leader," *The Business Journals*, September 12, 2014, https://gottareadsomethinggood.com /2019/03/28/how-to-create-alingment-within-your-company-in-order-to-succeed-by-marc -benioff/.

175 **"State of the American Manager"**: Jim Harter, "Obsolete Annual Reviews: Gallup's Advice," *Gallup*, January 30, 2023, www.gallup.com/workplace/236567/obsolete-annual-reviews-gallup -advice.aspx.

178 **which of three emails they would receive**: Bryar and Carr, *Working Backwards*, 63.

178 **"The NPI process was not beloved"**: Bryar and Carr, *Working Backwards*, 64.

179 **"duct tape and WD-40"**: Luke Timmerman, "Amazon's Top Techie, Werner Vogels, on How Web Services Follows the Retail Playbook," *Xconomy*, September 29, 2010, https://xconomy .com/seattle/2010/09/29/amazons-top-techie-werner-vogels-on-how-web-services-follows -the-retail-playbook/.

179 **"look like stoned hippies"**: David Streitfeld and Christine Haughney, "Expecting the Unexpected from Jeff Bezos," *New York Times*, August 17, 2013, www.nytimes.com/2013/08/18 /business/expecting-the-unexpected-from-jeff-bezos.html.

179 **"was so out there"**: chitchcock [Chris Hitchcock], "Stevey's Google Platforms Rant," *Gist*, accessed February 15, 2023, https://gist.github.com/chitchcock/1281611.

180 **"The [new, modular] Amazon development environment"**: Charlene O'Hanlon, "A Conversation with Werner Vogels," *ACM Queue*, May 1, 2006, https://dl.acm.org/doi/10.1145/1142055 .1142065.

180 **"Our annual employee poll"**: Satya Nadella, Greg Shaw, and Jill Tracie Nichols, *Hit Refresh* (New York: HarperCollins, 2017), 66–67.

181 **"find meaning in our work"**: Chris Ciaccia, "Satya Nadella Is Quoting Oscar Wilde in His First Email as Microsoft CEO," *TheStreet*, February 4, 2014, www.thestreet.com/technology /satya-nadella-is-quoting-oscar-wilde-in-his-first-email-as-microsoft-ceo-12305159.

182 **"debate and argument are essential"**: Nadella, Shaw, and Nichols, *Hit Refresh*, 81.

182 **"agility, agility, agility"**: Nadella, Shaw, and Nichols, *Hit Refresh*, 51.

182 **"Our culture had been rigid"**: Nadella, Shaw, and Nichols, *Hit Refresh*, 100.

183 **"extraordinary individual experience"**: Nadella, Shaw, and Nichols, *Hit Refresh*, 5.

183 **"Dr. Gervais was curious"**: Nadella, Shaw, and Nichols, *Hit Refresh*, 5.

183 **"personal passions and philosophies"**: Nadella, Shaw, and Nichols, *Hit Refresh*, 5–6.

184 **"War is older"**: John Tooby and Leda Cosmides, "Groups in Mind: The Coalitional Roots of War and Morality," in *Human Morality and Sociality: Evolutionary and Comparative Perspectives*, Henrik Høgh-Olesen, editor (London: Palgrave-Macmillan, 2010): 91–234.

185 **"pathetically easy to form"**: Robert Trivers, *The Folly of Fools: The Logic of Deceit and Self-Deception in Human Life* (New York: Basic Books, 2011).

186 **"In an intense prep session"**: Nadella, Shaw, and Nichols, *Hit Refresh*, 67.

Chapter 6: Speed

190 **an entirely new platform:** https://newsroom.vw.com/vehicles/the-electric-vehicle-module/.

190 **"intelligent design, identity, and visionary technologies"**: "First Member of the ID. Family Is Called ID.3," *Volkswagen*, accessed March 2, 2023, www.volkswagenag.com/en/news/2019/05 /VW_brand_ID3.html#.

190 **more than thirty-three thousand people:** Mark Kane, "Volkswagen ID.3 1st Reservations Hit 33,000," *InsideEVs*, September 13, 2019, https://insideevs.com/news/370583/33000-have-reserved -volkswagen-id3-1st/.

191 ***Manager Magazin* reported:** Michael Freitag, "Volkswagen AG: Elektroauto ID.3 MIT Massiven Softwareproblemen," *Manager Magazin*, December 19, 2019, www.manager-magazin.de /unternehmen/autoindustrie/volkswagen-ag-elektroauto-id-3-mit-massiven-softwareproblemen -a-1301896.html.

191 **Tesla had pioneered:** Steve Hanley, "Volkswagen Has 'Massive Difficulties' with ID.3 Software, Previews ID.7 Bulli," *CleanTechnica*, December 22, 2019, https://cleantechnica.com/2019/12/22 /volkswagen-has-massive-difficulties-with-id-3-software-previews-id-7-bulli/.

191 **frantic, all-hands-on-deck effort:** Michael Freitag, "(M+) Volkswagen AG: Herbert Diess Muss Den Start Des Id.3 Retten," *Manager Magazin*, February 20, 2020, www.manager-magazin.de /unternehmen/volkswagen-ag-herbert-diess-muss-den-start-des-id-3-retten-a-00000000-0002 -0001-0000-000169534497.

191 **"complete nonsense"**: R/Teslainvestorsclub, "More Problems at Volkswagen," *Reddit*, February 5, 2020, www.reddit.com/r/teslainvestorsclub/comments/f950gs/more_problems_at_volks wagen_translation_from/. Translation from *Manager Magazin*, "Volkswagen—Showdown in Hall 74."

191 **would not happen until September:** "ID.3 1st Deliveries Begin in Early September," *Volkswagen Newsroom*, June 10, 2020, www.volkswagen-newsroom.com/en/press-releases/id3-1st -deliveries-begin-in-early-september-6122.

191 **stripped Diess of his title:** "VW's Diess Was Stripped of Key Role amid Infighting, Reports Say," *Automotive News Europe*, June 9, 2020, https://europe.autonews.com/automakers/vws -diess-was-stripped-key-role-amid-infighting-reports-say.

191 **long rows of ID.3s:** Fred Lambert, "Tesla Updating Software of a Fleet in Parking Lot Looks Like the Aliens Are Coming," *Electrek*, February 7, 2021, https://electrek.co/2021/02/07/tesla -updating-software-fleet-parking-lot-aliens-coming/.

191 **"Effective immediately"**: "Volkswagen Introduces Over-the-Air Updates for All ID. Models," September 13, 2021, www.volkswagenag.com/en/news/2021/09/Volkswagen_introduces_Over -the-Air_Updates.html.

191 **"After months of delays"**: Stephen Menzel, "Digitalisierung Im Auto: ID-Modelle Von Volks-wagen Bekommen Endlich Neue Software," *Handelsblatt*, July 22, 2022, www.handelsblatt .com/unternehmen/industrie/digitalisierung-im-auto-id-modelle-von-volkswagen-bekommen -endlich-neue-software/28538284.html.

Notes

192 **Diess announced that he was stepping down:** Jay Ramey, "Here's Why VW Ousted Its CEO, Herbert Diess," *Autoweek,* July 25, 2022, www.autoweek.com/news/green-cars/a40706421/vw -ceo-herbert-diess-ouster-evs-cariad-electric-models/.

192 **"the state of the auto industry":** Stefan Nicola, "Porsches Postponed by Buggy Software Cost VW's CEO Herbert Diess His Job," Bloomberg, July 25, 2022, www.bloomberg.com/news/arti cles/2022-07-25/porsches-postponed-by-buggy-software-cost-vw-s-ceo-his-job#xj4y7vzkg.

192 **Tesla, meanwhile:** Steven Loveday, "How Often Does Tesla Send OTA Updates and How Important Are They?," *InsideEVs,* January 10, 2022, https://insideevs.com/news/559836/tesla -ota-updates-revealed-explained/.

192 **more substantial changes:** Bianca H., "A Timeline of All Software Updates: Tesla Model 3 Fleet," *Movia News,* January 21, 2021, https://movia.news/software-updates-model-3/.

192 **Failure rates have held steady:** Herb Krasner, "New Research: The Cost of Poor Software Qual- ity in the US: A 2020 Report," *CISQ,* Consortium for Information and Software Quality, accessed February 15, 2023, http://it-cisq.org/pdf/CPSQ-2020-report.pdf.

192 **"all but impossible":** Ralph Vartabedian, "Years of Delays, Billions in Overruns: The Dismal History of Big Infrastructure," *New York Times,* November 28, 2021, www.nytimes.com /2021/11/28/us/infrastructure-megaprojects.html.

193 **"Overly optimistic forecasts":** Daniel Kahneman, *Thinking, Fast and Slow* (New York: Farrar, Straus and Giroux, 2011), 250.

193 **talked to more than a dozen former employees:** Mikko-Pekka Heikkinen, "Knock, Knock, Nokia's Heavy Fall," *Dominies Communicate* (blog), February 15, 2016, https://dominies communicate.wordpress.com/2016/02/15/knock-knock-nokias-heavy-fall/amp/.

195 **When work began:** Kurt Eichenwald, "How Microsoft Lost Its Mojo: Steve Ballmer and Corpo- rate America's Most Spectacular Decline," *Vanity Fair,* July 24, 2012, www.vanityfair.com /news/business/2012/08/microsoft-lost-mojo-steve-ballmer.

195 **"this is the best Microsoft could do":** Don Tynan, "The 15 Biggest Tech Disappointments of 2007," *PCWorld,* December 16, 2007, https://web.archive.org/web/20071219030508/www .pcworld.com/printable/article/id,140583/printable.html.

195 **a few frank paragraphs:** Willie Brown, "When Warriors Travel to China, Ed Lee Will Follow," *San Francisco Chronicle,* July 27, 2013, www.sfgate.com/bayarea/williesworld/article/When -Warriors-travel-to-China-Ed-Lee-will-follow-4691101.php.

196 **initial budget for the Transbay Terminal:** Joshua Sabatini, "SF to Bail Out Transbay Project After Costs Nearly Double," *San Francisco Examiner,* April 28, 2016, www.sfexaminer.com /news/sf-to-bail-out-transbay-project-after-costs-nearly-double/article_15e626fd-3b00-5cb1 -878b-11ccd09b1e8a.html.

196 **workers found structural flaws:** Phil Matier and Andy Ross, "Transbay Transit Center Closed After Crack Found in Steel Beam," *San Francisco Chronicle,* September 25, 2018.

197 **so many big projects are completed late:** David N. Ford and John D. Sterman, "The Liar's Club: Concealing Rework in Concurrent Development," *Concurrent Engineering,* vol. 11, no. 3 (2003), 211–19, https://doi.org/10.1177/106329303038028.

197 **A manager they interviewed:** Ford and Sterman, "Liar's Club."

198 **"Estimates of the fraction of work completed":** Robert Laurence Baber, *Software Reflected* (New York: North-Holland, 1982).

203 **[One] executive engineer:** Ford and Sterman, "Liar's Club."

203 **"the consequence, of course":** Ford and Sterman, "Liar's Club."

204 **"small, three-day retreat":** Caroline Mimbs Nyce, "The Winter Getaway That Turned the Soft-

ware World Upside Down," *The Atlantic,* December 8, 2017, www.theatlantic.com/techno
logy/archive/2017/12/agile-manifesto-a-history/547715/.

205 **fully 75 percent failed:** Dean Leffingwell, *Scaling Software Agility: Best Practices for Large Enter-
prises* (Upper Saddle River, NJ: Addison-Wesley, 2008), 19.

205 **first described waterfall:** Winston W. Royce, "Managing the Development of Large Software
Systems: Concepts and Techniques," Proceedings, IEEE WESCon, August 1970, 1–9, https://
blog.jbrains.ca/assets/articles/royce1970.pdf.

206 **"A bigger gathering of organizational anarchists":** Nyce, "Winter Getaway."

206 **Bob Martin, who sent out the invitations:** Nyce, "Winter Getaway."

206 **The manifesto, which took shape:** "Manifesto for Agile Software Development," 2001, https://
agilemanifesto.org/.

208 **A 2015 survey:** Pedro Serrador and Jeffrey K. Pinto, "Does Agile Work? A Quantitative Analysis
of Agile Project Success," *International Journal of Project Management,* vol. 33, no. 5 (July 2015),
1040–51, https://doi.org/10.1016/j.ijproman.2015.01.006.

208 **"even badly done, Agile outperforms":** Nyce, "The Winter Getaway."

208 **Standish Group:** Anthony Mersino, "Why Agile Is Better Than Waterfall (Based on Standish
Group Chaos Report 2020)," November 1, 2021, https://vitalitychicago.com/blog/agile-projects
-are-more-successful-traditional-projects/.

208 **"Kanban only has two rules":** Alex Rehkopf, "What Is a Kanban Board?," *Atlassian,* accessed
February 15, 2023, www.atlassian.com/agile/kanban/boards.

210 **delayed the planned introduction:** Simon Hage, "VW-Aufsichtsrat Fürchtet Folgen des Softwarechaos im Wettbewerb mit Tesla," *Der Spiegel,* May 20, 2022, www.spiegel.de/wirtschaft
/unternehmen/vw-aufsichtsrat-fuerchtet-folgen-des-softwarechaos-im-wettbewerb-mit-tesla
-a-d28a2c76-6acf-436a-800a-f636cbe76b84.

210 **Porsche and Audi models:** Stefan Nicola, "Porsches Postponed by Buggy Software Cost VW's
CEO Herbert Diess His Job," Bloomberg, July 25, 2022, www.bloomberg.com/news/articles
/2022-07-25/porsches-postponed-by-buggy-software-cost-vw-s-ceo-his-job?sref=iW3WrQuv.

210 **A May 2022 story:** Hage, "VW-Aufsichtsrat Fürchtet Folgen Des Softwarechaos."

210 **simple exercise for small teams:** Peter Skillman, "The Design Challenge (Also Called Spaghetti
Tower)," *Medium,* April 14, 2019, https://medium.com/@peterskillman/the-design-challenge
-also-called-spaghetti-tower-cda62685e15b.

211 **2010 TED talk:** Tom Wujec, "Build a Tower, Build a Team," TED video, 00:50, accessed February 15, 2023, www.ted.com/talks/tom_wujec_build_a_tower_build_a_team?language=zh.

211 **"don't waste time":** "Peter Skillman Marshmallow Design Challenge," YouTube video, January
27, 2014. www.youtube.com/watch?v=1p5sBzMtB3Q.

211 **"Most people begin":** Wujec, "Build a Tower."

212 **"We do everything wrong":** Eric Ries, *The Lean Startup: How Today's Entrepreneurs Use Continuous Innovation to Create Radically Successful Businesses* (New York: Currency, 2011).

213 **something of a personal mantra:** Reid Hoffman (@reidhoffman), "You may have heard me say:
If you're not embarrassed by the first version of your product, you've launched too late [www
.linkedin.com/pulse/arent-any-typos-essay-we-launched-too-late-reid-hoffman]," Twitter March
29, 2017, 1:46 p.m., https://twitter.com/reidhoffman/status/847142924240379904?lang=en.

214 **in order to start his swing correctly:** Mark Mulvoy, "The Little Big Man," *Sports Illustrated,*
April 12, 1976, https://vault.si.com/vault/1976/04/12/the-little-big-man.

215 **"Anyone who travels very much on airlines":** Tom Wolfe, *The Right Stuff* (New York: Farrar,
Straus and Giroux, 1979).

215 **Craig administered painful electric shocks:** K. D. Craig and K. M. Prkachin, "Social Modeling Influences on Sensory Decision-Theory and Psychophysiological Indexes of Pain," *Journal of Personality and Social Psychology,* vol. 36, no. 8 (1978), 805–15.

217 **cultural evolution can be very fast:** Joseph Patrick Henrich, *The Secret of Our Success: How Culture Is Driving Human Evolution, Domesticating Our Species, and Making Us Smarter* (Princeton, NJ: Princeton University Press, 2016), 219–20.

219 **"It's our collective brains":** Henrich, *The Secret of Our Success,* 212.

219 **"Move Fast and Break Things":** Henry Blodget, "Mark Zuckerberg on Innovation," *BusinessInsider,* October 1, 2009, https://web.archive.org/web/20210209195313/www.businessinsider.com/mark-zuckerberg-innovation-2009-10?r=US&IR=T.

220 **"I've researched and consulted on megaprojects":** Bent Flyvbjerg, "Make Megaprojects More Modular," *Harvard Business Review,* November–December 2021, https://hbr.org/2021/11/make-megaprojects-more-modular.

220 **Copenhagen's City Circle Line:** Flyvbjerg, "Make Megaprojects More Modular."

220 *partially* **opened in 2017:** Nick Paumgarten, "The Second Avenue Subway Is Here!," *The New Yorker,* February 6, 2017, www.newyorker.com/magazine/2017/02/13/the-second-avenue-subway-is-here.

221 **"The tunnel modules":** Flyvbjerg, "Make Megaprojects More Modular."

222 **"The Tesla's stopping distance":** Patrick Olsen, "Tesla Model 3 Falls Short of a *CR* Recommendation," *Consumer Reports,* May 30, 2018, www.consumerreports.org/hybrids-evs/tesla-model-3-review-falls-short-of-consumer-reports-recommendation/.

222 **Musk tweeted:** Elon Musk (@elonmusk), replying to @ElectrekCo and @FredericLambert, Twitter May 21, 2018, 9:31 p.m., https://twitter.com/elonmusk/status/998738003668357120.

222 **"*CR* now recommends the Model 3":** Olsen, "Tesla Model 3 Falls Short."

222 **"To see something updated that quickly":** Neal E. Boudette, "Tesla Fixes Model 3 Flaw, Getting Consumer Reports to Change Review," *New York Times,* May 30, 2018, www.nytimes.com/2018/05/30/business/tesla-consumer-reports.html.

222 **two-thirds of all the payload:** Kate Duffy, "Elon Musk Says SpaceX Is Aiming to Launch Its Most-Used Rocket Once a Week on Average This Year," *Business Insider,* February 4, 2022, www.businessinsider.com/elon-musk-spacex-falcon-9-rocket-launch-every-week-payload-2022-2.

222 **2018 NASA report:** Harry Jones, "The Recent Large Reduction in Space Launch Cost," 48th International Conference on Environmental Systems, 2018.

223 **presentation Musk gave:** Dave Mosher, "Elon Musk Just Gave the Most Revealing Look Yet at the Rocket Ship SpaceX Is Building to Fly to the Moon and Mars," *Business Insider,* September 22, 2018, www.businessinsider.com/elon-musk-spacex-pictures-big-falcon-rocket-spaceship-2018-9.

223 **made out of stainless steel:** Ryan Whitwam, "Elon Musk Explains Why the Starship Will Be Stainless Steel," *ExtremeTech,* January 24, 2019, www.extremetech.com/extreme/284346-elon-musk-explains-why-the-starship-will-be-stainless-steel.

223 **"Everything for Starship":** Florian Kordina, "SLS vs. Starship: Why Do Both Programs Exist?," *Everyday Astronaut,* May 1, 2020, https://everydayastronaut.com/sls-vs-starship/.

224 **Kordina was right:** "List of SpaceX Starship Flight Tests," Wikipedia, February 5, 2023, https://en.wikipedia.org/wiki/List_of_SpaceX_Starship_flight_tests.

224 **$2.9 billion contract:** Kenneth Chang, "SpaceX Wins NASA $2.9 Billion Contract to Build

Moon Lander," *New York Times,* April 16, 2021, www.nytimes.com/2021/04/16/science/spacex -moon-nasa.html.

225 **maiden flight was originally scheduled for 2016:** Christopher Cokinos, "By the Numbers: The Space Launch System, NASA's Next Moon Rocket," *Astronomy,* September 2, 2022, https:// astronomy.com/news/2022/09/by-the-numbers-the-space-launch-system-nasas-next -moon-rocket.

225 **"no unusual engineering hurdles":** David W. Brown, "NASA's Last Rocket," *New York Times,* March 17, 2021, www.nytimes.com/2021/03/17/science/nasa-space-launch-system.html.

225 **delayed twenty-six times:** Joey Roulette and Steve Gorman, "NASA's Next-Generation Artemis Mission Heads to Moon on Debut Test Flight," *Reuters,* November 16, 2022, www.reuters.com /lifestyle/science/nasas-artemis-moon-rocket-begins-fueling-debut-launch-2022-11-15/.

225 **inspector general for NASA:** Eric Berger, "Finally, We Know Production Costs for SLS and Orion, and They're Wild," *Ars Technica,* March 1, 2022, https://arstechnica.com/science /2022/03/nasa-inspector-general-says-sls-costs-are-unsustainable/.

225 **more like $8 billion:** Berger, "Finally, We Know Production Costs."

225 **$150 to $250 million:** Ian Vorbach, "Is Starship Really Going to Revolutionize Launch Costs?," *SpaceDotBiz,* May 19, 2022, https://newsletter.spacedotbiz.com/p/starship-really-going-revolutionize -launch-costs.

225 **"*If a schedule is long, it's wrong*":** Elon Musk, *Wikiquote,* Wikimedia Foundation, https:// en.wikiquote.org/wiki/Elon_Musk.

226 **"the most influential military thinker":** Robert Coram, *Boyd: The Fighter Pilot Who Changed the Art of War* (New York: Little, Brown, 2002), 7.

226 **twenty-nine missions in the Korean War:** Coram, *Boyd,* 52.

227 **Boyd's approach to aerial warfare:** Harry Hillaker, "Tribute to John R. Boyd," *Code One,* January 28, 2015, www.codeonemagazine.com/f16_article.html?item_id=156.

227 **"While still a junior officer":** Coram, *Boyd,* 5–6.

228 **"We should operate at a faster tempo":** "The OODA Loop: How Fighter Pilots Make Fast and Accurate Decisions," *Farnam Street,* March 19, 2021, https://fs.blog/ooda-loop/.

228 **revised Desert Storm battle plan:** Coram, *Boyd,* 425.

228 **fewer than one hundred US soldiers were killed:** "Operation Desert Storm," *U.S. Army Center of Military History,* https://history.army.mil/html/bookshelves/resmat/desert-storm/index .html#:~:text=During%20air%20and%20ground%20operations,and%20105%20non%2Dhostile %20deaths.

229 **"the Iraqi army collapsed":** *Congressional Record,* vol. 143, no. 37 (March 20, 1997), www.govinfo .gov/content/pkg/CREC-1997-03-20/html/CREC-1997-03-20-pt1-PgS2610-2.htm.

229 **1991 testimony to Congress:** "Colonel John Boyd on OODA, People, Ideas, and Technology" (user clip of "U.S. Military Reform After Oper. Desert Storm," April 30, 1991), C-SPAN, December 23, 2019, www.c-span.org/video/?c4841785%2Fuser-clip-colonel-john-boyd-ooda -people-ideas-technology.

229 **when software is eating the world:** Marc Andreessen, "Why Software Is Eating the World," *Wall Street Journal,* August 22, 2011, www.wsj.com/articles/SB10001424053111903480904576 512250915629460.

230 **As he left his job:** Elisabeth Behrmann, "VW Software Issues Point to iOS and Android-Like Future for Cars," Bloomberg, September 14, 2022, www.bloomberg.com/news/articles/2022 -09-14/vw-software-issues-point-to-ios-and-android-like-future-for-cars.

Notes

Chapter 7: Openness

234 **"Client, public investor":** Barbara Ley Toffler and Jennifer Reingold, *Final Accounting: Ambition, Greed, and the Fall of Arthur Andersen* (New York: Broadway Books, 2004), loc. 3055–58, Kindle.

234 **"What's this $75,000?":** Toffler and Reingold, *Final Accounting,* loc. 56–60, Kindle.

235 **"not enough money in the city of Chicago":** Toffler and Reingold, *Final Accounting,* loc. 213–14, Kindle.

235 **AA partners were outspoken:** Flynn McRoberts, "The Fall of Andersen," *Chicago Tribune,* September 1, 2002, www.chicagotribune.com/news/chi-0209010315sep01-story.html.

235 **$82 million fine:** Reuters, "Andersen to Pay $82 Million in S. & L. Pact," *New York Times,* August 16, 1993, https://www.nytimes.com/1993/08/06/business/andersen-to-pay-82-million-in-s-l-pact.html.

236 **around eleven thousand largely elderly clients:** Toffler and Reingold, *Final Accounting,* loc. 2454, Kindle.

236 **$300 million in earnings:** Roni B. Robbins, "McKessonHBOC Crisis Engulfs Charles McCall," *Atlanta Business Chronicle,* June 21, 1999, www.bizjournals.com/atlanta/stories/1999/06/21/story8.html.

236 **Boston Chicken went bankrupt:** Bill Richards and Scott Thurn, "Boston Chicken's Andersen Suit Has Similarities to Enron Case," *Wall Street Journal,* March 13, 2002, www.wsj.com/articles/SB10159733244217920.

236 **special-purpose entity:** "Enron Lesson No. 2: Special Purpose Entities," *Credit Pulse,* accessed February 13, 2023, www.creditpulse.com/accountingfinance/lessons-enron/enron-lesson-no-2-special-purpose-entities.

236 **approximately three thousand SPEs:** "Enron Lesson No. 2."

236 **Andrew Fastow:** Toffler and Reingold, *Final Accounting,* loc. 3318–20, Kindle.

236 **internal AA memo:** Toffler and Reingold, *Final Accounting,* loc. 3328, Kindle.

236 **$100 million per year:** Toffler and Reingold, *Final Accounting,* loc. 3333–34, Kindle.

237 **Andersen wrote its own obituary:** Lisa Sanders, "Andersen Will Stop Public Audits," *CBS MarketWatch.com,* June 16, 2002, www.marketwatch.com/story/andersen-says-wont-audit-public-companies-any-more.

238 **"small masterpiece of hypocrisy":** Toffler and Reingold, *Final Accounting,* loc. 3678–81, Kindle.

239 **after one sales call in 1996:** Toffler and Reingold, *Final Accounting,* loc. 1623–25, Kindle.

239 **Univac I computer:** McRoberts, "The Fall of Andersen."

239 **40 percent of AA's revenue:** Toffler and Reingold, *Final Accounting,* loc. 1367–68, Kindle.

239 **Andersen's audit business was growing:** Toffler and Reingold, *Final Accounting,* loc. 1403–4, Kindle.

240 **"All of these guys have to fly first class":** Toffler and Reingold, *Final Accounting,* loc. 1450–51, Kindle.

240 **"In the New York offices":** Toffler and Reingold, *Final Accounting,* loc. 1394–1402, Kindle.

242 **Its norms include:** Chris Argyris, *Reasons and Rationalizations: The Limits to Organizational Knowledge* (Oxford: Oxford University Press, 2004), loc. 8–9, Kindle.

244 **"defensive reasoning mind-set":** Argyris, *Reasons and Rationalizations,* loc. 1–2, Kindle.

245 **"Defensive reasoning thrives":** Argyris, *Reasons and Rationalizations,* loc. 2, Kindle.

246 **"the ultimate business how-to":** Jack Welch and Suzy Welch, *Winning* (New York: HarperCollins, 2005).

246 **"a buzzy, vague, optimistic spin":** Thomas Gryta and Ted Mann, *Lights Out: Pride, Delusion, and the Fall of General Electric* (Boston: Mariner / Houghton Mifflin Harcourt, 2021), 4.

246 **"Immelt rarely folded his hand":** Gryta and Mann, *Lights Out,* 69.

247 **"no market for hard truths":** Gryta and Mann, *Lights Out,* 246.

247 **"I have to underscore":** Katie Paul, "Exclusive: Meta Slashes Hiring Plans, Girds for 'Fierce' Headwinds," *Reuters,* July 1, 2022, www.reuters.com/technology/exclusive-meta-girds-fierce -headwinds-slower-growth-second-half-memo-2022-06-30/.

249 **"one-way doors":** Jeff Bezos, 2016 Amazon letter to shareholders, www.sec.gov/Archives/edgar /data/1018724/000119312516530910/d168744dex991.htm.

250 **"a high capacity for self-reflection":** Argyris, *Reasons and Rationalizations,* loc. 15, Kindle.

251 **"The most serious problem":** Marc Andreessen (@pmarca), "The most serious problem facing any organization is the one that cannot be discussed," Twitter, March 11, 2022, 6:53 p.m., https://twitter.com/pmarca/status/1502432636865691648.

253 **Just Do It awards:** Craig Timberg and Jia Lynn Yang, "Jeff Bezos, the *Post*'s Incoming Owner, Known for a Demanding Management Style at Amazon," *Washington Post,* August 7, 2013, www.washingtonpost.com/business/technology/2013/08/07/b5ce5ee8-ff96-11e2-9711 -3708310f6f4d_story.html.

253 **2018 shareholder letter:** Jeff Bezos, "2018 Letter to Shareholders," April 4, 2019, www .aboutamazon.com/news/company-news/2018-letter-to-shareholders.

253 **"colossal failure":** Ron Amadeo, "Amazon Alexa Is a 'Colossal Failure,' on Pace to Lose $10 Bil- lion This Year," *Ars Technica,* November 21, 2022, https://arstechnica.com/gadgets/2022/11 /amazon-alexa-is-a-colossal-failure-on-pace-to-lose-10-billion-this-year/.

254 **YouTube, for example:** Dominic Basulto, "The 7 Greatest Pivots in Tech History," *Washington Post,* July 2, 2015, www.washingtonpost.com/news/innovations/wp/2015/07/02/the-7-greatest -pivots-in-tech-history/.

254 **more than 2.5 billion users:** Daniel Ruby, "YouTube Statistics (2023) — Trending Facts & Fig- ures Shared!," *Demand Sage,* January 5, 2023, www.demandsage.com/youtube-stats.

254 **Twitter, which started out:** John Koetsier, "The Legendary Pivot: How Twitter Flipped from Failure to Success," *VentureBeat,* November 19, 2012, https://venturebeat.com/entrepreneur/the -pivot-how-twitter-switch-from-failure-to-success-video/.

254 **Instagram, originally a location-based game:** Megan Garber, "Instagram Was First Called 'Burbn,'" *The Atlantic,* July 2, 2014, www.theatlantic.com/technology/archive/2014/07 /instagram-used-to-be-called-brbn/373815/.

254 **Slack, also born out of an unpopular game:** [Drew] Houston, "The Slack Story: How Pivoting Led to a $27 Billion Acquisition," *BAMF,* August 8, 2021, https://bamf.com/slack-story-how -pivoting-led-to-a-27-billion-acquisition/.

254 **Pinterest, which was originally a mobile shopping app:** Steve O'Hear and Natasha Lomas, "Five Super Successful Tech Pivots," *TechCrunch,* May 28, 2014, https://techcrunch.com /gallery/five-super-successful-tech-pivots/slide/2/.

254 **"Only the truth is funny":** Rick Reynolds: Only the Truth Is Funny, IMDb, accessed March 2, 2023, www.imdb.com/title/tt0251372/.

255 **the same purpose for HubSpot:** Dharmesh Shah, "The HubSpot Culture Code," *HubSpot Slides,* June 24, 2021, https://network.hubspot.com/slides/the-hubspot-culture-code-1f8v20t3a.

256 **Rangan joined HubSpot:** www.prnewswire.com/news-releases/hubspot-announces-first-ever -chief-customer-officer-yamini-rangan-300975698.html.

Notes

256 **took over from Halligan:** www.hubspot.com/company-news/yamini-rangan-ceo-brian-halligan -executive-chairman.

258 **Glassdoor's Best Places to Work:** www.glassdoor.com/Award/Best-Places-to-Work-LST _KQ0,19.htm.

259 **Best CEO for Women:** www.comparably.com/news/best-ceos-for-women-2022/.

259 **"Everyone has equal access":** Shah, "The HubSpot Culture Code."

259 **"All financial results":** Reed Hastings and Erin Meyer, *No Rules Rules: Netflix and the Culture of Reinvention* (New York: Penguin Press, 2020), 108–9.

260 **numerical feedback:** Richard Feloni, "Employees at the World's Largest Hedge Fund Use iPads to Rate Each Other's Performance in Real-Time—See How It Works," *Business Insider,* September 6, 2017, www.businessinsider.com/bridgewater-ray-dalio-radical-transparency-app-dots-2017-9.

260 **Hans Christian Andersen's:** "The Emperor's New Clothes," Hans Christian Andersen Centre, accessed March 2, 2023, https://andersen.sdu.dk/vaerk/hersholt/TheEmperorsNewClothes_e.html.

262 **a logic puzzle:** Morris T. Friedell, "On the Structure of Shared Awareness," *Systems Research and Behavioral Science,* vol. 14, no. 1 (December 31, 1968), 28–39, https://doi.org/10.1002/bs .3830140105.

265 **"A good argument for strong norms":** Dan Williams (@danwilliamsphil), Twitter, August 23, 2022, 7:42 a.m., https://twitter.com/danwilliamsphil/status/1562042572490657792.

266 **"thoughtful expertise":** Toffler and Reingold, *Final Accounting,* loc. 3982–83, Kindle.

266 **"not the me I used to know":** Toffler and Reingold, *Final Accounting,* loc. 3288–91, Kindle.

267 **65 percent of time:** R. I. M. Dunbar, "Gossip in Evolutionary Perspective," *Review of General Psychology,* vol. 8, no. 2 (June 2004), 100–110, https://doi.org/10.1037/1089-2680.8.2.100.

268 **"genuinely angry or sad":** Matthew D. Lieberman, *Social: Why Our Brains Are Wired to Connect* (New York: Crown/Archetype, 2013), 54.

268 **"wouldn't have been able to tell the difference":** Lieberman, *Social,* 58.

268 **daily dose of 1,000 milligrams:** C. N. DeWall, G. MacDonald, G. D. Webster, C. L. Masten, R. F. Baumeister, C. Powell, D. Combs, D. R. Schurtz, T. F. Stillman, D. M. Tice, and N. I. Eisenberger, "Acetaminophen Reduces Social Pain: Behavioral and Neural Evidence," *Psychological Science,* vol. 21 (2010), 931–7.

268 **"Our sensitivity to social rejection":** Lieberman, *Social,* 67.

269 **"assemblage of reasonable beings":** Augustine of Hippo, *Wikiquote,* Wikimedia Foundation, https://en.wikiquote.org/wiki/Augustine_of_Hippo.

269 **"common hatred for something":** Anton Chekhov, *Wikiquote,* Wikimedia Foundation, https:// en.wikiquote.org/wiki/Anton_Chekhov#Note-Book_of_Anton_Chekhov_(1921).

270 **"If you hang around a place long enough":** Toffler and Reingold, *Final Accounting,* loc. 3986–90, Kindle.

Conclusion

276 **650 million users:** L. Ceci, "Number of TikTok Users Worldwide from 2018 to 2022," *Statista,* September 5, 2022, www.statista.com/statistics/1327116/number-of-global-tiktok-users/.

276 **"most popular app":** Meghan Bobrowsky, Salvador Rodriguez, Sarah E. Needleman, and Georgia Wells, "TikTok's Stratospheric Rise: An Oral History," *Wall Street Journal,* updated November 5, 2022, www.wsj.com/articles/tiktoks-stratospheric-rise-an-oral-history-11667599696.

276 **"defining characteristic":** Mark Zuckerberg, "Founder's Letter: Our Next Chapter," *About Facebook,* October 28, 2021, https://about.fb.com/news/2021/10/founders-letter/.

277 **investment was $15 billion:** Martin Peers, "On Metaverse Spending, Zuckerberg Doesn't Care What Critics Say," *The Information,* October 26, 2022, www.theinformation.com/articles/on -metaverse-spending-zuckerberg-doesn-t-care-what-critics-say.

277 **two hundred thousand users:** Jeff Horwitz, Salvador Rodriguez, and Meghan Bobrowsky, "Company Documents Show Meta's Flagship Metaverse Falling Short," *Wall Street Journal,* October 15, 2022, www.wsj.com/articles/meta-metaverse-horizon-worlds-zuckerberg-facebook -internal-documents-11665778961.

277 **"Why don't we love the product":** Alex Heath, "Meta's Flagship Metaverse App Is Too Buggy and Employees Are Barely Using It, Says Exec in Charge," *The Verge,* October 6, 2022, www .theverge.com/2022/10/6/23391895/meta-facebook-horizon-worlds-vr-social-network -too-buggy-leaked-memo.

277 **from Adi Robertson:** Adi Robertson, "Meta Quest Pro Review: Get Me Out of Here," *The Verge,* updated November 22, 2022, www.theverge.com/23451629/meta-quest-pro-vr-headset-horizon -review.

277 **less than 60 percent:** Mike Isaac and Cade Metz, "Skepticism, Confusion, Frustration: Inside Mark Zuckerberg's Metaverse Struggles," *New York Times,* October 9, 2022, www.nytimes .com/2022/10/09/technology/meta-zuckerberg-metaverse.html.

278 **an open letter:** Meghan Bobrowsky, "Meta Investor Urges CEO Mark Zuckerberg to Slash Staff and Cut Costs," *Wall Street Journal,* October 24, 2022, www.wsj.com/articles/meta-investor -urges-ceo-mark-zuckerberg-to-slash-staff-and-cut-costs-11666634172.

278 **Zuckerberg holds:** Katie Canales, "'The Most Powerful Person Who's Ever Walked the Face of the Earth': How Mark Zuckerberg's Stranglehold on Facebook Could Put the Company at Risk," *Business Insider,* October 13, 2021, www.businessinsider.com/mark-zuckerberg-control -facebook-whistleblower-key-man-risk-2021-10.

278 **tried to back out:** Jacob Kastrenakes, "Elon Musk Officially Tries to Bail on Buying Twitter," *The Verge,* July 8, 2022, www.theverge.com/2022/7/8/23200961/elon-musk-files-back-out -twitter-deal-breach-of-contract.

278 **carrying a sink:** Elon Musk (@elonmusk), "Entering Twitter HQ—let that sink in!," Twitter, 2:45 p.m., October 26, 2022, https://twitter.com/elonmusk/status/1585341984679469056.

278 **verifying accounts:** Amanda Holpuch, "Why Does Twitter Verify Some Accounts?," *New York Times,* November 2, 2022, www.nytimes.com/2022/11/02/us/twitter-verification-elon-musk.html.

278 **with author Stephen King:** Elon Musk (@elonmusk), "We need to pay the bills somehow! Twit-ter cannot rely entirely on advertisers. How about $8?," Twitter, 1:16 a.m., November 1, 2022, https://twitter.com/elonmusk/status/1587312517679878144.

279 **Markey sent a letter:** Ashley Capoot, "Sen. Ed Markey Hits Back at Elon Musk After His Response to Questions About Impersonation," CNBC, November 13, 2022, www.cnbc .com/2022/11/13/sen-ed-markey-hits-back-at-elon-musk-after-his-response-to-questions-about -impersonation-.html.

279 **"impersonation issues":** Zoe Schiffer (@ZoeSchiffer), "NEW: Twitter has suspended the launch of Twitter Blue and is actively trying to stop people from subscribing 'to help address imperson-ation issues,' per an internal note," Twitter, 9:54 a.m., November 11, 2022, https://twitter.com /ZoeSchiffer/status/1591081913166745601.

279 **Omnicom recommended:** Mia Sato, "Another Major Ad Agency Recommends Pausing Twitter Ad Campaigns," *The Verge,* November 11, 2022, www.theverge.com/2022/11/11/23453575 /omnicom-media-group-twitter-advertising-pause.

279 **"thermonuclear name and shame"**: Elon Musk (@elonmusk), "Thank you. A thermonuclear name & shame is exactly what will happen if this continues," Twitter, 7:37 pm, November 4, 2022, https://twitter.com/elonmusk/status/1588676939463946241.

279 **90 percent of its revenue:** Clare Duffy and Catherine Thorbecke, "Elon Musk Said Twitter Has Seen a 'Massive Drop in Revenue' as More Brands Pause Ads," *CNN Business,* November 4, 2022, www.cnn.com/2022/11/04/tech/twitter-advertisers.

279 **"top 1 percent":** Elizabeth Dwoskin, "Musk Issues Ultimatum to Staff: Commit to 'Hardcore' Twitter or Take Severance," *Washington Post,* November 16, 2022, www.washingtonpost.com /technology/2022/11/16/musk-twitter-email-ultimatum-termination/?utm_source=pocket_saves.

280 **"History suggests":** Joseph Patrick Henrich, *The Secret of Our Success: How Culture Is Driving Human Evolution, Domesticating Our Species, and Making Us Smarter* (Princeton, NJ: Princeton University Press, 2016), loc. 3353, Kindle.

280 **wrote a blog post:** Brian Armstrong, "Coinbase Is a Mission Focused Company," *Coinbase* (blog), September 29, 2018, www.coinbase.com/blog/coinbase-is-a-mission-focused-company.

281 **More than one-third:** Casey Newton, "Inside the All-Hands Meeting That Led to a Third of Base-camp Employees Quitting," *The Verge,* May 3, 2021, www.theverge.com/2021/5/3/22418208 /basecamp-all-hands-meeting-employee-resignations-buyouts-implosion.

281 **made the right decision:** Brian Armstrong (@brian_armstrong), "1/ Wanted to share some thoughts on the recent Coinbase story around our mission," Twitter, 8:01 p.m., September 30, 2021, https://twitter.com/brian_armstrong/status/1443727729476530178.

282 **"lumbering bureaucracy":** Kevin Roose, "The Metaverse Is Mark Zuckerberg's Escape Hatch," *New York Times,* October 29, 2021, www.nytimes.com/2021/10/29/technology/meta-facebook -zuckerberg.html.

282 **a quarter of its workforce:** Clare Duffy, "Meta's Business Groups Cut in Latest Round of Layoffs," CNN, May 24, 2023, https://www.cnn.com/2023/05/24/tech/meta-layoffs-business -groups/index.html.

282 **"ways to be scrappier":** Naomi Nix, "Mark Zuckerberg Unveils 'Scrappier' Future at Meta After Layoffs," *Washington Post,* May 25, 2023, www.washingtonpost.com/technology/2023/05/25 /meta-layoffs-future-facebook-instagram-company/.

282 **"As we add different groups":** Mark Zuckerberg, "Update on Meta's Year of Efficiency," *About Facebook,* March 14, 2023, https://about.fb.com/news/2023/03/mark-zuckerberg-meta-year -of-efficiency/.

282 **"war against the bureaucracy":** Brad Stone, *Amazon Unbound: Jeff Bezos and the Invention of a Global Empire* (New York: Simon & Schuster, 2022), 264.

283 **advertising business:** Mark Di Stefano and Jessica Toonkel, "Amazon's Ad Staffers Flee amid Complaints of Bloat, Bureaucracy," *The Information,* June 24, 2022, www.theinformation.com /articles/amazons-ad-staffers-flee-amid-complaints-of-bloat-bureaucracy.

283 **at AWS:** Kevin McLaughlin, "AWS' New CEO Faces a Fresh Challenge: Bureaucracy," *The Information,* July 12, 2021, www.theinformation.com/articles/aws-new-ceo-faces-a-fresh -challenge-bureaucracy.

283 **"aging professional athletes":** Graham Averill, "The Secret to Athletic Longevity Is Surprisingly Simple," *Outside Online,* May 17, 2018, www.outsideonline.com/health/training-performance /athletic-longevity-secrets-play-on-book/.

Index

Note: Italic page numbers refer to illustrations.

<head
</header>

Index

About the Author

Andrew McAfee is a principal research scientist at the MIT Sloan School of Management and the cofounder of the MIT Initiative on the Digital Economy. He studies how technological progress changes the world. He lives in Cambridge, Massachusetts.